SEMBENE OUSMANE was born in Senegal in 1923. Essentially self-educated, he became a fisherman just like his father. He moved to Dakar until the outbreak of World War Two, when he was drafted into the French army and saw action in Italy and Germany. Returning to Senegal for a short time, Sembène realized that in order to further his literary ambitions he would have to move to France. He went to Marseilles where he worked as a docker, joined the French Communist Party, and became a union organizer. He also began writing.

His output has been prodigious. *Le Docker noir* appeared in 1956, a semi-autobiographical novel written in Marseilles, followed a year later by *Oh Pays, mon beau peuple!* about the problems of re-adaptation encountered by an African returning home with a French wife and new ideas. Three years later, *Les Bouts de bois de Dieu* was published. In 1962 Ousmane wrote *Voltaïque,* a volume of short stories which included the story 'La Noire de . . .', which he later turned into a prize-winning film. A fourth novel, *L'Harmattan,* was released in 1964, after which Ousmane had the opportunity to study at the Moscow film school. Two more short novels – *Véhi ciosane ou blanche genèse* and *Le Mandat* – followed, the latter becoming a film that won a prize at the Venice film festival and established Ousmane's reputation as a director. In 1973 another novel, *Xala,* was published, going on to become one of a series of successful films. In 1981 the massive two-volumed work *Le Dernier de l'empire* was published, followed by the novellas *Niiwam* and *Taaw* in 1987.

Heinemann publish several of Ousmane's novels in translation: *Les Bouts de bois de Dieu* as *God's Bits of Wood, Le Mandat et Véhi ciosane* as *The Money Order with White Genesis, Niiwam* and *Taaw* (in one volume) and *Xala. Le Docker noir* appeared in 1987, as *Black Docker.*

SEMBENE OUSMANE

GOD'S
BITS OF WOOD

Translated by Francis Price

Heinemann

Heinemann is a registered trademark of Pearson Education Limited,
a register company in England and Wales whose registered office is at
80 Strand, London, WC2R 0RL, United Kingdom,
company Registration number: 872828

Heinemann Publishers (Pty) Ltd
PO Box 781940, Sandton 2146, Johannesburg, South Africa

Les bouts de bois de Dieu
© 1960 Le Livre contemporain
This translation © 1962 Doubleday & Company Inc.
First published by Heinemann Educational Books
in the *African Writers Series* as AWS 63 in 1970
First published in this edition, 1995

British Library Cataloguing in Publication Data
Ousmane, Sembene
    God's bits of wood.——(African writers series)
    I. Title II. Les bouts de bois de Dieu. *English* III. Series
    843[F]   PQ 3989.08

Cover illustration by Fraser Taylor
Author photograph by George Hallet

ISBN: 978 0 435909 59 8

Printed in Malaysia (CTP-VVP)

20 19 18
28 27 26 25

Contents

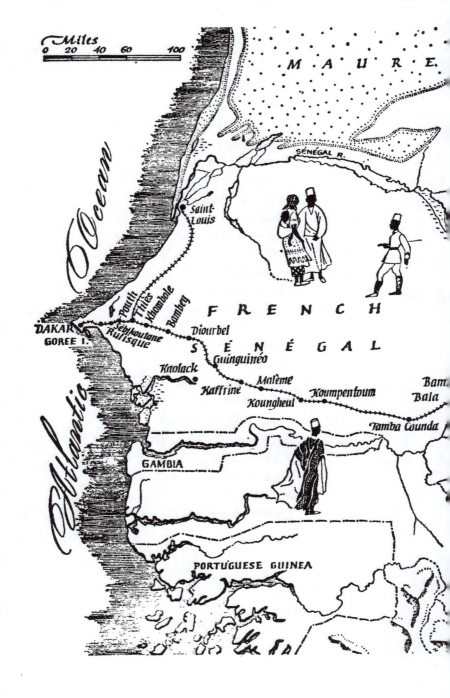

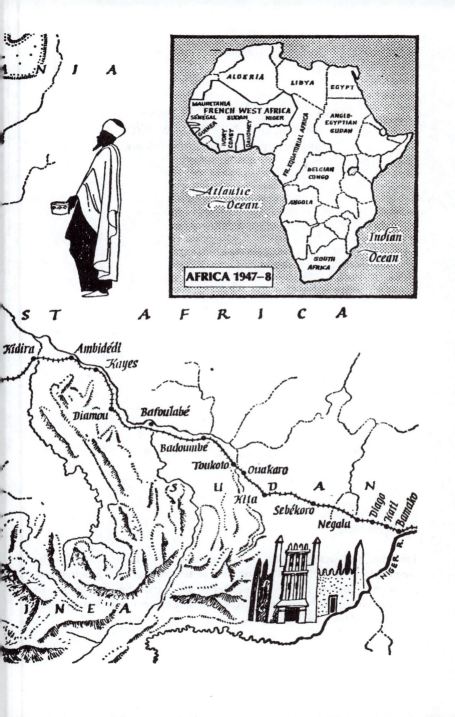

AFRICA 1947–8

MAURETANIA
ALGERIA
LIBYA
EGYPT
FRENCH WEST AFRICA
SENEGAL   SUDAN   NIGER
GUINEA
IVORY COAST   DAHOMEY
ANGLO-EGYPTIAN SUDAN
FR. EQUATORIAL AFRICA
BELGIAN CONGO
ANGOLA
SOUTH AFRICA
Atlantic Ocean
Indian Ocean

ST   AFRICA

Kidira   Ambidédi
Kayes
Diamou   Bafoulabé
Badoumbe
Toukoto   Ouakaro
SUDAN
Kita
Sebékoro
Negala   Dlago   Kati   Bamako
NIGER R.
GUINEA

Author's Note

The men and women who, from the tenth of October, 1947, to the nineteenth of March, 1948, took part in this struggle for a better way of life owe nothing to anyone: neither to any 'civilizing mission' nor to any parliament or parliamentarian. Their example was not in vain. Since then, Africa has made progress.

BAMAKO

Ad'jibid'ji

The last rays of the sun filtered through a shredded lacework of clouds. To the west, waves of mist spun slowly away, and at the very center of the vast mauve and indigo arch of sky the great crimson orb grew steadily larger. The roofs, the thorny minarets of the mosques, the trees – silk-cotton, flame, and mahogany – the walls, the ochered ground; all caught fire. Striking brutally through the cloud curtain, like the beam from some celestial projector, a single ray of light lashed at the Koulouba, the governor's residence, poised like a sugar castle on the heights that bore its name.

At the center of the belt of hills the groups of mud-walled houses and the dry grass, still scorched by the heat of noon, now swam in the red waters of the setting sun. A dry breeze from the northeast moved against the faces of the people, but they still sweated a little.

It was an afternoon in mid-October, at the end of the season of rains, and as was the custom at this time of day the women of the Bakayoko house were gathered in the courtyard. Only the women. As they went about their household tasks they chattered constantly, each of them completely indifferent to what the others were saying. Seated a little apart, with her back against the hard, clay wall, was old Niakoro.

Niakoro was very old indeed. On either side of her little, high-arched nose the drooping lids half covered her eyes. Her lips were tattooed – a souvenir of youthful vanity The line of her mouth was drawn back in a perpetual sucking motion, and her cheeks moved in and out to the rhythm of her breathing, so that she seemed always to be swallowing. Her head appeared linked to her body only by threads of flesh, and by the flabby dewlaps that drooped beneath her chin. And yet this ancient countenance had the serenity which comes to those who arrive at the end of a hard and virtuous life. From beneath an old and faded cloth, which came only to her thighs, her crooked little legs stuck out, and feet with toes widespaced and bent.

Old Niakoro was only half listening to the wives of the absent men. She seemed, rather, to be watching over them, like a shepherd not far distant from his flock. Only rarely did she take part in their gossiping; except, occasionally, to tell them a story of times when they were not yet born. But for some days now she had been worried. A serious thing had occupied her mind, and more serious than the thing itself was the fact that no one had noticed her suffering. It was this that disturbed and haunted her. In her time the young people undertook nothing without the advice of their elders, but now, alone, they were deciding on a strike. Did they even know what would happen? She, Niakoro, knew; she had seen one. A terrible strike, a savage memory for those who had lived through it; just one season of rains before the war. It had taken a husband and a son from her, but now no one even came to seek her advice. Were the ways of the old time gone forever? Ibrahim Bakayoko, her own son, had told her nothing!

At the time of that first strike it was true that she had been living in the west, in the country of the *toubabous dyions* – the slaves of the Europeans. She had been told enough about this Sénégal, about the work to be found there, the fortunes to be made, but she had brought back only mourning and sorrow. Since then she had called the Senegalese 'the slaves', and when she spoke of her younger son she said, 'He seems like one of the Ouolof people, one of the westerners; he has the bearing, and the manners.'

'But now,' Niakoro thought, sucking at her cheeks, 'I want to hear no more of those people. Slaves, and sons of slaves, they are nothing but liars – will the Bambaras never learn that? The Bambaras have never run before an enemy; we speak honestly, and we do as we say we will do. And now these brainless workers on the trains want another strike, and it will be the Sudanese who are killed, just as it was the last time!

'What was the name of that one who came here two weeks ago? I knew his father; he was a good Ouolof. He came to see Ibrahim. They know the Bambaras, the men of Ibrahim Bakayoko; even the white men know the Bambaras. And Ibrahim, my son – everyone knows my son. Ever since his father's death he has never been content to stay in one place. He was restless even while I still carried him, but then it gave me pleasure. And now he is preaching a strike – why? It is dangerous, and I would feel better about it if the westerners were not involved. I don't trust them. They are all liars and cheats.'

Weary with thinking, weary of all these memories whispering in her skull, Niakoro lifted her head to look at the women, seated now along the wall of the enclosure, trying to escape the sun. In the middle of the courtyard stood the little platform used for drying seeds. Bunches of red

2

pimentos and sheaves of millet dangled from each of its posts. In one corner the children were playing. Suddenly Fatoumata laughed; a sort of loud, neighing sound. 'What an ugly voice,' old Niakoro thought. 'That awful giggling. How can a decent woman laugh like that? The neighbors will wonder what is happening. That Fatoumata has no shame.'

But what did old Niakoro mean to these women, occupied only with the passing hour? She was just a leftover from a vanished time, slowly being forgotten.

A baby crawled toward her on hands and knees, and Niakoro bent her old back to pick it up, but the child began to scream.

'Be quiet, be quiet,' she said, and when the baby just screamed louder she began to sing a very old lullaby, wrinkling up her face to illustrate the words. This upset the child even more, and Fatoumata, the woman with the vulgar laugh, came to take it away. The manner in which she seized the infant and carried it off displeased Niakoro. 'She might have calmed it a little and given it back to me,' she thought. And again she felt the burden of age and memories.

'Ad'jibid'ji, Ad'jibid'ji,' she called, and when she received no reply she called loudly again.

'She is doing her schoolwork,' said Assitan, walking over from the group of women. 'What did you want, *m'ba*?'

'Put the iron in the fire for me,' Niakoro replied.

'Right away, Grandmother.'

Old Niakoro could never let the afternoon go by without doing something. Sometimes she mended or darned, and sometimes she would work at ornamenting gourds. 'I will never understand your carelessness,' she often said to the other women. 'Why do you never think to decorate your utensils? And don't you know that your iron pots destroy the virility of the men?'

Assitan brought her the white-hot iron marker. Niakoro took up a medium-sized gourd, which she clasped between her thighs, and with a steady hand began to trace a design of arabesques. The iron made a little crackling sound, but Niakoro's eyes remained fixed on the movement of her hand. After a moment she stopped, put the iron aside, and turned the gourd around. Satisfied with her work, she sucked at her cheeks and began again on the other side, a pattern of diamond shapes studded with big dots.

On the horizon the sun was disappearing, but the heat remained. In the shade at the foot of the platform, a few cocks and hens stood motionless, beaks hanging open, eyelids drawn down.

3

'Ad'jibid'ji, come here.'

The child stopped short and turned to come back.

'In the first place,' old Niakoro said, 'why do you leave the house without a word; and next, where are you going in such a hurry?'

'To the gathering of the men.'

Ad'jibid'ji must have been eight or nine years old, but she was tall for her age. She had the same features as Assitan, her mother, and the same fine nose, for they were nobly descended, from the Peuls and the Berbers. Her thick black hair was gathered in four twists and caught with four slender amulets.

'To the gathering of the men!' Niakoro repeated. She had set her work in a little pile beside her; for today she had done enough. She swallowed noisily. 'Why are you always poking your nose in the affairs of the men? They are preparing a strike, and that is not a thing for you. Can't you stay here, for once?'

'Yes, but today I must take this book to Fa Keïta,' the child responded, holding out a schoolbook that was clutched in her hand.

'It is not a place for a woman, and even less for a child your age. Why must you spend all of your time with the men?'

'Petit père always used to take me with him, and besides, I am learning.' Ad'jibid'ji was Ibrahim Bakayoko's adopted daughter, and she always referred to him as her 'little father.'

'Learning – learning what?' Niakoro demanded, and there was both mockery and sadness in her voice. 'If I call you I am told not to disturb you – and why? Because you are learning the white man's language. What use is the white man's language to a woman? To be a good mother you have no need of that. Among my people, who are your father's people, too, no one speaks the white man's language, and no one has died of it! Ever since I was born – and God knows that was a long time ago – I have never heard of a white man who had learned to speak Bambara, or any other language of this country. But you rootless people think only of learning his, while our language dies.'

Niakoro stopped for a moment to catch her breath, and her cheeks puffed out like rising dough. 'In my time we learned only some verses of the Koran, for our prayers.'

Through all of this Ad'jibid'ji had been standing on one foot scratching her right leg with the big toe of her left, her slender neck twisted to the side, her eyes fixed on the ground. There were two generations between her grandmother and herself, but Ad'jibid'ji was neither disrespectful nor

4

impudent. On the contrary, her maturity, her quickness, and her intelligence astounded everyone – and Niakoro most of all.

She passed the book from one hand into the other and asked respectfully, 'May I go, Grandmother?'

'But don't you know that today is the day of the big meeting, on the strike?'

'Yes.'

'You have never seen a strike! Your "little father" saw one, when he was still a child. Soldiers will come, and there will be shooting. And you – in the middle of the men you will be like a sheep in a stampede of camels. Are you not afraid?'

'Of what, Grandmother?'

'Of what? You ask of what? But what do you have in your head?'

'Thoughts, Grandmother, nothing but thoughts.' Ad'jibid'ji's hands were clasped behind her back, and she was balancing carefully, first on one foot, and then the other. Her slight body seemed almost lost in the cotton dress that was much too big for her.

For an instant the old scarred lips formed an incredulous O, without making a sound. Then Niakoro said sarcastically, 'You don't even know how to prepare a *couscous*. That's what comes of always hanging about with the men, instead of staying beside your mother, where you belong.'

The last phrase stung the child to the quick. 'This morning I went to the river alone to do the washing,' she stammered, 'and then I went to the market. For three days we have been grinding, and I was always there. And tonight I cleaned up from the meal. *Alors?*'

Ad'jibid'ji had spoken the last word in French.

'*Aloss, aloss!*' her grandmother screamed, as if trying to wrench the words from the child's lips. 'You speak to me, to your father's mother, and you say "*aloss*"! The white men say "*aloss*" when they call their dogs, and my granddaughter talks to me in the same way!'

Old Niakoro had never spoken to a white man, but for some reason this word had always grated on her ears. Without knowing why she thought it vulgar, and in the mouth of a child who should have lowered her voice when she spoke to her, it was worse than that.

'*Aloss, aloss,*' she repeated. 'I speak to you in Bambara, and you answer me in a language of savages!'

'The word just came out, Grandmother.'

Ad'jibid'ji was honestly confused. She hadn't meant to hurt the old woman. She glanced over toward her mother, and tears flowed from the almond ovals of her eyes. The knowledge of her fault upset her, but even

5

as she thought about it she wanted to cry out that she was free and independent. She wished she might explain that word – independence.

As for Niakoro, she was more stunned than hurt. She could not understand how the child could be unaffected by what she had said. And as Ad'jibid'ji continued to cry, the other women ceased their gossiping.

'Ad'jibid'ji,' Assitan exclaimed, 'your father forbade you to use that word!'

'I know, Mother, I know. But I didn't do it on purpose.'

'Go bring me the *nguégué*,' Assitan said, putting down her fan.

A moment later the child came back, carrying a whip. Assitan took it from her hands. Ad'jibid'ji regarded her mother gravely, and before turning around she asked, 'Is it to hurt me, Mother, or to make me better?'

The uplifted arm remained motionless.

The education she had received from her *petit père* had made Ad'jibid'ji a precocious child, and she had learned very quickly to make a distinction among punishments. If she knew she was at fault she withstood the most severe correction with a disarming, almost impersonal attitude, and there were even times when she could be heard talking with herself about her mistakes.

Dumbfounded, Assitan stared at the naked little bottom and then reached out and dropped the cotton dress, as if she were lowering a curtain. She adored Ad'jibid'ji, as did all of her neighbors, and could find nothing to complain of in the child. She helped with the work of the house, and she ran the errands, but there were moments, such as this, when Assitan would have preferred to have a son.

'Go over there, in the corner,' she said.

Head bowed, the child went to the opposite corner of the courtyard, and after a little while the women appeared to have forgotten the incident. It was Fatoumata, the woman with the man's voice, who found a means of freeing Ad'jibid'ji.

'Go and look for Fa Keïta,' she said, 'and tell him to give me some money. I asked him for it already.'

'May I go, Mother?'

'Yes,' Assitan replied, shaking her head.

Walking very slowly, Ad'jibid'ji left the house. In her corner, old Niakoro was sleeping, or pretending to sleep.

◆

The building occupied by the union was just next door to the prison. Low and solidly built of hard clay, it was surrounded by a thick mud wall the height of a man's head. For some days now it had been a beehive of activity, with workers from all of the locals arriving or departing, and with men from every corner of the district coming in search of news. But on this day, from one hour to the next, ever since dawn, the crowd had grown constantly larger. The trainmen were going to call a strike, and each man knew that such a decision would involve them all. Inside the courtyard some squatted on their heels, while others remained standing, or leaned against the wall. There were men in the branches of the trees, and sitting astride the wall. Swiftly, the courtyard had become too small, and the mass of bodies now pressed against the gate of the prison and overflowed into the fields. Everyone was waiting for the speaker who had been announced.

As soon as she was in the street, Ad'jibid'ji gathered up the too long skirt and began to run, her feet stirring little clouds of dust at every step. She crossed the Kati road, passing the police barracks, and when she reached the prison a militiaman who had recognized her called out to her, but she paid no attention. Soldiers, looking like watchdogs, with their weapons beside them, and militiamen in leggings and khaki shirts and shorts, with heavy whips in their hands, were there to keep an eye on the workers.

Once she had passed the prison, Ad'jibid'ji collided with the mob that surrounded the union building, but she was accustomed to this sort of thing and had perfected a means of getting through. She would thrust her hands, and then her head, between the bodies of the men, look up at them, and murmur, '*Pardon*', and slip by. Everyone knew her; they called her the *soungoutou* of the union – their 'little daughter' – and as soon as she had passed on, the crowd closed again behind her. As she made her way forward she could hear snatches of the speech of Fa Keïta, who was talking about wages and the cost of living. Someone in the crowd, whom she had disturbed, cried, 'Shhh', and the sound was taken up by the others. For a moment Ad'jibid'ji waited and then began her little game again: a timid upward glance, a little smile, a coaxing wink of the eye, and once again she slipped through. In this manner she finally reached the door.

On either side of a central aisle the crowd before her pressed solidly up to the foot of the stage – a collection of bodies and heads, of shaven skulls and woolly ones, of rags blackened by axle grease. The faces seemed to have lost all trace of personality. As if some giant eraser had rubbed out their individual traits they had taken on a common mask, the anonymous mask of a crowd. The hall was ventilated by four windows, but tonight these were serving as seats or as resting places for the audience. A heavy odor of sweat and of stale smoke rose like a fog.

On the wall behind the stage hung a large banner:

7

TREAT AS A FRIEND WHO TREATS YOU AS A FRIEND
TREAT YOUR MASTER AS AN ENEMY

Stepping over the legs of the seated men, and pushing between their shoulders, Ad'jibid'ji made her way to the foot of the stage and sat down on the hard-packed ground, between two men. From time to time she sniffed and glanced disgustedly at the man on her right, whose filthy, sore-covered feet gave out a fetid odor. But he was too preoccupied with the words of the Old One to pay any attention to the child.

Mamadou Keïta, or the Old One, as he was respectfully known, was standing at the left of the stage. A sleeveless tunic revealed his long, emaciated arms. The narrow, angular head perched above his meager body was entirely shaved, except for a sparse white beard of which he was fiercely proud. He spoke slowly, but precisely, evoking the laying of the first rails. At that time he had not yet been born, but later he had seen the completion of the railroad at Koulikoro. Then he spoke of the epidemics, of the famines, and of the seizure of tribal lands by the company.

Mamadou Keïta paused, and his bloodshot, deep brown eyes studied the crowd thoughtfully. From his forehead three ritual scars ran down to his chin, crossed at intervals by little horizontal gashes. He saw Ad'jibid'ji and began to speak again.

'It is true that we have our trade, but it does not bring us what it should. We are being robbed. Our wages are so low that there is no longer any difference between ourselves and animals. Years ago the men of Thiès went out on strike, and that was only settled by deaths, by deaths on our side. And now it begins again. At this very moment meetings like this one are taking place from Koulikoro to Dakar. Men have come to this same platform before me, and other men will follow. Are you ready to call a strike – yes or no? Before you do, you must think.'

From the hall Tiémoko interrupted him.

'We're the ones who do the work,' he roared, 'the same work the white men do. Why then should they be paid more? Because they are white? And when they are sick, why should they be taken care of while we and our families are left to starve? Because we are black? In what way is a white child better than a black child? In what way is a white worker better than a black worker? They tell us we have the same rights, but it is a lie, nothing but a lie! Only the engines we run tell the truth – and they don't know the difference between a white man and a black. It does no good just to look at our pay slips and say that our wages are too small. If we want to live decently we must fight!'

All through the hall clenched fists were raised, and voices cried out, 'Yes, we must strike! Strike!' Then, from the hall into the courtyard, and from the courtyard to the neighboring streets there seemed to be only one voice, crying, 'Strike!' Everyone wanted to present his evidence, to give his opinion, and the din became indescribable.

Tiémoko, who had interrupted the Old One, got up from his seat, his brutish head thrust forward. He was a thirty-year-old colossus with a thick-muscled body, enormous shoulders, and a bull neck on which the veins pulsed angrily. From his left ear hung a heavy ring of twisted gold. His yellow undershirt was soaked with sweat.

Disconcerted by the tumult he had unleashed, Mamadou Keïta waited silently, but the disorder only increased. In the deepening uproar the hall seemed suddenly smaller. It was no longer possible to hear anyone; there was just a clamor of voices. A sickly-looking youth, arguing with someone, tried to climb up on a bench, but it collapsed and crashed against the shins of the men around him. Almost immediately, six, eight, ten voices began to curse, and angry cries and oaths filled the air. Outside, the crowd was growing restless, too, and a vague, rumbling sound poured in through the door and the windows. Through it all, one word could be heard, endlessly repeated: 'Strike!'

In the street, the militiamen fidgeted with their whips, and the soldiers adjusted their weapons. The officers surveyed the excited mob uneasily.

Ad'jibid'ji took advantage of the confusion to climb up on the stage with the Old One. She gave him Fatoumata's message, and he told her to stand against the wall at the back, beneath the banner. She was taking in the noisy spectacle with more interest than amusement, when suddenly a little smile lit up her face. The memory of a story Ibrahim Bakayoko had told her raced through her mind. 'In the days before we had the union the men used to sit on the ground, in the middle of a discussion, and demand that we give them benches. We gave them benches, and what happened? When they wanted to argue they all stood up, as if the benches weren't even there!' Remembering, Ad'jibid'ji suppressed a laugh.

On the stage the officials murmured among themselves, and several times Keïta called for silence. Little by little the uproar died down, and the men began to take their places again. When someone refused to sit down, the others pulled him by the tunic, or pushed him down by the shoulders. Diara, the ticket collector on the railroad, was trying to worm his way into a better place and had managed, by adroit maneuvering, to move up several rows before he got an elbow in his belly and fell down. In the midst of the general laughter Mamadou Keïta was at last able to resume his interrupted speech.

'I did not say that I was against the strike. I said only that a decision of this importance has never before been taken here, and that we must think about it carefully. I am your oldest member, and I have never seen such a thing here. Your enthusiasm frightens me and makes we wish that Ibrahim Bakayoko was with us today. He knows how to speak to us, and all of us listen to him. Do you remember – the last time he spoke to us of strike-breakers . . .'

'We'll take care of traitors!'

Again it was Tiémoko who interrupted. His supporters rose with him from their bench. The Old One stopped speaking and bowed his head. Tiémoko looked like a wild animal preparing to charge, and Ad'jibid'ji regarded him breathlessly. She did not like Tiémoko, and now, in her heart, she could sense the birth of hatred for this man.

Someone, overcome by nausea, ran out of the hall with a hand clasped to his mouth. The heat was becoming unbearable.

Konaté, the secretary of the union, tried to intervene. 'Tiémoko, let the Old One speak, so that we can get to the vote . . .'

A voice from the courtyard stopped him. 'Hey, in there! You are late – some of us are already on strike!'

It was three of the locomotive workers who had just arrived, their clothes still covered with grease and coal dust. A frantic burst of applause rattled through the room. Arms were held out to them, and they were lifted up and carried through a window, to be stared at as if they had accomplished some miracle which was impossible to other humans. Pleased and proud, their faces creased with laughter, they drank in this adulation.

After that, no one could speak. A vote was taken, and the strike was called unanimously, for the next morning at dawn.

◆

Like the closing of the lid on a kettle, night covered the earth, but the heat remained. In the day it had burned down from above, searing the skull, and now it rose from the ground, seeped through cracks in the walls, and welled up from the terraces.

The hall was a long time in emptying, as the men still argued passionately among themselves. The kerosene lamps were lit, throwing faces shining with sweat into a smoky relief. The odor of kerosene mingled with that of steaming bodies. At last, however, they began to tire, and the crowd broke up into little groups, still talking and gesturing. The Old One made his way home, accompanied by Diara and Konaté, with Ad'jibid'ji trotting at their heels. They were silent, each one thinking his own thoughts. Occasionally Mamadou Keïta would turn around, and the child would say simply, 'I am here, Grandfather.'

In the sky a few stars shone. Suddenly, from very far away, the sound of drums broke through the night, beating out the rhythm of a Bambara dance. The three men separated at the square. Ad'jibid'ji took the hand of Mamadou Keïta and the old man and the little girl went into the house. Lying about on the straw matting, surrounded by all the children, the women were humming a song.

'God be praised, God be praised,' Niakoro said. 'We have heard no shooting.'

The old man echoed her gratitude in Arabic. '*Alhamdou Li lah*,' he said. 'There has been no shooting, and no fighting. This strike will not last. Two or three days at most.'

He sat down next to Niakoro.

Fatoumata brought in the supper and said, 'A blessing for your care.'

'And to you, wife, a blessing for your care. Has everyone had supper?'

'Everyone except yourself and Ad'jibid'ji.'

Fatoumata seated herself behind her husband, where she would remain throughout the meal, as a sign of courtesy. Mamadou Keïta and the child washed their hands.

'When will Ibrahim Bakayoko return?' Niakoro asked.

'Ah, God knows I cannot say! And you, child, do you know when your father will come back?'

Ad'jibid'ji withdrew her hand from the dish and finished what she was eating before replying. 'I do not know, Grandfather. He promised to write each week.'

'And he has not told you how long he thinks the strike will last?'

'No, Grandfather; but he did not seem to think it would be long, and I think he will be here for the time when the men go back.'

'*Perhaps Tiémoko knows something*,' the old man thought, and even as he ate he wondered.

'*Hi Allah*,' Niakoro said, seeming to read his thoughts, even in the darkness. 'Don't you believe that these children are making a mistake? How can you, a wise man, listen to the words of infants?'

'Niakoro,' the old man replied, 'even we old people must learn, and recognize that the things people know today were not born with us. No,

11

knowledge is not a hereditary thing. For months I have been learning that – and with regret, believe me.'

'*Vai!* Lies! Whatever a child knows a grown person knows better.'

'You do not work, Niakoro. You do not know that there are all sorts of new machines – and I do not know them either. But tomorrow, tomorrow, Niakoro – what do you know of tomorrow? At the union building, just now, if I had spoken the words you have just spoken they would have thrown me out.'

'And your white hairs? Of what use are they then?'

'Do not confuse respect with knowledge. Do you remember the old saying – "Before one has white hairs, one must first have them black"?'

'Bah,' old Niakoro said and relapsed again into silence.

When he had finished eating, Mamadou Keïta washed his hands and rendered thanks to Allah. He gave a portion of his cola nut to Niakoro and then said to Ad'jibid'ji, 'Child, you do not like Tiémoko?'

'No, Grandfather, I do not like him.'

'Why?'

'*What can I say to him?*' the child thought, as she washed her hands. '*How can I explain that to me he is a bully; that I didn't like the way he spoke; that even though he is a friend of father's . . .*'

'I just don't know, Grandfather.'

'And yet, he gets along well with your father, and you like to hear him sing.'

'I do like his voice,' the child said, hoping to cut off these questions. 'I would like to go to bed, Grandfather. Grandmother, I would like to go to bed.'

'Go, and pass the night in peace, and may you live to be older than your grandmother.'

'May everyone pass the night in peace.'

Ad'jibid'ji disappeared down the corridor, and the old people were left alone with their thoughts and their fears. The night no longer brought them rest. At the moment the eyes of the body closed, the eyes of the mind were opened. On the threshold of every dwelling place, people listened fearfully to the distant rhythm of the dance. In the darkness that enclosed the city the deep-toned drumming seemed now to come from everywhere at once, twisting and turning through the heads of those to whom sleep would not come.

THIÈS

The City

Hovels. A few rickety shacks, some upturned tombs, walls of bamboo or
millet stalks, iron barbs, and rotting fences. Thiès: a vast, uncertain plain
where all the rot of the city has gathered – stakes and crossties, locomotive
wheels, rusty shafts, knocked-in jerricans, old mattress springs, bruised
and lacerated sheets of steel. And then, a little farther on, on the goat path
that leads to the Bambara quarter, piles of old tin cans, heaps of excrement,
little mountains of broken pottery and cooking tools, dismantled railway
cars, skeletons of motors buried in the dust, and the tiny remains of cats,
of rats, of chickens, disputed by the birds. Thiès: in the midst of this
corruption, a few meager bushes – wild tomato, dwarf peppers, and okra
– whose pitiful fruits were harvested by the women. Bald-sided goats and
sheep, clotted with filth, came here to graze – to graze on what? – the air?
Constantly hungry, naked children, with sunken chests and swollen bellies,
argued with the vultures. Thiès: a place where everyone – man, woman,
and child – had a face the color of the earth.

Still a little farther on, at Dialav, there were houses made of wood.
Unsteady houses, shored up with beams or trunks of trees, ready to fall
down at the first gust of wind, but houses just the same. The roofs were
held together by stones and iron bars and old jugs filled with earth, and
the holes in the tarpaulin of the outhouses were plugged with rags and
cardboard, but they were houses.

Beyond this were the homes of the more fortunate, who had acquired
obsolete freight or passenger cars from the railway and mounted them on
crossties.

From Randoulène to the watchmen's barracks, from the outskirts of
Thiès to Dialav, the houses, the trees, and the land itself lay buried in a
thick coating of black dust spewed out by the locomotives. The maintenance and repair shops were located here, as well as the headquarters of
both the railroad company and the union. Every inhabitant of Thiès, no

matter who he was, depended on the railroad, and on the traffic between Koulikoro and Dakar.

SAMBA N'DOULOUGOU

One by one the stars faded into the light of morning, and the rising sun restored to objects their true outlines. The workmen rose early that morning. In truth, they had scarcely closed their eyes. The night before they had made a decision, and today they must abide by it, but there was not one of them who did not experience a feeling of uneasiness, a void in the pit of his stomach.

The first ones to go out pushed through the hedges and rapped lightly against a neighboring wall of wood or zinc, to be answered by a voice still heavy with sleep, and then another man would leave his house. Like a column of military ants they invaded the paths and streets, shaking hands with each other as they met, exchanging meaningless greetings. Little by little, the jangling of bicycle bells and the sputter of motor scooters roused them from their torpor, but they spoke hardly at all. Even the young men, usually noisy and exuberant, were silent; and what laughter there was was forced. No one dared ask the question that burned on all their lips – 'What do you think of the strike?' – because no one would have dared to answer.

When they came to the grade crossing they stopped, and Boubacar, who was one of the ironworkers, said, 'Look – here comes "the station gazette."'

Approaching them, at the head of a little group of men, was Samba N'Doulougou, who was known to everyone as a regular walking newspaper. He was a curious little man, and ordinarily the sight of him was enough to cause laughter among the others. He dressed always in old American khakis, with the shirt hanging out over the pants, and the pants, which were much too long, falling in pleats around his sandals. He tugged constantly at an old cap with a broken visor.

'I don't see why you are hesitating,' he said, speaking to all the uneasy faces he saw before him. 'Last night was the time to give your opinion. It's too late to turn back now.'

It was Bachirou, 'the bureaucrat', a man who worked on the office staff of the railway, who answered. 'Perhaps the night has made us wiser. We must look at things squarely; our union is still not very strong, and perhaps we have not examined all the consequences of a strike.'

'What do you mean? Everything was examined, studied, and discussed last night! Look at things squarely, you say? Very well – squarely in front

14

of us are the workshops. If you are afraid of blood you cannot be a butcher, but without butchers there would be no meat.'

'That's a lot of nonsense!'

'And what you are saying is not?' Samba was growing angry. A crowd had gathered around the two men, listening, knowing that this argument between two of their own number was an expression of their own troubled thoughts. 'What you are saying is not nonsense? Then you should have said it last night, and not this morning – but last night you were not there. And why? I will tell you why – because you work in their office, and you think you are one of them. You go everywhere, saying, "I am part of the office staff." That is why you want this strike to fail.'

'So you've been spying on me! If I didn't come last night it was because . . .'

'Listen, Bachirou. At heart, you are not even happy with yourself – you keep wondering where you really belong. With the workers? The bosses will get rid of you. With the bosses? Then you would be a foreigner to us. And in this strike that is what you are – you are more of a foreigner than *Monsieur le directeur* himself!'

In this way the discussion went on until the group of men had arrived at the market place. The air had grown very still. In the east the sun was climbing the slope of the sky.

The market place covered all of the station plaza, the square at the grade crossing, and the Place Aly N'Guer. A constant, hive-like buzzing and the clouds of powdery dust greeted everyone who entered the area. Almost anything could be found here: bread in whole loaves or portions; local pastries, and sugar, in crystals or in powder; cigarettes of every make, in packages or separately; smoking tobacco as well as snuff; even flints, and cigarette lighters made by the machinists in the railway shops.

On the Place Aly N'Guer were the stalls of the women who sold foodstuffs. Standing behind their counters, neatly dressed, they called out to the passers-by, trying to tempt them with the variety of their offerings: papayas, earthnuts, and fritters of all kinds; fish or meat balls; sweet potatoes, fried or raw; steaming porridges of maize and of millet; rootstocks of cassava, roasted in hot ashes or cooked in sauce like kidney beans and served to the customer in bowls. It could all be bought on credit – 'on the back of the month', as the saying went.

And everywhere swarmed the market's most numerous denizens – the beggars and the flies. There were beggars of every age, crying their misery aloud, while the great, blue-green flies floated between the dishes on the foodstalls and the sores on the faces and limbs of the beggars. If they were brushed away they simply went elsewhere, moving in small, black clouds.

Dieynaba had set up her stand a little apart from the market proper, on the corner nearest the workshops. Seated on her bench, her legs stretched out comfortably, she was smoking a long clay pipe and studying the crowd through half-closed eyes. On the stand before her was an enormous gourd filled with porridge. To her right there was a pile of smaller gourds, and to her left a bowl in which spoons were soaking in a bubbling, blackish water. Dieynaba never solicited customers, as the other women did, but simply waited for them to come to her, puffing calmly at her pipe, wreathed in a cloud of smoke. When one of the workmen came up, she would rise to serve him, and as he ate she would scratch out his name on her list and then go back to waiting.

Dieynaba's neighbor was Maïmouna, and the two women got along well. Maïmouna was blind, but this is not to say that she was pitiable. Far from it. She held her splendid, smooth-skinned body like some goddess of the night, her head high, her vacant glance seeming to contemplate an area above people, beyond the world. Seated now, with her legs crossed, she had opened a threadbare cotton blouse and was nursing one of her twins. The other, held between her thighs, made little paddling motions with its arms, trying to reach her. No one knew anything about Maïmouna, except that she was blind, but everyone liked to hear her sing, and throughout the day there would be people who had stopped to listen. On this morning she was singing the legend of Goumba N'Diaye, the woman who had measured her strength against that of men, before she lost her sight. The rhythms of the old chant could be heard above the noise of the crowd.

Samba N'Doulougou came up, followed by his little band of workmen.

'You are late, Samba,' Dieynaba said. 'The smelters and the iron-workers have already been here. Here, take the list and see the names I have marked.'

Samba took the list, and as Dieynaba filled gourds for the others he wrote down their names.

'You seem to be scratching out more than you are writing,' said Bachirou. There were beady grains of porridge dripping down his chin.

'They have names that could derail a train.'

'Do you want me to take your place?' asked Boubacar, pretending to reach for the pencil.

'You? No one would be able to read it,' Samba replied, knowing very well that Boubacar could neither read nor write. 'Ah, there's Magatte! Come here, my boy, and rescue an old man.'

16

For a moment Samba watched the boy, whose wrist seemed hardly to move as he wrote, and then, as the others began to discuss the strike again, he walked over toward Maïmouna.

The whole body of the blind woman stiffened, her normally gentle features contracted, and hot tears seemed to well in the naked cavities of her eyes.

'Don't touch the children,' she said softly.

Samba, who had not opened his mouth, drew back. Dieynaba had watched the fleeting little drama with astonishment, but she said nothing. Like everyone else, she had no idea who was the father of the twins.

◆

When they had finished eating, the men began to gather in front of the gate, and soon there was a tangle of bicycles and motor scooters leaning against the fence that surrounded the yards. On a normal day they would have gone quickly to their respective shops, but today they just hung about at the entrance. They were all there – the men who worked on the trains themselves and the laborers from the marshaling yards, the switchmen and the office workers – those who should have been on duty and those who were not.

The great gate was open, but in the main court there was just one man. Leaning heavily on his cane, Sounkaré, the head watchman, surveyed the crowd with an expression of astonishment on his face and then made his way, in his awkward, crab-like gait, toward a group of the old men, who were standing by themselves.

'This is strange,' he said, after greeting them.

'Very strange, indeed,' Bakary replied, between two fits of coughing. 'But soon we will know what is going to happen.'

Bakary was tuberculous, and no one who saw him could have failed to know it. The years behind the firebox of the trains had turned the skin of his face to gray and covered it with tough film, like callus.

'So they are not going to work?' the watchman muttered. 'They have short memories, these children! But you . . .' he turned to the group of old men. 'Surely you will not follow them?'

'That's just what we were talking about. Some of them came to see us this morning, to ask if we agreed with their demands.'

'What demands?' asked Sounkaré. 'I have demanded nothing.' He paused and laughed. 'But then, I don't have much longer to live.'

'You are not as ill as I am, Sounkaré,' Bakary said. 'The sickness in my chest will be with me always. I thought they were talking just about

17

salaries, but I went to their meetings, and I found that they were talking about a pension, too – a pension that would affect us, and not just the young ones. Look around you . . .' he coughed and turned his head to spit a little ball of black phlegm into the dust. 'Look around you. There are not very many of us any more. Where are all the others – Aliou Samba, and Abdoulaye, and Coulibaly, and the Davids who came from the island of Gorée – they had no pension, and now they are dead. Soon it will be our turn, and what are we to live on? And the fathers of the white men, the ones who taught us our trade – the Edouards and the Henris and the Delacollines – where are they? They are living at home again, and they have their pensions. Why should we not have this pension, too? That is what the young ones are asking.'

'Ha! I can see that these children have led you astray. God in His wisdom may help you, Bakary, but the *toubabs* may refuse. From here to Koulikoro, everything that moves belongs to them. Even our lives belong to them.'

'Don't mix religion in this. Perhaps it is true that it is the will of God, but we must live. And it is not written, "God loves to help him who strives to help himself"!'

A new fit of coughing racked Bakary, and he was forced to stop. He squatted on the ground, hands pressed against his temples, looking like a little old toad.

At this moment Boubacar, the ironworker, came over to greet the old men.

'Is it true, Boubacar, that you are not going to work today?' the watchman asked.

'Don't you see, *père* Sounkaré, that no one has passed through your gate?'

'But if you aren't going to work, why did you come here?'

The question was unexpected, and it perplexed the old men as much as it did Boubacar.

And then the waiting began; a long wait, broken into minutes, into seconds. The words that had been spoken were spoken again, and all the words that had been heard were pondered and studied again. Little by little, anxiety came, and a fear that settled heavily in their stomachs. It was a fear not unmixed with an ill-defined hope, the sort of hope a man who does not believe in God might place in divine intervention. As the time ran on they became a prey to the minutes and the seconds, and the great gate, standing open before them, seemed to be waiting, too.

The intolerable silence was broken by Bachirou, 'the bureaucrat'. He was wearing a white linen suit, which fitted badly over a crooked left shoulder. The pockets sagged beneath the constant weight of his hands.

'When you think about it,' he said, 'the thing has been badly done. We should never have started a strike in the middle of the month.'

'That is true,' said one of the workmen, whose name was Sow. 'I cannot even pay my debts. I have been ill, and already I owe all of my salary for four months. This is not the time to start a strike.'

'That is a special case, a personal thing; but what of the rest of us? Where does it get us?'

A man who was sitting on a motorcycle spoke up. 'Last night we were lucky that the soldiers didn't interfere, but now the whole place will be surrounded, and there is sure to be fighting.'

In the midst of this uneasiness, of these doubts and conflicting questions, Samba N'Doulougou moved from group to group, rallying those who were undecided, rebuking the defectors. He deserved the nickname of 'station gazette;' he knew everyone, and he had the latest news on everything.

He rejoined Boubacar in front of the gate. The enormous smith and the little carpenter were old friends.

'I can smell out the cowards a hundred meters off,' he said. 'It's too bad Bakayoko isn't here; if he were, they wouldn't talk like that! I'd like to crack their stupid skulls for them!' He waved a tiny fist, and the giant Boubacar laughed.

Not far from where they stood, Bachirou was going on with his harangue. 'Suppose they refuse everything: the pay raise, the pensions, the auxiliary workmen, everything? What can we do? It would be madness to go on – it would just be stupidity!'

Samba hitched up his pants and tugged at the visor of his cap. 'Why are you trying to discourage them, Bachirou? Because you are on the staff, and the idea of any of the rest of us being on it, too, is enough to make you piss in your pants? Because you're jealous of everyone, and think only about yourself? Sow – you were sick, weren't you? And who gave you money when you needed it? Bachirou, your boss? Do you know what he did when Gaye and Lahbib were on the night shift? He made them pay a kickback to him, on their overtime! He only hands out money when there's a collection for a death, because everyone would know if he didn't. This is our first strike, and we're going through with it! Bachirou is a coward!'

'Me, a coward! No! But don't forget about 1938. Let's wait for the delegates . . .'

It was Boubacar who interrupted now. 'We have thought about 1938, but that was before the war! If you ever came to the union meetings you would know that we had talked about it, and we know everything that happened.' The blacksmith's voice was harsh. Without quite knowing why, he hated Bachirou from the bottom of his heart – hated his posturing and his obsequious manners.

'We have to hang on,' Samba said. 'We have to know what we want, and we have to stand together.'

'And we ought to pull up our pants!' Bachirou laughed.

Samba refused to be annoyed by the joke. 'Bakayoko has told us: "It isn't those who are taken by force, put in chains and sold as slaves who are the real slaves: it is those who will accept it, morally and physically."'

'Oh yes, I know. "The Bambara" is a great one for theory, but we've got to be practical, too. He goes around making speeches, but where is he now?' Bachirou looked at Boubacar. 'It doesn't matter to me, though. I don't belong to the lowest classes.'

'And you think that I do? I am a smith, by birth and by trade; and even if my parents did have to accept a menial place, that doesn't mean that I will be anyone's slave.'

'Oh, forget it,' Samba said. 'Can't you see that this pen pusher is afraid?'

'You're both out to get me,' Bachirou said.

Boubacar thrust his great body toward him. 'If you ever try anything, I'll kill you!'

◆

But at that moment a noise which they had all noticed a moment earlier grew suddenly louder, and every head turned to watch, putting an end to the quarrel. With a rhythmic thudding of boots and a clash of metal, a troop of soldiers was marching in from the highway. Above the ordered ranks of men the steel of bayonets flashed, reflecting the rays of the sun, like some great, upended harrowing machine; and the workmen's eyes were caught by the gleaming movement. In the market place, before the workshops, and in the streets, all other noise had ceased. The shopkeepers hastily gathered together their merchandise, without bothering about what they left behind, and even the beggars had vanished. Bakary withdrew into the crowd, and Magatte, the apprentice, began herding the other young men toward the grade crossing. Only Maïmouna, the prisoner of her infirmity, queen of her shadowy realm, had not moved. She was singing a new verse in the legend of Goumba N'Diaye:

20

'I have come to take a wife,' the stranger said.
'My bridegroom must be stronger than I,
There are my father's fields,
And there are the abandoned scythes,'
                    replied Goumba N'Diaye.
And the stranger took up a scythe.
Two days each week, and still they came not to the end,
But the man could not vanquish the girl.

In the midst of the abruptly silent crowd, only the voice of Maïmouna was still heard, muting the sounds of spiked boots and the shuffling of naked feet. The men were going round in circles, huddling together like frightened animals being led into a trap. With their weapons held ready, the soldiers spread out in a thin line, stationing themselves between the fence and the crowd of workers.

'There are the delegates!' cried Bachirou suddenly, as if even he had been hoping for the arrival of some savior.

At the sight of their own leaders, the crowd seemed to forget its anxiety, the tense faces relaxed, and the closed fists opened. As one man, the workers rushed to greet the seven newcomers, holding out their hands to them, frenziedly.

Doudou, the secretary-general, was preparing to make some kind of an announcement, but his voice was suddenly drowned out by the shrieking of the siren, and immediately the anxiety returned: sweat ran down their faces and oozed in the hollow of their hands, their eyes went dull, their thick-lipped mouths hung open. The first blast of the siren seemed longer than usual. The silence gripped them again; a silence which rendered movement, and even thought, impossible.

The great entrance gate still stood open, but no one moved toward it. When the siren screamed again, a shudder went through the crowd. The sound seemed to enter into their bodies, to mingle with their blood. For as long as they could remember, that sound had meant obedience. As children they had seen their fathers, and even their grandfathers, begin to run when they heard it call. It had always told them when to leave their houses, and to walk up here and pass through the gate, and it had punctuated their working day.

Sounkaré, the lame watchman, went back into the courtyard and disappeared. Bakary was not even coughing any longer, as if his illness had suddenly left him. Bachirou, the hesitant; Boubacar, the smith; and Doudou himself remained silent. Magatte and the other apprentices studied the supply of pebbles they had gathered together between the rails. But Maïmouna, the mother of children without a father, continued to sing:

> For two moons they cleared the land,
> And neither the stranger nor Goumba N'Diaye
> Would confess to being vanquished.
> Beat on all the drums!
> 'Stranger,' demanded Goumba N'Diaye,
> 'From what country do you come?'
> And the stranger replied, 'I am from every country.
> I am a man like every man.'
> 'It is not true,' said Goumba N'Diaye.
> 'For many seasons, men have fled from me.
> Men are not alike.'

And while Maïmouna sang thus, in praise of living, one of the twins left her lap and began to crawl toward the bicycles.

◆

It was Samba N'Doulougou – a difficult name to remember, but more difficult still to forget – who was the first to recover. Jumping up onto Boubacar's shoulders, he cried out, 'Hurrah for the strike!' – and then, perched on his friend's back, he began shouting to the crowd in Bambara.

That was when the soldiers charged.

The battle was joined in an instant, and with every available weapon: the butt ends of muskets, the tips of bayonets, the soles of heavy boots, and tear-gas bombs. Cries of rage, of pain, and of fear mingled in single clamor, rising to the morning sky. The crowd fell back, breaking into terrified segments, then regrouped, wavered, and fell back again. Dieynaba had rallied the women of the market place, and like a band of Amazons they came to the rescue, armed with clubs, with iron bars, and bottles. From the grade crossing, Magatte and the apprentices had opened up a regular barrage of pebbles. Everything that could be picked up was flying through the air. The officer in command of the detachment of soldiers had lost his helmet, and his forehead was bleeding. One soldier had been caught by a group of workers, and his screams could be heard above the tumult. In the market place itself, not a single stall remained standing; the conflict was everywhere at once.

Maïmouna no longer sang. The twin which had escaped from her lap was playing with the spokes of a bicycle wheel, when a fleeing man seized the handle bar and tried to pull the machine away. The child screamed, and the man dropped the bicycle, which fell across the baby's body. At this moment Bachirou came running up, pursued by some militiamen. He cleared the bicycle with a single leap, but the heavy boots of the soldiers came down on the frame and the rear wheel, whose axle rested squarely on the child's head. With a little cry, like that of a wounded animal, the wailing stopped.

Holding the second baby in one arm, and with her other hand stretched out before her, Maïmouna heard the cry, but just as she did she was knocked from her feet by a running man. She fell forward, clutching the child against her breast, and stayed there, on hands and knees, her arched back forming a shield, her head moving swiftly from left to right, like an animal seized by panic.

Farther on, two soldiers had driven Demba, the smelter, up against the fence and were raining blows of their rifles and bayonets on his head and abdomen. In his flight, Bachirou collided with Dieynaba.

'Where are you going, coward?' she said, handing him a rock to throw; but he just stammered something and ran off again.

From the height of the roadbed at the grade crossing, Magatte and the apprentices were still launching salvos of stones. The riot had spread through all of Thiès. Other men had come from the market to help the workers, but more armed men had also arrived, from the airfield and the watchmen's barracks. Finally, toward the middle of the morning, the conflict stopped, but not the turmoil. The strikers held the market place, the grade crossing, the station square, and the fringes of the marshaling yards, but the station and the workshops themselves were guarded by soldiers, ready to shoot. The noisy mass of people was so dense that carts and automobiles were forced to detour around the center of the city and rejoin the highway farther on.

THIÈS

Maïmouna

The directors of the union had set up their headquarters in the office of the works inspector, a single room in which the confusion was now so great that it frightened them a little. Everyone was there – at least everyone who had not been too badly injured in the clash with the soldiers. Samba N'Doulougou was recounting his own version of the troops' assault and demonstrating graphically how he had seized a tear-gas grenade from one the soldiers and hurled it back at the same man a moment later. A ribbon of slowly congealing blood trickled around Boubacar's right ear and ran down his neck, but he was watching his friend's performance delightedly. Old Bakary, the eldest of them all, was there, too, and he was completely exhausted. His eyes were bruised and swollen, he coughed constantly, and with each new spasm tears mingled in the film of sweat that masked his face.

Doudou, the secretary-general, was talking distractedly with his assistant, Lahbib. Doudou was uneasy. His wide-set, deep brown eyes wandered over the faces before him, and then his attention passed to the scene outside the window; the courtyard and roofs of the workshops, the great chimneys, the silvery gleam of the railroad tracks, the miserable huts, and the groups of workers arguing in the shade of the trees. Doudou knew that he should speak to them, but nothing in the landscape or the sight of the men themselves encouraged him. Fear slumbered in his breast, like a tightly coiled serpent, and he was afraid of awakening it.

His thoughts carried him away from the little room and the hubbub of voices, back to the time several years ago, just after the war, when everything was rationed and hunger was everywhere. It was at that time that the employees of the company put forth their first demands, and there was talk of forming a union. Doudou, Lahbib, and Bakayoko, who was the most popular of the trainmen, were the founders of the movement, and because his work as a fitter and lathe operator kept him always in one place Doudou had been named secretary-general. From the very first the

24

directors of the company had opposed the formation of the union, and when the unanimous pressure of the workers had brought it into being they refused to recognize it. Doudou remembered all of this very clearly. He also remembered that there had never been any money in the treasury, because no one ever paid his dues ... At last, though, all of the work of organization had been completed, and the machinery for operation of the union had been set up. Now it only remained to be seen how it would function. And it was precisely this of which Doudou was afraid.

Coming out of his reverie, he glanced at Lahbib, who was standing beside him, chewing thoughtfully at his moustache. In the first row of the men before him, motionless as a block of coal, was the enormous smith, Boubacar, and next to him Samba, who was still talking.

'Yes, my friends, the ninth of October, 1947, is a day that will be celebrated in the history of the movement ...'

'The tenth of October,' Bachirou interrupted.

Samba N'Doulougou studied the 'bureaucrat's' bandaged forehead. 'Have you had a meeting with *Monsieur le directeur*, Bachirou, or are you just coming back from Mecca?'

'We have better things to do than listen to your jabbering,' Bachirou said.

'Yes, and stop jumping around like a bean in a stew pot,' said Gaye, whose right arm was in a sling.

'The men are waiting,' Lahbib said, nudging Doudou.

The latter rose slowly to his feet. 'I think it would be best to hold a meeting tomorrow, as we originally planned,' he said. 'For today at least it is clear that the management is not ready to give in ...' He paused for a moment. 'And tonight the men must go to their homes peacefully. I can see soldiers and watchmen from here, and there are others. Stay away from them. And by the way – how many were wounded or killed?'

It was Gaye who answered, unfolding a sheet of paper. 'The dead? There is Badara, the smelter, and ...'

'No, Gaye, no names,' Doudou interrupted, frowning.

'Well, then, there are eight dead, and a quantity of wounded – men, women, and some of the apprentices.'

'Tomorrow, after the funeral services,' Doudou said, 'we will hold a general meeting. Tonight, you, Lahbib, and the elders will come with me to see the widows. Is there any news from the other stations?'

'Nothing, except that there was also some fighting at Dakar.'

'Papa Bakary, have you had any news from your nephew?'

'Before leaving Bamako he wrote that he was coming here, but the other day a kinsman who arrived from down there told me that he was no longer there. And now that there are no more trains only God knows when we will see Ibrahim Bakayoko!'

'We will wait for him,' Doudou said. 'But, for the time being, we must organize a permanent watch, beginning tonight. Samba, you and Boubacar will be on guard, with Lahbib. The strike committee will meet here tomorrow morning at six o'clock. Now let me pass, so I can make the announcement to the men.'

A few minutes later the workers began to disperse and go home, each one carrying within himself an echo of the tumult that had risen from the black dust of Thiès.

◆

As soon as calm had returned to the market place, Maïmouna, the blind woman, began groping her way about in search of her child, not knowing that the little body had been carried away when the dead and wounded were gathered up. She had been beaten, pushed, and trampled until her body was bruised and stiff in every joint. Her clothes were in shreds: the cotton blouse, ripped in two, was held together only at the neck; from her naked breast little drops of red trickled down to the knot which fastened the cloth around her waist, and the cloth itself was split up the front above her knees. The handkerchief was gone from her head, and her short-cut hair was as tangled as a grain field after a storm. She clutched the second twin close against her breast and bent her head from time to time to listen for its irregular breathing. As she tried to make her way forward, she stumbled constantly over the wreckage of the market stalls. She could hear the soldiers talking, and from their accent she knew that they had been brought in from another district. Staggering as though she were drunk, she managed at last to get out of the market place and took the road to Thivaouane. Quite suddenly then, she sensed that someone was watching her.

'It's all right – you can come out!' cried a young, strong voice. 'It's not one of the soldiers!' It was Magatte, the apprentice, who had just seen the blind woman. The apprentices were playing at being soldiers, along the sides of the ravine, and Magatte was their chief.

'Where are you going, Maïmouna?' he demanded, in the tone of his role in the game.

'Ah, it's you – I recognize your voice! You are from the workshops.'

26

'That's right. I'm the apprentice of Doudou, the secretary-general of the strike,' Magatte replied, surveying his comrades proudly.

'I want to go to Dieynaba's house . . . Do you know Dieynaba?'

'Do I know Dieynaba? Everyone knows Dieynaba! Corporal Gorgui!' Magatte called.

One of the youngsters came forward. 'Yes, *seneral*?'

'Don't say *seneral*! The word is general!'

'Yes, general,' Gorgui said, detaching the syllables carefully. He was standing at attention, holding back his head. The top of it had been painted blue, because of a bad case of ringworm.

'I have a mission for you. You are to conduct Maïmouna to your mother's house. And don't fall into the hands of the enemy! Understood? In two hours we are going to attack!' Magatte tapped at his wrist, as if he had been wearing a watch.

'Very well, *seneral*,' Gorgui said.

'General!' Magatte repeated.

'Please, my children, hurry,' Maïmouna pleaded. And to herself she added, 'I no longer know even where I am.'

'Don't attack before I get back,' Gorgui said, tugging at a strip of the blind woman's blouse.

◆

Dieynaba lived just outside of the city, in a cabin hidden at the edge of the woods. From a distance it could not be seen, since it was completely surrounded by a hedge of millet stalks. As soon as she returned from the market, Dieynaba had transformed the house into an infirmary. She had torn up every piece of material she could lay her hands on and was bathing the wounded with salted water. Mariame Sonko was helping her.

'Go empty this water in the sump,' Dieynaba said, 'and bring back some fresh. Fetch some plantain leaves, too, but put lots of salt in the water before you soak the leaves.'

It was just as she was saying this that Gorgui appeared on the summit of the little ridge that sheltered the house, leading the blind woman.

'What am I seeing?' Dieynaba cried. 'God forgive me, I had forgotten Maïmouna! Come here! Everyone come here!' Even as the words came out she was running toward the blind woman. 'What have I done? How could I have deserted you down there? Gorgui! Go back to your friends!'

With infinite gentleness, almost ceremonially, she helped the blind woman into the house; and from Maïmouna's ceaseless, disjointed mur-

murings she learned that the other twin had been left in the market place. Dumbfounded, the others simply stared at the blind woman, as though she had been the solitary victim of the battle. Dieynaba finally made her sit down, on the blackened bottom of an old stone cooking vessel.

'Give me the child,' she said.

Tears welled in the blind woman's eyes. 'I cannot,' she said. 'I don't want to.'

'I know you don't want to, Maïmouna, but give her to me just the same. Can't you see that you are bleeding . . . Oh God, I don't even know what I am saying! You are bleeding, do you hear me? I have to wash off the dirt, and I have to see if the child is injured.'

Mariame Sonko came into the room, carrying a bowl of water in which leaves were floating.

'Gorgui!' Dieynaba called. 'Gorgui! Where is that little devil? There's a strike on . . . no one is working. He should be here!'

'But you told him yourself to go back to his friends,' Mariame said.

'Men!' Dieynaba said. 'Whenever you need them they are nowhere around. Put that down here, and go into my room and bring me my old red and yellow blouse, and the checked waistcloth.'

'Don't get so excited, Dieynaba,' Mariame said. 'If you had stayed calm, everything would already be done.'

'Me, excited? You don't know what you're talking about, Mariame. Now come and help me, all of you; and you, Maïmouna, give me the child, or I will take her from you.'

Maïmouna knew that this time Dieynaba meant what she said and allowed her to take the child. Dieynaba handed the baby to one of the other women and began herself to bathe the cuts and bruises of the blind woman.

◆

The office of Monsieur Dejean, the regional director of the railway company, was on the second floor of the company's administration building. It was a spacious room, with cream-colored walls hung with large framed photographs. The six windows opened out to a view of the warehouse and the workshops. From the ceiling hung a big-bladed, slowly turning fan, and in one corner of the room, on a table, there was a scale model of the whole railway network, complete to a miniature train.

Dejean was walking aimlessly from one end of the office to the other, first clasping his hands behind his back and then digging them into his pockets. He was a stocky little man, completely bald, with a sloping, sharp-featured skull. Thick-lensed, concave glasses sat firmly astride his stubby nose. On his left lapel was the thin, red ribbon of the Legion of Honor.

Twenty years before, Dejean had been an ambitious clerk, who arrived in the colony with the intention of making his fortune in the shortest possible time. He had climbed the first rungs of the ladder very quickly, and there had even been a time when he dreamed of founding his own company. At that time there were few Europeans who remained long in the colony, but Dejean had returned home only twice, and his longest absence – it was for his wedding – was less than two months. In addition to all this, he was reliable, and he didn't drink. In 1938, when he was deputy chief clerk, the metalworkers in the shops had made their first attempt at a strike. Dejean had crushed the disturbance almost immediately and as a reward he had been named chief clerk. Then the Second World War had come, and the German occupation of France, and the colony, like France itself, was divided into two camps. When the representatives of the Vichy government took control of the railway, the regional director had simply disappeared. He was not a *Pétainist*. Dejean had replaced him, and he had held the position ever since.

An unreasoning anger stirred in him now, as he walked back and forth, like a bear in a cage. That very morning he had refused to see the representatives of the workers. He knew that among them were the sons of the same men whose movement he had crushed nine years before, and he had no intention of yielding now. It was not a question of agreement or disagreement. First they must go back to work; that was all there was to it.

The sound of the telephone rang out in the empty office, and Dejean ran to his desk, sank into the leather armchair, and took up the receiver.

'Hello, hello . . . yes, speaking . . . No, they haven't gone back yet. . . . No, I won't see them today, or tomorrow either . . . What are they asking? A raise in the pay scale, four thousand auxiliary workmen, family allowances, and a pension plan! . . . I'm sorry, I don't think I heard you . . . Give family allowances to these people? The minute they have some money they go out and buy themselves another wife, and the children multiply like flies! . . . Oh no, I assure you . . .'

Dejean's voice was deferential. It was obvious that he was talking to someone of importance. 'The soldiers? Yes, they are here . . . Wounded? There are some, but at the moment I can't tell you exactly how many . . . Dead? No, there are no dead. The soldiers have been ordered just to

frighten them . . . Reinforce the troop? Yes, that's a good idea – thank you
. . . I'll take care of the natives . . . Thank you, I'm grateful for your
confidence; and don't worry, it will be just like the last time . . . If they
persist? In that case, we have a powerful ally – hunger . . . I'm waiting for
my assistants now. I sent them out to see what is happening, and then we
will make our plans . . . I beg your pardon?. . . But I know them, I assure
you, they are children. Twenty years out here – I've had experience with
them . . . Yes, you are right, there must be a few fanatics behind it – men
who have worked them up and are using them for their own purposes. But
they are all alike; they're more interested in titles than in money. I know
my Africans; they're all rotten with pride . . . Right, I'll call you tomorrow
at the same time. And don't worry, it won't go beyond this district . . .
Yes, of course, and thanks again for your confidence . . . Remember me to
Madame. As soon as this is over we must get together and go tuna fishing
again . . . Thanks again.'

Dejean hung up and leaned back in his chair, staring up at a rectangle
of sky visible through one of the windows. He could hear the pacing of
the sentinels on guard outside the building, their heavy tread muffled by
distance and the murmur of the fan. In the garden a watchman was
watering the lawn. A miniature rainbow floated above the spray from the
hose. The sun was descending toward the horizon, slowly, as if it regretted
being forced to leave the peaceful spectacle of the white villas and flower
gardens of the residential quarter, and the pink-cheeked children playing
on the steps of the verandas.

Dejean wiped off his glasses and was reaching across his desk to take up
a file when someone knocked on the door.

'Come in,' he called, adopting once again the sharp tone of a man who
is completely sure of himself.

Three men came in, one behind the other: Victor, Dejean's chief
assistant, Isnard, the director of the repair shop, an 'old hand' in the
colonies, and Leblanc.

'Sit down, gentlemen,' Dejean said, playing with a penholder, 'and tell
me the news.'

'There's nothing really new,' said Victor, 'except that we are sure now
that Doudou is the one who is behind it. But they don't seem to be paying
him.'

'Whether they pay him or not is their business; I don't give a damn!'
Dejean said sharply.

Victor went on as though he hadn't heard him. 'They have installed
their headquarters in the inspection office. There is a second ring-leader –

the most important one, perhaps – Bakayoko, the conductor. He is their orator. He travels up and down the line, making speeches to the men. Right now he is at Kayes . . .'

'Gentlemen, I had Dakar on the phone just a few minutes ago. They will support us in whatever we do, but we must make sure that this business doesn't drag on. I need every bit of information possible. I know the natives here. In just a few days there will be some who want to go back to work. Perhaps even sooner. But we have to start planning right now the measures to be taken if it should go on. The first is simple: cutting off the most necessary provisions – rice, millet, maize. The shopkeepers must be told. As for you, gentlemen, I want information; I want every scrap of information you can get.'

It was Leblanc, the youngest of them, who answered. 'I was told that a good many of the natives didn't approve of this strike, but that this Doudou and Lahbib and Bakayoko are honest men, and they trust them.'

At these words Dejean was seized by a fit of anger so intense that his face turned a bright purple. 'Honest! Leblanc, you make me laugh! You're just a youngster out here. You can buy every one of these Negroes! Do you hear me? Any of them, and all of them!'

Leblanc slid down in his chair, like a child who is caught in a mistake and hopes that the storm will pass if he can make himself small enough.

'And you, Isnard?' Dejean demanded, still angrily. 'You know something about them – what do you think?'

Isnard squared his shoulders. His bush jacket, left open at the front, exposed a neck reddened by the sun to the color of brick, and on his chest and forearms was a thick matting of reddish hair. Isnard was the subject of a legend in the colony, and he nourished it carefully. In the first place he was one of the few of the 'old hands', but in addition to this he had had an experience which every newcomer learned about almost before he was off the ship. One night someone had knocked at his door, and when he opened it he found a Negro woman on the point of giving birth on his threshold. There was no doctor available at that time for such a case – the thing was usually handled by native midwives – and the woman had not enough time left even to return to her own home. Isnard had taken her in and helped her: he had cut the umbilical cord with his teeth and then had bathed the baby and cared for the woman. He invariably concluded his account of this experience with the statement that 'both mother and child are doing well!'

'To my way of thinking,' he said, uncrossing his legs and leaning forward deliberately, 'we can't reason now the way we did in '38. There's

31

a good deal in what they are saying – and moreover, the line is very long, and they have a good start on us. We must act carefully . . .'

'And give in to their demands?' Dejean said dryly.

'No, of course not, but avoid any rough stuff. We can either buy off the most important leaders – for a price, in return, of course – or work on some of the others and try to build up a rival union.'

'Buying off the leaders would be simpler,' Victor said.

'I don't think so,' Dejean said. 'The second plan is better – and it also has the big advantage of looking to the future. Isnard, do you know anyone you could contact about this second union?'

'I've already been working on two of them. It wouldn't surprise me if they went along with us.'

'Good, get on with it. Now, one other thing: how many wounded were there, among the troops and the watchmen?'

'Six, including two officers and two native ratings. A third officer is dead.'

'The savages! Victor, I want you to telephone to the other stations and tell them they are to do nothing at all until they receive further orders. As for you, Isnard, see those two contacts again as soon as possible, and get them to work! Now, gentlemen, if you will excuse me, I have work to do myself.'

As soon as the door had closed behind the three men, Dejean picked up the telephone. 'Get me Dakar,' he said.

◆

Slowly, the sun went down, and blue-black shadows lengthened across the motionless locomotives and railway cars, the silent workshops and yards, the white villas and the mud-walled houses, the sheds and the hovels. From somewhere in the watchmen's barracks came the call of a bugle.

And so the strike came to Thiès. An unlimited strike, which, for many, along the whole length of the railroad, was a time for suffering, but for many was also a time for thought. When the smoke from the trains no longer drifted above the savanna, they realized that an age had ended – an age their elders had told them about, when all of Africa was just a garden for food. Now the machine ruled over their lands, and when they forced every machine within a thousand miles to halt they became conscious of their strength, but conscious also of their dependence. They began to understand that the machine was making of them a whole new breed of

32

men. It did not belong to them; it was they who belonged to it. When it stopped, it taught them that lesson.

The days passed, and the nights. There was no news, except what every passing hour brought to every home, and that was always the same: the foodstuffs were gone, the meager savings eaten up, and there was no money in the house. They could go and ask for credit, but they knew what the storekeeper would say. 'You already owe me this much, and as it is I won't have enough to pay my own bills. Why don't you do as they say? Why don't you go back to work?'

Then they would have to fall back once more on the machine and carry off the motor scooters and the bicycles and the watches to a moneylender. After that it was the turn of whatever jewelry there was, and of any clothing of value, the ceremonial tunics that were worn only on important occasions. Hunger set in; and men, women, and children grew thinner. But they held on. Meetings were held more frequently, the directors of the union intensified their activities, and everyone swore not to give in.

The days passed, and the nights. And then, to everyone's surprise, the trains began to run again. The locomotives were driven by mechanics brought from Europe, and soldiers and sailors became station masters and trainmen. The big, gardenlike squares before the stations became fortresses, surrounded by barbed wire and guarded by sentinels, night and day. And after the hunger, fear set in.

Among the strikers, it was a formless thing; a further astonishment at the forces they had set in motion, and an uncertainty as to how they should be nourished – with hope, or with resignation. Among the whites, it was a simple obsession with numbers. How could such a small minority feel safe in the midst of these sullen masses? Those few members of the two races who had had relations based on friendship avoided seeing each other. The white women went to the market only if there was a policeman at their side; and there had even been cases when the black women refused to sell to them.

The days passed, and the nights. In this country, the men often had several wives, and it was perhaps because of this that, at the beginning, they were scarcely conscious of the help the women gave them. But soon they began to understand that, here, too, the age to come would have a different countenance. When a man came back from a meeting, with bowed head and empty pockets, the first things he saw were always the unfired stove, the useless cooking vessels, the bowls and gourds ranged in a corner, empty. Then he would seek the arms of his wife, without thinking, or caring, whether she was the first or the third. And seeing the burdened shoulders, the listless walk, the women became conscious that a change was coming for them as well.

But if they were beginning to feel closer to the lives of their men, what was happening to the children? In this country, they were many, so many that they were seldom counted. But now they were there, idling in the courtyards or clinging to the women's waistcloths, their bones seeming naked, their eyes deep-sunk, and on their lips a constant, heart-bruising question: 'Mother, will there be something to eat today?' Then the mothers would gather together, by fours perhaps, or tens, the infants slung across their backs, the brood of older children following; and the wandering from house to house began. Someone would say, 'Let's go to see so-and-so. Perhaps she still has a little millet.' But most of the time so-and-so could only answer, 'No, I have nothing more. Wait, and I'll come with you.' Then, carrying a baby against a flaccid breast, she would join the procession.

The days were mournful, and the nights were mournful, and the simple mewing of a cat set people trembling.

One morning a woman rose and wrapped her cloth firmly around her waist and said, 'Today, I will bring back something to eat.'

And the men began to understand that if the times were bringing forth a new breed of men, they were also bringing forth a new breed of women.

DAKAR

Daouda-Beaugosse

The shutters on the window banged back noisily, and the morning light swept across the sleepy face of the man who had pushed them open. He yawned. Leaning his naked torso across the low, iron railing, he looked out, to the right and to the left. It was still very early, and only a few men who worked for the city were going about their business. Buses were coming in from the native quarters, loaded, and returning empty. Dakar was waking up.

For a long moment the man remained leaning out, gazing absently down the length of the rue Blanchot. He shivered suddenly and contracted his muscles to warm himself.

From behind him, the voice of a man still half asleep called out irritably. 'Beaugosse, Beaugosse! Close that window, damn it!'

All the familiar noises of the Avenue William-Ponty – the thin patter of Turkish slippers, the clack of wooden heels, the coughing of motors, the bark of a dog who had doubtless just been kicked – began to fill the room in the union office where the three men had been sleeping. The one who was called Beaugosse turned his back to the window. The other two were still rolled in sleep on their camp beds, smothered in army blankets.

'Come on, get up!' Beaugosse said. 'It's five minutes after six; and we have to get things cleaned up. It'll be seven o'clock before you know it. And, Deune, tonight you are going to leave those sandals outside. You'll asphyxiate us!'

'That's right, you are going to leave your sandals outside the door.' It was a gentle, almost musical voice from the second bed that was speaking now. 'But you, Beaugosse, are going to close that window.'

The occupant of the bed on the left turned over and curled up even tighter, as if this embryonic position would help him to stay warm. He was no longer asleep, but he was determined to take advantage of these last minutes.

On the white and yellow tiles of the floor an old sheet of newspaper held an untidy heap of cigarette butts, used matches, little balls of paper, and a pair of sandals. Clothing and caps were strewn across the chairs.

'You played cards until two o'clock in the morning, instead of going to bed at a decent hour,' Beaugosse said, beginning to take his cot apart.

'If you're going to carry on like this, I'll never stand a watch with you again,' the voice from the first bed said. A black arm came out from beneath the cover, and the fingers groped along the floor in search of a cigarette. Then the cover was thrown back, and a face appeared, or at least the upper part of a face: a high-arched, protruding brow, above bloodshot eyes swimming in cavernous sockets. 'Throw me my matches,' Deune said.

Beaugosse, still in his shorts, went on shaking out his blanket. His real name was Daouda, but he deserved the nickname Beaugosse. In the midst of a generally unpleasant world, he was extremely pleasant to look at. Four months earlier he had graduated from the trade school, with a diploma as a lathe operator. His first contacts with the other workers had been difficult, because of his passion for clothes. His entire salary seemed to be spent on the gratification of a desire to be always 'in style', and he insisted on being properly dressed, no matter what the circumstances or the place. In spite of this, however, he had been appointed assistant to Alioune, the local director of the strike committee, because he had received an elementary education.

'Beaugosse, give me the box of matches,' Deune repeated.

'It's empty,' Beaugosse said, throwing the matches at him and missing, so that the box smashed against the plaster wall.

Deune stretched out his legs, and the thick toes and dirty, broken nails of his feet appeared from beneath the cover. Beaugosse put on a pair of trousers of a light fabric, cut in the baggy, Turkish fashion, and studied the holes in his socks sadly, muttering to himself in French.

'Shit; what luck! The last pair I have!'

The gentle voice from the heap of blankets on the second bed said, 'Only people who eat every day can afford to worry about shoes and socks.'

'You only say that, Arona, because you never had a pair like this!'

'Wa lahi! By my father's sash, that's the truth!'

Deune, still comfortably stretched on his back, watched Beaugosse and tried to repress a smile.

'Come on, Arona, get up,' Beaugosse said. 'It's your turn to clean out the latrine. It's twenty minutes to seven now, and if I know Alioune he'll be here at seven on the dot. I don't want to have my head chopped off because of you.' Shaking his head unhappily, he pulled on the worn-out socks.

Arona stretched lazily and began to murmur some verses of the Koran. Deune had sat up. With one hand he was scratching his loins, and with the other attempting to knuckle the night's mucous deposits from his eyes. At last he stood up, dropping the blanket, and Arona turned away.

'Nakedness in the morning brings bad luck,' he said. 'At least cover up your backside; it's as black as the bottom of a pot!'

Deune paid no attention to him and walked across the room toward the window. Beaugosse threw his blanket at him. 'Are you crazy?' he demanded. 'Do you want them to slap a summons on us? This is hardly the time!'

'Ha!' Deune said. 'How did I ever get in a spot like this – between a true believer who doesn't like to see anyone naked in the morning and a black *toubab*! If anyone doesn't want to see, all he has to do is mind his own business and not look at me!'

'If you go on like that,' Arona said, sitting up and putting his feet on the floor, 'your heirs will be simple-minded.'

'You've been listening to the women again. And how do you do it with your women, by the way?'

'That's enough of your dirt,' Beaugosse said.

Deune changed the subject. 'Beaugosse,' he said, deceptively softly, 'you know, I saw the little Portuguese last night. She has some coffee ready for you!'

'What?' Beaugosse demanded in surprise. 'I don't remember asking her to do that.'

'I know, I know. But you like coffee, and so do I, and so does Arona. If this girl is willing to provide us with it, especially during the strike, why should we stop her?'

'Listen, Deune,' Beaugosse said. 'You are older than I am, and I respect you for that – but I don't like your doing this!'

Arona, who had finished dressing and was looking for his sandals, came over to him. 'Now wait a minute, little one,' he said quietly. 'This is a good child ... I mean, at this particular time, she is really something special. She brings us water, for instance. Perhaps because of what is happening, but also because of you. It hurts me, too, to exploit her, to use her this way, but I ask you – have we the right to refuse her?'

'Do you realize what you are making of me right now?' Beaugosse demanded. 'A prostitute!' He repeated the word in French. 'Now I understand,' he went on, at last. 'Now I understand all of those meals that are brought to us.' Beaugosse was a young man of principles, and the matter troubled him.

Deune opened his mouth to say something, but Arona stepped on his foot.

'Very well,' Beaugosse said. 'I'll go out. I'll do the latrines myself, Arona, but when I come back everything had better be in order here!'

'Certainly, corporal,' Deune said, digging his elbow into Arona's ribs.

When the boy had gone out, they both began to laugh, but they did as he said and bathed and shaved and swept out the office.

Beaugosse came back carrying an aluminium coffee pot, three cups, and some bread and sugar. Deune whistled joyfully and ran his tongue across his lips. 'We're going to have a feast! It's a blessing from heaven to have a . . . well, you know what I mean . . .'

'I haven't any idea what you mean,' Arona said, taking a cup and three lumps of sugar.

'Three lumps for one cup?' Deune said. 'That's not coffee; it's syrup.'

They divided up the bread, and Beaugosse spread out a newspaper on the desk so they could eat more comfortably. Deune was chewing thoughtfully and looking out at the sky, when quite suddenly he said, 'It's odd. It's very odd, and I still don't really understand . . .'

'What's odd?' Arona asked.

Deune stared into his empty cup, holding his chin in his hands. 'This business of the help we've been getting from outside. I don't understand it. The support from the French unions, for instance. You have Europeans who have come all the way from up there, just to break the strike, and then there are other Europeans who send us money to go on with it. Don't you think it's odd?'

'There are other things that are even odder – those guys from Dahomey who sent us money. I certainly never expected that!'

'Neither did I. I never would have thought of them. But you know – now, even if it was just for their sake and had nothing to do with us, I'd like to see that louse of a Dejean get beaten.'

The coffee pot was empty. Arona leaned back against the wall. Beaugosse had been listening to them, saying nothing, but occasionally shaking his head, as if he were thinking what fools they were.

Deune began pulling apart some butts, looking for enough tobacco to roll another cigarette, and went on. 'I used to make fun of people from Dahomey before – and do you know why?'

Arona opened his eyes wide, seemingly in perfect candor. 'No,' he said, 'why?'

'Because I thought I was better than they are, that's why. Do you remember the talk Bakayoko gave, on "the pitfalls of citizenship"? Well, now I understand what he was talking about, and I'm ashamed of myself. Bakayoko is right – this strike has taught us a lot of things.'

'Bakayoko, Bakayoko!' Beaugosse exclaimed. 'All day long I hear nothing but that name – as if he were some kind of prophet!'

'Ha! Ask N'Deye Touti . . .'

'That's enough of that, Deune! Keep her name out of this! To listen to you, anyone would think that man was running the strike all by himself. It's Doudou who's the secretary-general, after all!'

'All right, all right, Beaugosse; you don't have to shout. Everybody knows that.'

The interruption had come from the door, and all three of them turned around. Alioune, the local director, came in, followed by several workers. Alioune was not much older than Beaugosse. He was wearing a green tunic and a heavy cap, which he placed on the desk.

'Anything new last night?'

'Nothing at all.'

'Well, the guard is getting spoiled. By the way, Beaugosse, the little Portuguese told me yesterday that her family had killed a pig for some occasion or other, and that she was going to prepare a *catioupa*.'

Deune and Arona looked at each other, and Deune, unable to contain himself, burst out laughing.

'What are you laughing at?' Alioune asked.

Beaugosse bit his lips.

'Well, in any case,' Alioune continued, seating himself on a corner of the desk. 'I know that you eat pork, and so do I, for that matter, and so does Deune, on the sly.'

Deune seemed unable to control his hilarity. Every time he looked at Beaugosse he burst out laughing again, and Alioune was forced to wait until the fit had passed before he could go on.

'Idrissa also eats it, so the noon meal would seem to be taken care of. The others will have to go home. One more thing, Beaugosse: N'Deye Touti is in the city this morning with Bineta and Mame Sofi. They are going back at noon. As for you, Deune, your wife said to tell you that everything is all right.'

'Do you know what she told me day before yesterday? – "If you go back to work before the others, I'll cut off your thing!"'

'From what I know of my cousin, she's quite capable of it,' Alioune said.

'I don't think I'll have lunch here,' Beaugosse said abruptly. 'I'm going back to the house. Deune, what are you muttering about now?'

'I wasn't muttering, I was singing. Listen – it's the striker's song!'

'Never mind – I've heard enough of it. I'll see you tonight.'

'Don't kid him too much, Deune,' Alioune said, when Beaugosse had gone. 'He's only been in the shops for a few months, and besides, he's having a rough time with N'Deye Touti.'

'Ah, so that's why he doesn't like to hear Bakayoko's name mentioned!' Idrissa said.

They didn't pursue the subject of Bakayoko and Beaugosse and N'Deye Touti, however, because now the workers were beginning to come in, one by one, hoping for news.

◆

It was a habit with Ramatoulaye on her walks never to move far away from the millet or bamboo fences. In this way she could pause before the entrance to each house and greet its inhabitants; and invariably the greeting became the occasion for an interminable exchange of courtesies and news. She knew everyone, by their first names and their family names; she knew all of their relatives, and the blood lines of all the men, for generations back. She was, in fact, a walking encyclopedia of every family in the district.

Today, however, Ramatoulaye did not pause at all. Her sturdy legs pumped steadily forward, beneath a long, shapeless cloth which bulged in front from the mass of amulets she wore around her neck. Her arms, as far up as her elbows, were circled with fetish bracelets of red and yellow and black.

Since the beginning of the strike Ramatoulaye had become more withdrawn, and perhaps more stern. There was no longer time for gossiping. Her responsibilities had become very great, because the house of which she was the eldest was large: there were no less than twenty of 'God's bits of wood.' It would never have occurred to Ramatoulaye to count the members of her household in any but the old way; to give them names might attract the attention of some evil that would fatefully alter their lives.

Although it was only nine o'clock in the morning the heat was already oppressive. Ramatoulaye passed a group of quarreling children, but today even this could not distract her. She turned to the left and entered the Place de Djouma, a vast stretch of hard-packed sand dominated by the mass of the cathedral-mosque. The crescents atop its twin minarets glittered fiercely in the sun, pointing to the sky. On every side of the square there were sheds with roofs of tile, and unfinished buildings, slashed with sand-paved streets and alleys.

Ramatoulaye wiped her face with a corner of her dress. The handkerchief around her head was soaked with sweat, and sand clung to her feet. On the stone bench before the mosque there was a large group of women, telling their morning beads, and out of courtesy she made a genuflection. Some of the women returned the greeting with a gesture of their rosary, others just by bowing their heads, and then they returned to their dialogue with the All Powerful. Ramatoulaye crossed one of the streets and entered a building known to every housewife in the neighborhood as 'the hen roost'.

Hadramé the Moor's shop had received its nickname because of the dirt that pervaded everything in it, but it was the largest one in the whole district. There were three entrances from the street, and an enormous wooden counter, covered with a mixture of grease and dust, ran the entire length of the store. On either side of a haberdashery showcase there were scales, of different sizes. At one end of the counter there were fly-specked jars of sweets, and at the other a sort of cage of metallic gauze, containing loaves of stale bread. A cockroach was climbing slowly up its inner frame. The whole rear wall of the shop was covered by rickety shelves, held together with wire and piled with rolls of cloth of every kind, from the cheapest calicoes to silks, side by side with boxes of candles and squares of tallow. Between the counter and the row of shelves there was a narrow pathway, littered with bags of rice and salt and cases of tinned sardines and tomatoes. The floor surrounding the big cask of oil was thick with grease. And, as if this glut of merchandise was not enough, Hadramé had succeeded in wedging three tailors into a corner at the back. They sat in the shop all day, measuring, cutting, and sewing.

Ramatoulaye entered by the center door. 'Have you passed the night in peace?' she asked, and since the tailors, bent over their work, did not reply, she called, 'Hadramé, Hadramé!'

One of the men stopped his pedaling to look up, and when he recognized her, he said, 'Hadramé is in the back, Rama. He will be here in a minute.' Then he returned to the murmur of his sewing-machine.

The sun, coming through the doors, sketched geometric patterns on the floor, but the light at the back of the shop was the murky green of an aquarium. Ramatoulaye was ferreting about in the jumble of merchandise, rapidly growing impatient, when suddenly her glance came to rest on the

41

pair of scales. Like the spark of a flint in darkness, an idea flashed through her mind – an old idea, as a matter of fact, stored for a long time in the back of her head. She walked over to the scale, but just as she was about to put her hand on the balance to test its accuracy the red curtain which screened a door at the rear of the shop was drawn aside, and Hadramé came in. He saw her gesture; and his expression hardened.

'Hadramé,' Ramatoulaye said, without any prefatory greeting, 'I want ten pounds of rice. No oil, no sugar – just rice.'

'Just rice!' the shopkeeper repeated, shaking his head so violently that the uncombed thickets of his hair seemed to jump. 'I told you yesterday, Rama, that I couldn't do anything more for you, or for any of the strikers' families. I can't even give you any more credit, or they will cut off my own supplies. As it is, they want to close my store. And I have to live myself!'

'Hadramé, you know I have always paid what I owe. And you are the one who bought our jewelry – you can give me five pounds at least.'

While she spoke, the Moor had walked away, and she could see the blue lines left on his arms and the back of his neck by the indigo dye of his tunic. At the other end of the counter he pulled up a stool and sat down, scratching the calf of his leg indifferently. Ramatoulaye remained leaning against the counter, gazing at the sacks of rice. When she looked up, her glance crossed Hadramé's, and she thought, 'If I stay, I'll make him give me. I can persuade him, I know, if I just hold on.'

The designs sketched by the sun moved across the floor until they reached the counter, and several clients came and went, but Ramatoulaye never changed her position. Her silent presence began to wear on the shopkeeper's nerves, and he got up and went into the little office at the back. Hidden behind the half-opened door, he watched the woman through a gap in the red curtain. It seemed to him that Ramatoulaye and her silence filled his shop from wall to wall. Finally he could stand it no longer and thrust his head around the curtain.

'I cannot do it, Rama,' he said mournfully. 'I just cannot! They know everything I do here!'

Ramatoulaye did not reply.

'Tell our men to go back to work,' Hadramé said. From the sound of his voice he seemed really to be suffering. 'You will all die of hunger. This strike is a war of eggs against stones!'

Ramatoulaye still said nothing, and Hadramé tried again. 'I cannot – I cannot! They'll close my shop! Tell the men to go back.'

'*Bilahi*, Hadramé,' Ramatoulaye said then, 'you have no heart, and you also have a short memory! Give me two pounds – just enough to cheat the hunger.'

'*Valahi* – I cannot,' the shopkeeper said again, casting a pleading glance at the tailors, as though they might help him.

At this moment two boys came into the shop, breathless from running. The older one greeted Ramatoulaye politely and then spoke to the shopkeeper. 'My father sent me for the rice,' he said.

Hadramé weighed out the rice and emptied the balance from the scale into a square of cloth the boy had spread on the counter. As soon as they had left, Ramatoulaye resumed her pleading.

'Hadramé, for the love of God, give me just two pounds of rice. Don't listen to the *toubabs*! It's true that the men are on strike, but what have we to do with that? We are just the mothers. And the children? What can they do?'

'I cannot do it,' Hadramé repeated, trying to avoid her eyes.

Ramatoulaye was at the end of her strength, and, without realizing it, she was almost shouting. 'For us there is nothing – for us you can do nothing! But for Mabigué! Oh yes, you can do it for him!'

Hadramé grimaced, as if he had a cramp in his stomach. 'Why don't you go to see him?' he said. 'He is your brother, and he is the chief of the district.'

'You and he – you are both on the side of the *toubabs*. But the strike will end some day, Hadramé; nothing lasts forever. I'll be back – if they haven't brought anything from the city, I'll come back, Hadramé. Be sure that your hen roost is closed up well, or I shall have my rice.'

And with a polite farewell to the tailors, who had been watching her in astonishment, Ramatoulaye left the shop.

◆

The sun's rays flowed across the Place de Djouma like molten lead, transforming it into a furnace. Ramatoulaye branched off to the right and saw her brother Mabigué approaching, followed by his ram. She took shelter in the shadow of a fence and waited.

El Hadji Mabigué was dressed as if he were on his way to some ceremony. He wore both an inner and an outer tunic, and his red fez was wrapped with a scarf, in the fashion of Mecca. His soft Turkish slippers were lemon yellow, and he was protected from the sun by an umbrella of iridescent pink. Since he could not avoid his sister, he greeted her and inquired politely, 'Does all go well with those of your house?'

'We ate nothing yesterday, and I cannot yet say whether we will eat today.'

'The designs of Providence are unfathomable,' El Hadji Mabigué said, turning up the pink, delicately lined palm of a hand that was soft and plump as a woman's. The ram, Vendredi, stood quietly at his side. He had magnificent curling horns, and his fleece, white at its roots and yellowed by the sun at its tips, had been carefully combed and brushed. He had been castrated, to make him more sleek, and his imposing bulk was the terror of every woman in the neighborhood.

Mabigué made a gesture of farewell, but Ramatoulaye detained him. 'I don't like to ask favors,' she said, 'and especially of you, but I have just come from Hadramé's shop, and he refuses to give us any more credit. Will you guarantee him the price of a hundred pounds of rice? You know the position we are in – and I know that you can do it.'

'I?' Mabigué's face was an astonished mask of soft, black wax. 'I? *Lah ilaha ilaha!* He doesn't even give me credit! Hadramé is not a good neighbor, and I have been meaning to speak to the authorities about having him moved to another district.'

Ramatoulaye stared at him, thrusting out her tattooed lower lip imperceptibly. 'Mabigué, God loves only the truth! If you had said, "I do not wish to", I would have believed you; but when you say, "I cannot", you are lying. I have just come from the shop. Your younger son was there, and Hadramé gave him rice, in your name.'

Mabigué was taken aback. The loose sleeves of his tunics flapped like the wings of a long-legged bird preparing for flight. Shifting his umbrella from one hand to the other, he stammered, 'God is my witness that I paid for that rice!' Then, toying nervously with the wristband of his tunic, he added, 'All this could probably be arranged, if the men would just go back to work.'

'The men have not consulted their women, and it is not the task of the women to urge them to go back. They are men, and they know what they are doing. But the women must still eat, and the children, too.'

'I know, I know. But if the women should refuse to support them, they would soon return to the shops. Do you really think that the *toubabs* will give in? I know better – I know that they will have the last word. Everything here belongs to them – the shops, and the merchandise in the shops, even the water we drink. This strike is like a band of monkeys deserting a fertile plain – who gains from that? The owner of the plain! It is not our part in life to resist the will of heaven. I know that life is often hard, but that should not cause us to turn our backs on God. He has

44

assigned a rank, a place, and a certain role to every man, and it is blasphemous to think of changing His design. The *toubabs* are here because that is the will of God. Strength is a gift of God, and Allah has given it to them. We cannot fight against it – why, look, they have even turned off the water . . .'

Exhausted and unnerved by this tirade, Ramatoulaye interrupted him brutally. 'You are in league with them, Mabigué – and you are a fornicator as well!'

'*Asta-Fourlah!* May God forgive you! It is true that I am your brother, but I am also an El Hadji, and I must ask you to remember that I have made a pilgrimage to Mecca and to use my proper title before pronouncing my name.' He paused a moment, and when he spoke again his voice was heavy. 'Out of courtesy first, but also in your own interest!'

'You are a thief, in addition, Mabigué. You stole my allotment by saying that I was an illegitimate child, so by your own words there is no relationship between us. Do you know what I wish? . . .'

Mabigué raised his eyebrows.

'I wish that you should not be present at my funeral, and that if my house should be destroyed by fire you would fan the flames rather than throw water on them! And as for that one . . .' she turned towards the ram. 'If he enters my house again, I will kill him with my own hands. And now, as God is my witness, I have spoken my last word. I shall never speak to you again.'

And she turned and left him, to go on with her quest, looking in at all of the shops and stopping at every street fountain. As she walked, the events of the morning whirled through her head, and she muttered constantly to herself: 'Ah – I no longer even know what I am doing! How could I have told Hadramé that I would be back? And if I went back, what could I do? I'm not capable of setting fire to his shop – I must have said that in a moment of anger. But why should I have threatened him? Is all this because of the strike – or is it perhaps because I am evil? No, I know that is not so, I am not evil – it is just that we are hungry. And Mabigué – that old she-goat! I didn't lie to him – I don't want him at my funeral, and I will be sure that everyone knows it. He is the lowest creature I know . . . But it is enough to drive one mad – no rice, not even any water – but I can't go back empty-handed, with a whole family to take care of. Once, I would have found a way out – I would have sold candles, I would have found some way; but now . . . and all because of the strike . . . I don't know about the strike . . . It is hard, yes, but the thing is that it gives us too much to think about . . .'

The sun was at its zenith, and Ramatoulaye was walking on her own shadow when she came to the street fountain in her neighborhood.

A child was waiting there, sitting comfortably on the stone shaft of the fountain, with a straw basket over her head in place of a hat. She was the 'watcher', appointed by the women and charged with alerting them when the water was turned on. From beneath the mouth of the fountain stretched a queue of weirdly dissimilar objects, over a hundred feet in length. There were old baskets, frying pans, big stones, and earthenware jugs; and each object represented the place in line of a family. Around the fountain itself a sort of platform of hard clay had been formed by the constant pounding of wet feet in the earth, and from the platform a web of tiny trenches reached out to the gates of the near-by courtyards. Now the trenches were dried out and filled with refuse, old rags and bits of paper, and the skeletons of rats, decomposing in the sun.

'Still nothing, Anta?' Ramatoulaye asked.

'Nothing,' the child said, lifting the basket and revealing a dark face marked with even darker stripes, where the rays of the sun had filtered through her makeshift hat.

'You heard no sound from the pipe?'

'No, and I'm sitting right on top of it. I would have heard it even if I had been sleeping.'

'And if the noise was in your own backside?'

For a moment the child was embarrassed, but then she put down the basket and smiled. 'It's not the same thing. When the noise comes from the pipes you can hear it in your head.'

Anta got down from her perch, turned the handle of the pump, and put her ear against the fountain. Ramatoulaye did the same, but neither of them heard a sound.

'It's after noon,' Ramatoulaye said, straightening up, 'and I don't remember ever having seen a distribution of water in the afternoon. Come with me, and we'll walk over and see if we can find Mame Sofi.'

Obediently the child followed the woman, walking beside the fences.

◆

A rain of blows came down on the horse's meager flanks, and the driver cracked his tongue as loudly as his whip, trying to force the animal on. On the third attempt the wheels ground against the slight ridge that marked the footpath. The horse whinnied pitifully and dropped his head. A glue-like foam dripped from his mouth, and his nostrils flared open. The cart was in no better shape than he: the axles were ungreased, and the wheels struck the angles of a dance. At every jolt, the occupants – the driver and three women – were hurled against each other, shoulder to shoulder. The horse pulled with every ounce of strength he had, the harness stretched and groaned, biting into old, blue-painted scars, but both his hoofs and the wheels of the wagon slipped and sank into the sand at every step.

Relentlessly, the sun sought out their faces, the backs of their necks, their arms, their legs – every corner where their flesh was naked. The waves of heat rising from the sand distorted their vision, and from a nearby dumping ground fragments of broken glass, old tin cans, and empty bottles threw back a merciless light. They sweated as though they were in a great vat, hermetically sealed and heated from every side.

In a desperate effort to escape from this hell, the man lashed out again, under the horse's belly, and the frightened animal plunged forward. The three women had not exchanged a word; they were too busy trying to hold their soaking garments away from their skin.

Mame Sofi was seated beside the driver, and the other two – Bineta, the second wife of Mame Sofi's husband, and N'Deye Touti – were on the seat in the rear, with their backs to her. Her great protuberant eyes and the sweat, rolling in sheets down her black and shining face, made her look like a seal emerging from the water. The leather cords that held the fetishes and amulets around her neck showed through the opening of her blouse, seeming glued to her skin.

'*Ouvai, ouvai,*' she said, passing her forearm across her forehead and upsetting the careful arrangement of her starched headcloth, which she had knotted so that two corners of it stood up arrogantly, like horns.

She turned toward N'Deye Touti. 'You go to school – you must have some ideas about the strike?'

'You know that I don't, Aunt. It's too complicated for me.'

'Well, what do they teach you in school then?'

'Everything – everything about life.'

'And the strike is not part of life? Closing the shops and turning off the water – that is not part of life?'

Overcome with the heat, N'Deye Touti said nothing, and Mame Sofi changed the subject. 'When is Bakayoko coming back? Does he still want to marry you? For my part, I think you would be better off with Beaugosse. With Beaugosse, we could have a real celebration, but with the other one . . . I'm not saying that he isn't a good man, but he's a little heavy-handed. Besides, he is already married, isn't he?'

'Yes, he is married.'

'For a young girl, a married man is like a warmed-over dinner!' She turned to the driver. 'If that horse doesn't move he is going to dissolve in his own sweat!' Then, turning back to the girl, she said, 'You'll see – the men will consult us before they go out on another strike. Before this, they thought they owned the earth just because they fed us, and now it is the women who are feeding them. Ours ...' Mame Sofi said 'ours' because she shared Deune, the guard at the union headquarters, with Bineta – 'I told ours the other night, "If you go back to work before the others, I'll cut off the only thing that makes you a man". And do you know what he said?'

'No,' said N'Deye Touti.

'He said, "How would you do it?" "It's easy", I told him. "You sleep like a wooden leg, so all I have to do is wait for the proper time. A good shoemaker's knife, and wham! One good slice, and there's nothing left!" And all he said then was, "And what would you do after that?" Would you believe it?'

N'Deye Touti smiled, but Bineta shook her head disapprovingly. 'You have no shame, Mame Sofi!'

At this moment, the cart, which had finally passed the dumping ground, turned into a cross street, and they saw Ramatoulaye and Anta coming to meet them.

'Have you traveled in peace?' Ramatoulaye asked.

'And only in peace,' Mame Sofi answered, trying to extricate her considerable bulk from the shaky cart. A corner of her white cotton skirt caught on a nail, and the driver reached over hastily to unhook it.

'Good for you,' Mame Sofi said. 'If this miserable hearse of yours had torn the last rag I own I would have killed that dried fish you call a horse!' She turned to Ramatoulaye. 'Is there any water?'

'Nothing. Not a drop. I told the child she could leave. And you? Has Providence been favorable?'

'God be praised, we have ten pounds of rice, a can of milk for Strike, and some earthnut cakes – all thanks to our *mad'mizelle* N'Deye Touti.'

The latter, who had also climbed down from the cart, was a lovely girl of about twenty, in the full bloom of youth and health. Her skin was shiny smooth, and so black that it seemed almost blue. Her most striking features, though, were her eyes – shadowed by long, thick lashes – and her full, finely drawn mouth. Her lower lip had been slightly darkened with antimony. Her hair was carefully braided into a little crown at the top of her head, revealing a clear, high forehead. She was wearing a simple, one-piece dress, gathered in at the waist and cut low across the shoulders. Her breasts, in a brassière that was a little too tight, clung boldly to the material.

When Bineta had joined them, Mame Sofi announced, in a tone she might have used to issue a challenge, 'We're going to baptize this baby, and we're going to name him Strike! The men will die of shame!'

'And where are we going to find wood to make a fire?' Bineta demanded. 'And flour, and oil, and sugar? Mame Sofi, you can't ask a blind man to jump across a ditch. We have more important things to do than to think of celebrations. First we have to manage to stay alive!'

No matter what they may have thought, or wished, they all knew that she was right, so they gathered together their belongings and turned back toward their homes, followed by Anta, the little 'watcher'.

DAKAR

Houdia M'Baye

The compound that was known as N'Diayène, the motherhouse of Ramatoulaye, and of all her progeny and family, centered around a big, shed-like structure, painted the color of earth and standing on a foundation of bricks. The central part of the house was taken up by three large rooms, flanked by two smaller ones under the eaves. The roof was of tiles and had been extended outward by a sheeting of zinc to form a veranda. There were also two huts of mud and straw, whose crumbling walls were held in place with old fishing nets, and five other cabins, of wood and tarpaper. Standing before the gate in the wall which surrounded the entire compound was a latticework screen – the *m'bague gathié*, or 'protection from dishonour' – which prevented passers-by from looking into the central courtyard. Behind the main house was a smaller courtyard for the women and the lean-to which served as a kitchen.

On a big iron bed in one of the three principal rooms of the house, the baby Mame Sofi had called Strike waved his hands and feet in the air in a fretful, cycling movement. Houdia M'Baye, Anta's mother, knotted the cloth around her waist, watching her last-born child. The bed, shared at night by all of the children, was covered with a patchwork spread of a dozen different materials and colors. The only other furnishings in the room were two wooden trunks, doubling as chairs, and a big clothes cupboard. Hung from nails above the door was a collection of fetishes to bar the entrance to misfortune or an evil eye – there were bits of paper cut out in the form of arabesques, sashes and bracelets, and animal horns still bearing tufts of hair.

Houdia M'Baye took the baby in her arms and went out into the central room. In addition to being the living and dining area for the whole house, this was also N'Deye Touti's room, and it bore the stamp of the girl's personality. The two doors, one opening on the central courtyard, and the other on the smaller courtyard at the rear, gave ample light to the walls, and she had pinned snapshots and photographs from magazines everywhere. The bed was covered in a gaily colored, striped material, and the table was littered with books.

Crossing through this room, and passing the curtain which closed off Ramatoulaye's room, Houdia M'Baye went out to the veranda. She had brought nine of 'God's bits of wood' into the world, and her successive pregnancies had made her dull and listless. And now she was a widow; her husband, Badiane, had been one of the victims of the very first fighting in the strike. His other wives had already gone back to their families, but although Houdia M'Baye would have liked to return to her own village, she had been unable to make the journey, because of the strike and because she was again on the point of giving birth. When the baby was born he should have been named Badiane-the-Little, but Mame Sofi had insisted on calling him Strike, and now the absurd, circumstantial name seemed likely to stay with him.

A white-headed cat rubbed against Houdia M'Baye's legs, arching its back, and she pushed it away. Indolently, the cat strolled off, its yellow eyes flickering over the brood of children coming into the courtyard. There had been no distribution of water all day, so once again they had gone unwashed. Their scaly, dried-out skin was streaked with dirty cracks, and their eyelashes were caked back against their brows. Houdia M'Baye studied them all anxiously, but her primary concern was for N'Dole, her next-to-last. The child wobbled unsteadily forward, on a pair of rickety legs. His shining belly was so distended that it appeared to precede him, giving the impression that the skin might, at any moment, burst like a too full bladder.

'You've been eating dirt again,' Houdia M'Baye said.

N'Dole rummaged in a nostril with one of his fingers, then sucked thoughtfully at the snotty, filthy object, keeping a safe distance from his mother.

'Stop that!' she cried. 'Stop eating that!'

'I'm hungry,' the child screamed, bursting into tears.

'Wait until Ramatoulaye returns – you will all have something to eat. But why have none of you washed?'

'There was no water, Mother,' said Abdou, the eldest boy, reaching out to seize the cat by the tail.

'Let that animal alone, Abdou; he'll scratch you.' Her tone was empty, as though her mind was already somewhere else. 'And Ramatoulaye doesn't like people to tease her cat.'

Abdou obeyed her and went to join his brothers and sisters, who had formed a little circle in a far corner of the courtyard. Houdia M'Baye remained where she was, rocking the baby in her arms, thinking. This ceaseless hunger, which swelled the bellies of the children while it defleshed their limbs and bent their shoulders, called up pictures in her mind, pictures of an earlier, happier time. In eight years of life together, her husband, Badiane, had deceived her only once – and once in eight years was nothing to speak of. Badiane had had two other wives, but in spite of this there had always been contentment and harmony in the house.

The story of that single deception went back to the early days of their marriage, just ten or twelve moons after she had become part of the family of N'Diaye. The day it happened, it was her turn to do the cooking, and it was also the day Badiane received his pay. All the preceding night she had been planning the ingredients for the *couscous* she would prepare, and when she returned from the market in the morning she was carrying such an incredible quantity of condiments, and spices of every sort, that every housewife in the district had come by to observe and marvel. The entire day had been spent in preparation and cooking. From time to time the neighbors handed little bowls or gourds across the walls, asking to taste the sauce; and all of the children had gathered in the courtyard near the kitchen, waiting impatiently for the moment when they would be given the big cooking pot to scrape.

At last the night had come, and with it came the return of the men. Their nostrils had caught the pungent scents from the kitchen as soon as they entered the door, and with shouts and laughter they gathered around the enormous vessel containing the *couscous* and the caldron in which the sauce still simmered.

'This,' said Deune, who was famous for his appetite, 'this, woman, is not worthy of a beggar's palate – but tonight I will be your beggar!'

As silently as if the sight of the *couscous* had robbed them of speech, the men plunged their hands into the common vessel, their agile fingers forming the meat and grain into little balls, dipping them swiftly in the sauce and carrying them to their mouths. Houdia M'Baye had watched every movement, listening with delight to the compliments and expressions of appreciation and thinking to herself that tonight she would surely be the happiest of wives. Suddenly then, she heard Badiane's voice.

'Woman,' he said, 'it is very good.' He belched loudly and began again, speaking now to his neighbor. 'But tell me, Deune – haven't you noticed that there seems to be something missing?'

Houdia M'Baye had not even waited to hear the answer. In the depths of humiliation and deception, she fled to her room and spent the entire night forming plans to return to Kaolack, her native village. 'Never again will I try to please a man!' she told herself. 'Never again!'

It was a long time before Houdia M'Baye brought herself to recognize that Badiane's remark had been intended simply to tease her, and in the meantime it had become a sort of family joke. 'Haven't you noticed that there is something missing?' It was a joke that belonged to a happy time, but now it had taken on a sinister meaning. The 'something missing' was their daily bread.

Suddenly Houdia M'Baye recalled the tone of Ramatoulaye's voice, that very morning, when she had said, 'Real misfortune is not just a matter of being hungry and thirsty; it is a matter of knowing that there are people who want you to be hungry and thirsty – and that is the way it is with us.'

Strike began to cry, and Houdia M'Baye interrupted her journeying in the past to give him her breast – now nothing more than a slack and empty parcel of flesh. The baby seized at it with his tiny fists, sucking greedily, his eyes closed, his head jerking awkwardly back and forth. The breast was already so riddled with scars and pricks that it seemed to have been stuck with pins, and he hurt her. She moved him from one arm to the other and put his mouth to her other breast, but she knew that it would serve no purpose; her milk was exhausted. The thought of the strike ran through her like a sickness. She tried to shift her stiffening legs and glanced over at the corner of the courtyard where the children had gathered.

'Stop eating that dirt!' she cried again; but the only answer she received was a slight turning of emaciated heads, a glimpse of sunken eyes.

The heat was becoming intolerable again. The cat had gone back to sleep, and Strike moaned feebly in her arms. From far off she could hear the grinding sound of the motor of a truck stalled in the sand, and from somewhere close at hand the bleating of Vendredi, El Hadji Mabigué's ram. Then, just outside the wall of the compound, there was the cry of a water carrier. '*Kiô dieu n'da n'do?*' 'Water, water, who will buy?'

'Abdou,' Houdia M'Baye called. 'Go and bring that water carrier here.'

Abdou dashed out immediately, almost knocking over N'Deye Touti and Anta, who were just coming through the gate.

'Why doesn't the little fool look where he's going?' N'Deye Touti said irritably. She took Strike's little fists in her hands and carried them to her lips, whistling softly, trying to make him laugh. 'I have some milk for you,' she said, holding out a can of condensed milk to Houdia M'Baye, and then, when the baby went on crying, she said, 'All right, all right – I'll leave you alone, you ungrateful little man!'

'Has Providence been more favorable today?' Houdia M'Baye asked.

'Yes. We have some rice, some earthnut cakes, and the can of milk.'

'Is Ramatoulaye coming back?'

'Aunt Ramatoulaye is coming with Aunt Bineta,' Anta said.

At the sight of the can of milk, the other children had gathered eagerly around their mother. 'This is for your brother,' Houdia M'Baye said, 'but you will all have something to eat soon.'

At this moment Abdou came back, followed by the water carrier. He was a member of that indeterminate race which the purebred Ouolofs called Toucouleur; a very tall man made even taller by a slender tin jug he carried on his head. He was wearing nothing but a sweaty undershirt and baggy trousers cut off to a ragged edge around his knees.

'How much do you ask for the jug of water?' Houdia M'Baye asked.

'Five pieces, of five francs each, woman.'

'Five pieces? The price has gone up again?'

'Woman, I must now go all the way to Pikine to find water, and Pikine is far.'

'That makes two times in a single month that the price has been raised. What will happen to us – you know that we cannot pay such a price. Give me just half of it, then, for two pieces of five francs.'

'But I can't sell my water that way, woman. You know that I sell it only by the jug.'

The other women had come into the courtyard while the discussion was going on. Bineta went directly to her cabin, and Ramatoulaye, hot and out of breath, dropped her basket and sat down by one of the veranda posts, wearily caressing the cat, which had leaped onto her outstretched legs. Mame Sofi listened to Houdia M'Baye's explanation of the crisis with the water carrier and stared fixedly at the man for a long moment. Then she said, 'Follow me.'

The Toucouleur was forced to bend almost double to cross the veranda and enter the house. Mame Sofi led him into the dining area and pointed out a huge earthenware jar, standing in a shallow basin filled with sand.

Lifting the jar's raffia cover, she said, 'Pour it in there.'

With no apparent effort the man brought the mouth of the heavy jug against that of the jar, and a crystal sheet of water began to flow from one vessel to the other. The children gathered expectantly around the jar, their eyes riveted to the sight, pushing at each other to get a better view, their mouths open, a tip of each tongue protruding.

'Just wait a minute,' Mame Sofi admonished. 'You will all have a chance to drink.' When the water carrier had straightened from his task, she said,

'Wait for me outside – I will be there in a minute. Now, children, come over here.'

As they approached, she filled an old chipped cup from the jar and passed it to each one in turn. Then she went out to the veranda again, carrying water to the astonished women.

When each of them had had a proper share she turned to the Toucouleur and said abruptly, 'Do you believe in God?' Her expression gave no slightest hint of trickery.

'Who, me?' the man stammered, disconcerted by this unexpected question.

'Yes, you.'

'*Ouai*, of course I believe in God.'

'*Al Hamdou lilah*,' Mame Sofi said, as if the answer had relieved her of a great burden. Then she added, 'I owe you five pieces, of five francs each.'

'*Ouai, Koni!*' The exclamation seemed to burst from the dumbfounded man. 'But, woman! I didn't say that I would sell you my water on credit!'

'That is true – you did not say it, but I must owe you for this water just the same. I live in this house, so you will have no trouble finding me. And if, for some reason, I do not pay you in this world, then I shall pay you in the other, before I can hope to enter Paradise.'

The water carrier was completely taken aback. 'If this is a joke,' he said, 'it is not to my liking. Don't waste my time, woman. Give me my money and we will say no more about it.'

The flesh of Mame Sofi's face was normally soft and glossy, but when she was angry it became somehow harder, tougher, more like the hide of an animal. It looked like that now. With one hand clutched to her throat, and the other still distractedly stroking the cat, Ramatoulaye watched the scene in amazement, wondering what would happen next. She did not approve of what Mame Sofi had done, but at the same time she could not help thinking that today at least there would be water to drink and food to eat, since there was water to cook the rice. N'Deye Touti, who had come back to the veranda after changing into a work dress, looked on indifferently – an argument over some water seemed of little interest to her. Houdia M'Baye was terrified. She could not take her eyes from the water carrier's powerful hands; she was sure that at any moment one of them would crash against Mame Sofi's head. Her arms tightened protectively around the baby. Bineta, too, had come out of her cabin and gone to stand beside her husband's first wife, watching silently, a plug of tobacco wedged carefully between her teeth and her lower lip.

'I swear that I will pay you,' Mame Sofi was shouting. 'On the tombs of my mother and my ancestors, I swear that you will be paid! But it cannot be today – I haven't a sou. But by the sash of my father, who was the best of men, that water will not leave this house! You say you believe in God, and yet you would let these children die of thirst?' She swept an arm toward the little group that had gathered to watch the spectacle from a safe distance.

The poor man's efforts to speak made him look like a goat, chewing on its cud. His face was contorted with nervous tics. Sensing her advantage, Mame Sofi moved toward him, her great hands planted resolutely on her buttocks. Her waistcloth was stretched tight across her body, revealing the outlines of her ham-like thighs and knees.

'I tell you that you will be paid,' she said, 'and I tell you again that it cannot be today.'

'Woman, pay me for my water and stop insulting me! Oh, if only you were like other women! If you will not pay me, let me take what is left of the water. That woman,' he pointed to Houdia M'Baye, 'has two pieces of five francs. I will take those to pay for the water you have already used.'

'Two pieces – for what little we drank? And tonight you will come back and ask for more!' Mame Sofi moved closer to the man and clapped her hands together within an inch of his face, so loudly that he jumped.

'I shall pray to God,' he swore, 'that this water should be the last you will ever drink! Let it poison your offspring for a hundred generations and make all your descendants into blind men and cripples and lepers!'

'Bastard! Son of a she-dog! If I were a *toubab* I would have you dragged through the streets by the heels!'

The children and the other women all descended on the water carrier now. Bineta seized his undershirt and ripped it open from top to bottom, while Mame Sofi slapped him hard across the face, screaming at the same time, 'Help! Help! Everyone, help! A man is attacking us!'

From all the neighboring courtyards men and women came running to help, and the Toucouleur fled precipitately, leaving to the victorious women not only the water but his undershirt and the tin jug.

Then peace returned to a rejoicing N'Diayène. There was water enough for everyone, and the chipped cup was passed around again.

◆

N'Deye Touti prepared the milk for Strike, as Ramatoulaye had ordered, but as soon as the baby was fed she began to dress to go out. Leaving the topmost buttons of her blouse open, and pushing the sleeves up above her elbows, she adjusted her skirt and considered her sandals critically. They were too large for her small, well-shaped feet. She lifted her shoulders in resignation and picked up a green, polka-dot foulard to wear on her head, knotting it carefully beneath her chin.

N'Deye, as everyone called her, was pretty, and she knew very well the stir she caused among all the boys in the district. Before the strike, she had gone to the teachers' training school, which gave her a considerable advantage over the boys, but at the same time made her the public scribe for the whole neighborhood. And it was hard to fill out tax forms, and write letters applying for jobs, and even love letters, for all of your family and friends without beginning to feel more and more remote from them. She lived in a kind of separate world; the reading she did, the films she saw, made her part of a universe in which her own people had no place, and by the same token she no longer had a place in theirs. She went through the normal acts of everyday living as if she were dreaming, and it was a dream that was constantly filled with the image of some Prince Charming from her books. N'Deye was not at all sure who this Prince Charming would be, nor what color his skin would have, but she knew that he would come some day, and that he would bring her love. The people among whom she lived were polygamous, and it had not taken her long to realize that this kind of union had nothing to do with love – at least not with love as she imagined it. And this, in turn, had made her recognize what she now called the 'lack of civilization' of her own people. In the books she had read, love was something that went with parties and costume balls, weekends in the country and trips in automobiles, yachting trips and vacations abroad, elegant anniversary presents and the fall showings at the great *couturiers*. Real life was there; not here, in this wretched corner, where she was confronted with beggars and cripples at every turning. When N'Deye came out of a theatre where she had seen visions of mountain chalets deep in snow, of beaches where the great of the world lay in the sun, of cities where the nights flashed with many-coloured lights, and walked from this world back into her own, she would be seized with a kind of nausea, a mixture of rage and shame.

One day she had made a mistake on the date of a film she wanted to see and gone into a theatre where a documentary film on a tribe of Pygmies was being shown. She had felt as if she were being hurled backward, and down to the level of these dwarfs, and had an insane desire to run out of the theatre, crying aloud, 'No, no! These are not the real Africans!' And on another day, when a film of the ruins of the Parthenon appeared on the screen, two men seated behind her had begun talking loudly. N'Deye had turned on them like an avenging fury and cried in French, 'Be quiet, you ignorant fools! If you don't understand, get out!' N'Deye herself knew far more about Europe than she did about Africa; she had won the prize in geography several times in the years when she was going to school. But she had never read a book by an African author – she was quite sure that they could teach her nothing.

Now, as she approached the gate in the wall around N'Diayène, she suddenly remembered the day when she had experienced for the first time what she called her own 'approach to civilization'. It was during her first years in school, at a time when she used to keep a diary, which she had long since torn up, because 'nothing really interesting ever happens here'. It was also the time when her young breasts had first begun to form. One day, in the sewing class at school, she made herself a brassière, and as long as she was among her classmates she had worn it proudly, with no feeling of embarrassment, but when she went home for the holidays she had put it away. Beneath the covers at night, she would measure the growth of her breasts with a finger and torture herself with the thought that some day they would fall, and lie flat against her, like those of the older women. She would watch them secretly and observe how their breasts tossed about beneath the loose cloth they wore, and the thought that this might happen to her made her almost ill. One night, through forgetfulness, she had gone back to the house still wearing the brassière, and the sharp-tongued Mame Sofi had noticed it at once.

'Ha! Come look, come look!' she had called to everyone. 'There is a cow in the house, walking on two feet, and all dressed up!'

In spite of the sympathy of Ramatoulaye, who had told her to keep the brassière if it gave her pleasure, N'Deye Touti had wept with shame. And ever since that day she had considered herself a prisoner in the place that should have been her home.

She was still thinking of this, when she heard a feminine voice calling her name. She turned around and saw a friend of hers, a girl named Arame, hurrying to catch up with her. Arame was the same age as she, but maternity had hardened her features, and there was little about her now to instill desire in a man. A baby, slung awkwardly across her hip, clutched at her waist with his skinny arms.

'I went to N'Diayène to see you,' she gasped, 'but Houdia M'Baye told me you were going into town. I had to talk to you.' Then, since N'Deye Touti said nothing, she went on with her story. 'I want you to answer a letter for me. My husband wrote that he had sent me a money order a month ago . . .'

'Where is he?' N'Deye asked.

'In *Madame Caspar* . . .'

'Arame! You know perfectly well that it's not *Madame Caspar* – it's Madagascar!'

Arame shrugged. 'He's been made a sergeant-in-chief, or something like that, and he wants me and the children to come and join him.'

'Well, why don't you go?' There was a note of envy in N'Deye Touti's voice.

'*Vaï, vaï!* Do you think it's that simple? I went to the district military office – the one they've had since the strike – and they told me that I'm not even married, according to the *toubab*'s laws. The marriage in the church doesn't count unless you're married in one of their offices, too. It's as if I had been living with my husband all this time and never been married. If you could have seen me! In front of all those *toubabs* – I was so ashamed! It seems I have to go to the city hall, and even to the central military office. They gave me some papers to fill out – that's why I had to see you. I want you to write to my husband and tell him about all this, and that the children have nothing to eat, and they aren't well. I'm not well myself. And don't forget to tell him about this awful strike, and that we have to live for three days on one day's food, and . . .'

'Wait a minute, Arame! I'm not writing the letter now. I'll come to your house in a little while.'

'No, I'll come to see you. One of the soldiers gave me some paper with the stamps already on it, so I don't have to pay the tax, thank God. But if you come to my house my husband's family will want to write the letter themselves – they do it all the time. It makes me furious, but there's nothing I can do.'

N'Deye Touti was getting restless. Arame's prattling irritated her, but the girl didn't seem to notice. 'Have you seen Beaugosse?' she asked. 'He was at your house, looking for you. I wish I could be at your wedding – it will be a wonderful one.'

'What makes you think we are going to be married?'

'Everybody knows that he's courting you – and he's very good-looking, and always well dressed, so he must be rich.'

'You're talking nonsense.'

'Well, what *is* happening?'

'Nothing,' N'Deye Touti said, speaking Ouolof for the first time. 'Before there can be a wedding I have to give my consent.'

'Well, if I were you I would marry him. He will be working again, and you know how to read and write, so you can work, too. I wish I had gone

59

to school. When do you think the strike will be over – is there any talk yet of going back? You know that man – the Bambara – don't you? I can't think of his name. Everybody says that he could end the strike if he wanted to. Is that true?'

'I don't think so. His name is Bakayoko.'

'Is it true that he is courting you, too? Personally, I wouldn't want to marry a foreigner.' Arame shrugged again. 'Look – there's Beaugosse coming now. My, he looks handsome. Don't you think so, really?'

'Do you want me to tell him that you think so?'

Beaugosse was wearing a new tunic, a plaid of black, white, and red, woven into squares as large as a man's hand. He was carrying his hat under his arm.

'Good evening, Beaugosse,' Arame said, with a smile she hoped would be noticed. She turned to N'Deye Touti. 'I'll keep your place at the fountain.'

When she had gone, and the two young people were alone, they walked on slowly, not saying anything. Children were playing silently in the gutters, the air was soft, and in the sky the clouds spun out toward the ocean, like shining threads.

The women were now gathered at the street fountain where Anta had waited through the morning – women of all ages, seated on the vessels which they hoped to fill with water, or standing about, talking quietly. N'Deye and Beaugosse greeted them politely and, almost unconsciously, hastened to be away from the spot. When they came to a little flagstone bridge in the middle of an open area that was used as a sports field, N'Deye sat down on the low parapet.

'Arame told me you had been to the house,' she said.

'Yes. I left the others on duty at the office this morning.' Beaugosse's voice was serious, but he seemed ill at ease. He was standing before her, studying the crumbling masonry of the bridge.

N'Deye Touti smoothed out her skirt and pulled it down to cover her knees. 'Is there any news at the union office?' she asked.

'Nothing at all. This strike is just damned stupidity. It's been going on for two months now, and we're still right where we were when it started. I told Alioune at the beginning it would never work, but I didn't realize myself ... Listen, I read in the paper that there are jobs open as storekeepers, for Africans who know how to read.'

'You mean you want to quit now? What would Alioune say?'

'They'll try to make me change my mind. But, look at it – at one of the stations they've just thrown a lot more people into prison; and besides, we'll starve to death if it goes on!'

'Do you have any news from Doudou, at Thiès? Or from Bakayoko?'

'Bakayoko, Bakayoko!' Beaugosse repeated. 'That man is beginning to get on my nerves.'

'You don't even know him, so how can he get on your nerves?'

It was not so much the question as the mocking tone of N'Deye's voice that made Beaugosse lose his temper. 'You've never told me what there is between you and him,' he said harshly.

N'Deye Touti brushed the foulard scarf back from her hair and drew her feet up to the parapet. Crossing her arms around her knees, she stared absently at the scene around her, as if seeking an answer. At the end of the avenue El-Hadji-Malic-Sy the sky was propped against an uneven wall of rooftops. The clouds were gathering into a long, ash-gray pool, ringed with little islands, shadowed in purple, and being pushed into the pool by the wind. On the highway, two cows were coming back from the fields, followed by a man waving a stick. Then a bus went by, sounding its horn, and the noise brought N'Deye Touti back to reality.

'What were you saying?' she asked.

'I asked you what there is between you and Bakayoko.'

A light seemed to dance across the girl's eyes. She smiled suddenly, and Beaugosse could feel his jealousy gnawing at him.

'It's hard to explain, you know. You want to marry me – you've already told me so – but he has told me nothing. And I can't really tell you anything, because there are only two things I am sure of myself – I admire him, and at the same time I'm almost afraid of him. Is that love, or some kind of sickness? I don't know.'

'But you know that he is already married, and you've told me a hundred times that you hated polygamy.'

On the highway, the man and the cows had disappeared and been replaced by a cyclist, whose loose white tunic floated behind him like a sail. The clouds had all gathered now, in a vast, gray-black sea that threatened to swallow up the city.

'I told you that I wasn't at all sure of my feelings about him,' N'Deye said, 'but I am sure of one thing. I'll never share my husband with any other woman.'

Beaugosse fidgeted irritably with his hat and then sat down on the wall beside her. The toes of her sandals pressed against his thigh.

'After all, I didn't ask you to marry me,' N'Deye went on, 'but with you men it's always the same – you hardly know a girl, and you want to get

61

married. Maybe if you had been in bed with me already, you wouldn't be in such a rush to get married.'

'You've been reading too many books.'

N'Deye burst out laughing. 'You say I've read too many books, and Bakayoko says I don't read enough, and the books I do read are bad ones!'

'N'Deye! I wanted to talk to you seriously . . . and you're just making fun of me.'

'No, I'm not doing that, or at least I didn't mean to. In fact, I wanted you to know . . . You know, I like you.'

'And I love you. I'm going to see about that thing in the paper, and then in two months we can be married. You can't go to the school any more, so . . .'

'Now, wait a minute – let's not go so fast! I told you I like you, and I do. You're a very handsome boy . . . but let's wait a little while.'

'Wait for what? Until he comes back?'

'You're being stupid . . . but I have to see him again.'

'To find out if he wants to marry you?'

'He is against polygamy, too.'

'Well, then . . . is he going to leave his wife?'

'From what I know of him, it would surprise me very much if he did.'

'But if he doesn't want to leave his wife, and he doesn't want to have more than one wife, and you won't share him with anyone else anyway – then what? You are really confused!'

Beaugosse could not help thinking that there was something the girl did not want to tell him, and an agonizing feeling that he was somehow being betrayed mingled with his jealousy. For her part, N'Deye Touti felt trapped between her unresolved feelings about Bakayoko and her genuine desire not to hurt Beaugosse.

'I met Bakayoko before I even knew you,' she said slowly. 'It was at Saint-Louis, during the Easter holidays. I went there with some of the girls from school, for the wedding of one of our classmates. I don't know who had invited him, but he was there, too – and he's not the sort of person who goes unnoticed. At night, when we all got together to talk, he always brought the discussion around to the problems of the workers. But he talked about all sorts of things – unemployment, the educational system, the war in Indochina; he talked about France and Spain, and even about countries as far away as America and Russia. Nobody seemed to know much about him, and everyone was asking where he came from. I remember that the first thing I asked him when I met him was, "Where do you come from?" and he said, "From the railway station," and I thought he was joking.

'On the afternoon of the day after the wedding all of the boys and girls who were there decided to go swimming and have a picnic on the beach. After we had been there for a while, I wanted to be by myself, so I went for a walk and came across him, lying in the sand, holding out a stick and watching the ants climb up on it, trying to get across. I had a daisy in my hand, and I was pulling out the petals, automatically. He looked at me rudely – or at least I thought at the time that he was being rude – and said, "Don't you know that in this country we don't decide such things by pulling the petals off a flower?"

'"Well, what should we do then?" I asked him.

'"Just say, 'Shall I sleep with him, or shall I not?' It's more poetic, isn't it?"

'He was lying on his stomach in the sand the whole time and never even turned around when he spoke, but two days later, when we were leaving, he said to me, "There are so many beautiful customs right here that there is no reason to bring in foreign ones – especially when there is so much we still have to learn, about things that can be useful to our country."

'I don't think I really understood what he meant, but at school, every time I saw a daisy, either a real one or just a picture in a book, I thought about him. Then, during the summer holidays, he came to the house with a friend of his, a great brute named Tiémoko. He came to see Alioune, and not because of me, but he recognized me and said, "Well, if it isn't the girl with the daisy!" and Tiémoko made some stupid remark about what beautiful eyes I had. When he comes to Dakar now, I often see him . . . I can't explain what happens, but whenever he is with me I can't seem to say a word.'

'Maybe it's the effect of an amulet, or some kind of spell he has put on you.'

'Oh Beaugosse, don't be stupid! I've been out with him several times now, but it was a long time before I got used to his habit of sometimes not saying anything at all and other times saying things so sharp that they hurt; but I've learned a lot about him. He has even told me about his marriage.'

'Well, if he can't marry you, that's just what I was saying . . . What are you laughing at? I don't see anything funny about it.'

'Laughter isn't always a sign of gaiety. Have you noticed that in the whole time we have been talking we haven't spoken a single word in Ouolof?'

63

'Well, what of it?'

N'Deye burst out laughing again. 'He has a daughter, Ad'jibid'ji, who always says that in French, and it infuriates her grandmother, his mother. But he doesn't like it either if I always speak French. He's not easy to get along with, you know . . .'

'N'Deye, tell me something . . .' Beaugosse hesitated. 'Tell me . . .'

'Tell you what?'

'Have you ever been to bed with him?'

'You want to know if I am a virgin? Is that really important to you?'

Beaugosse had regretted the question the instant he asked it. He was silent for a moment and then stood up, turning away from the girl. 'I have to go,' he said abruptly. 'If I'm going to quit the railway and the union I have to let Alioune know.'

He strode off rapidly, his thoughts twisted bitterly around the image of Bakayoko. Who was this man whose shadow reached into every house, touching every object? His words and his ideas were everywhere, and even his name filled the air like an echo.

DAKAR

Ramatoulaye

After Beaugosse had gone, N'Deye Touti walked back to the street fountain. Arame, seeing her approach, came over to join her.

'Still no water,' she said, and then added abruptly, 'You know, you should say yes.'

'Say yes to what?'

'For your wedding.'

'You have a screw loose somewhere, my girl.'

'What is that supposed to mean?'

'I read it in a book,' N'Deye said. 'It means that you have something missing up here.' She tapped a finger against her forehead.

The two girls joined the women who were gathered around the fountain, weary with waiting. In the days before the strike the trip to the fountain for water had been the occasion for an exchange of all kinds of gossip, for the spreading of news, and even for arguments; but now there was only a gloomy silence, a stillness that was a reflection of impatience worn down by fatigue. There was also a sullen kind of fear, mingled with hatred of this instrument the white men could shut off whenever they wished. The whole system belonged to them, from the water-purification plant through the labyrinth of pipes to the faucet on the fountain itself.

Suddenly they heard a little gurgling sound, followed by a deep moaning in the pipes. There was a general rustle of movement, and the child Anta hurriedly turned the knob of the pump. Nothing happened.

'Another false alarm,' said a woman who was chewing on a toothpick. 'The *toubabs* are trying to kill us, little by little. There isn't a drop of water from here to Pikine.'

All of the women were now crowded around the fountain, holding out pots and jugs, clutching at the babies on their backs to prevent them from falling. Their mouths hung open, and their eyes were fixed hungrily on a single drop of water which had appeared on the spout of the faucet, like a pearl held in the beak of a bird. From somewhere within the fountain they heard the gurgling sound again – was it water or only air – then there was a little sucking noise, and after that silence.

'Let Anta climb up and see if she can hear anything,' the woman with the toothpick said, and the child was lifted to the top of the stone column.

'Can you feel anything? Is there water coming through the pipe?'

'I can feel something – it feels like it was turning – but I think it's just my stomach. Yes, it is – it's just the rumbling of my stomach.'

Once again the women relapsed into silence, and the brief hope that had flickered in their eyes disappeared. They were roused by the sight of Houdia M'Baye running toward them, sweating and out of breath, her flaccid breasts jogging frantically up and down.

'Why on earth are you running like that?' Ramatoulaye demanded. 'Have you gone crazy?'

'*Kaye, kaye,*' Houdia M'Baye stammered. 'Come with me – come and see!'

'See what?'

'Just come and see!'

In spite of Houdia's urging, Ramatoulaye took her time, pausing on the way to rebuke N'Deye Touti and Oulymata, one of El Hadji Mabigué's wives, who were arguing over a place in the queue.

'N'Deye,' she said, 'stop arguing with this woman at once; and you, Oulymata, stay in your place. If your husband didn't tell lies to the *toubabs* about us, the fountains would not be turned off. So hold your peace!'

Ramatoulaye walked home calmly enough, but the spectacle she beheld on entering the house almost made her choke with fury. In the smaller courtyard a few grains of dirty rice and the remains of the earthnut cakes were strewn across the ground, and fragments of gourds were scattered everywhere. In the kitchen, all of the cooking pots on the unused stove had been overturned. Ramatoulaye's enormous nostrils quivered, and words came from her throat as though she were strangling.

'Who did this?' she finally managed to ask.

'It was Vendredi,' Houdia M'Baye said.

'Vendredi, Vendredi! Where is he?'

'He was still here when I ran out to find you.'

At this moment, from somewhere near at hand, they heard the animal bleating. Ramatoulaye, who rarely hurried, raced into the larger courtyard like an avenging fury. From the veranda of the main house she saw the ram coming out of Bineta's cabin, chewing contentedly on a piece of red and white striped material. Ramatoulaye tightened her waistcloth around her hips and knotted the handkerchief on her head firmly in place.

66

'Stay right where you are, all of you!' she called to the women and children, who had gathered around her. 'Abdou, bring me the big knife! And hurry! No one in this house will go to bed hungry tonight – if you don't have ram's meat to eat, there will at least be mine!'

The boy brought her a rusty old kitchen knife, scarred with use, and Ramatoulaye walked down the steps, staring fixedly at the animal. Seeing her approach, Vendredi moved warily backward, drawing his head down between his shoulders, so that the long hairs from his chin dragged on the ground and his curling horns pointed directly forward. He stopped chewing on the piece of cloth, his eyes glittered wickedly, and his hind legs bent and stiffened, ready to propel himself forward like an uncoiled spring.

Clutching the knife in her hand, Ramatoulaye kept her eyes on the animal's massive neck. Sweat oozed from every pore of her body, and yet her blood seemed to have turned to ice. She could feel the nerve ends pulsing against the drum-taut flesh of her stomach.

Houdia M'Baye and the children were completely stunned. Wide-eyed and openmouthed, they could only stare helplessly, first at the woman and then at the ram. The frightened cat thrust its head between the crooked legs of little N'Dole.

Vendredi pawed briefly at the ground with his hoofs, and then he charged. His horns and head seemed to bury themselves in Ramatoulaye's body, and animal and woman hurtled against the wall of one of the cabins, shattering a wooden panel with the force of their impact. Ramatoulaye succeeded in linking her arms around the ram's neck, and he wheeled viciously, tossing his head in a violent attempt to shake her off, but she clung desperately to her hold, managing to get one leg across his back, while the other dragged along the ground. The knife had fallen from her hand, and most of the clothing had been torn from her body.

Houdia M'Baye, seeing her almost naked, sent the children into the house, just as Bineta arrived in the courtyard. At the sight of the eldest member of the family struggling with the ram, and covered with blood and dirt, her hands went to her mouth and she cried, '*Lah ilaha ilaha,*' but she had the presence of mind to gather up Ramatoulaye's clothes and cover her nakedness.

'Get the knife, Bineta!' Ramatoulaye gasped. 'Get me the knife! I won't die from being naked!'

Bineta found the weapon, but then she just stood there, her eyes bulging fearfully.

'What are you waiting for? Cut open his throat!'

Bineta managed, somehow, to plunge the knife into the animal's side and then recoiled in horror as blood spurted from the open wound. The knife dangled uselessly in her hand, and she seemed rooted to the spot. The ram lurched forward and fell, almost at her feet.

'Give me the knife, Bineta,' Ramatoulaye said and called out, 'Abdou, Abdou!'

Houdia M'Baye opened the door of the house, and the boy ran out to the old woman.

'Hold him by the hoofs,' Ramatoulaye said, and when he had done as she ordered she plunged the knife three times into the ram's neck. The blood spurted out again, spraying over the trembling figure of Bineta. Ramatoulaye wiped the blade clean on the animal's heavy fleece and stood up at last. There was neither pride nor arrogance in her attitude, but just a kind of satisfaction, as if what she had done had been only a duty she could not avoid. For the first time she seemed to notice that she was bleeding, and she turned and went silently into the house.

Although the scene had lasted only a matter of minutes, the neighbors had already begun to gather, and there was even a rumor that Vendredi had killed Ramatoulaye. Now, as men and women came into the courtyard and saw the carcass of the ram, they dipped their fingers in its blood and marked their foreheads with a little circle of red. El Hadji Mabigué was no better liked by the people of the district than he was by his own relatives, and it was generally agreed that someone should have killed Vendredi before this, instead of allowing him to grow fat at their expense. In the midst of the discussion, a voice called out, 'Let us cut him up properly, and everyone will have a share.'

The two Sow brothers volunteered to skin and butcher the animal, and the woman with the toothpick said, 'God's goodness is unbounded. This morning we could hope for nothing – not even a handful of rice – and now there is fresh meat for all. Mame Sofi, you will even be able to put some away for the children.'

'Providence has indeed been kind,' Mame Sofi said, 'but everyone must have his proper share. Send the children and fetch all the water you can, because there is none here. Empty everything you have – we will need lots of water. We'll boil the meat, and that way there will be both food and drink.'

When she went into the big house, Mame Sofi found Bineta, who was trying to wipe the blood from her face with a cloth.

'I told you this morning that we would baptize Strike today,' she said triumphantly. 'Now we will do it with a feast of mutton.'

She went over to Ramatoulaye, who was stretched out on the mattress, but did not seem to be suffering badly. She had pains in her stomach – from the shock, she said – but the cuts and scratches on her body were not serious. Houdia M'Baye was weeping and sniffling at her side, and the terrified cat was cowering so close to its mistress's side that only its head could be seen.

'Why did you do it?' Mame Sofi demanded. 'You might have been killed. *Vaï!* – if there was nothing to eat today, we would have eaten tomorrow. Our friends haven't yet let us die of hunger.'

'I knew that God was with me,' Ramatoulaye said, 'and I knew that it is possible to die of hunger, and that Houdia M'baye had no more milk. God knows all of these things, too ... I told my brother Mabigué this morning that I would kill Vendredi, but God is my witness that it was not because of that I did it. It was because we were hungry – we were all too hungry for it to go on. The men know it, too, but they go away in the morning and don't come back until the night has come and they do not see ... Being the head of a family is a heavy burden – too heavy for a woman. We must have help.'

Ramatoulaye was silent for a moment, and the women around her were silent, too, listening to her words as though they were hearing a confession.

'When you know that the life and the spirit of others depend on your life and your spirit, you have no right to be afraid – even when you are terribly afraid. In the cruel times we are living through we must find our own strength, somehow, and force ourselves to be hard. If Vendredi had not destroyed the only hope we had for today he would still be alive; and if he had killed me, you would have wept – but in weeping you might have forgotten your hunger, at least for today. Oh yes. God knows that these times are hard and strange!'

For a long time there was silence in the room, broken only by Houdia M'Baye's weeping, and then N'Deye Touti said, 'I'll go to the post office and try to telephone Alioune. He should be told. Lend me ten francs, will you, Houdia M'Baye?'

Houdia M'Baye reached into her blouse and brought out a coin from a little sack hung around her neck like an amulet.

'Don't tell him too much of what happened,' Ramatoulaye said feebly, 'but say that we will send them some boiled meat tonight. They need it, too.'

Just as N'Deye was leaving the room, another woman came in seeming very agitated. She had come to tell them that Mabigué had heard the news and had gone in search of the police.

'Well,' Mame Sofi said, 'if that's the case, let us get ready to receive them,' and she began to fill an empty bottle with sand. The other women were soon busy, copying her, and in the courtyard the men hastened to complete their work of butchering the carcass of the ram.

◆

At the union office, Deune was joking carelessly with Arona, while he opened some letters that had just come in. There was nothing very much for them to do, and Arona had already leafed through the pages of the newspaper at least a dozen times. Seated at the table, Alioune was drawing up a situation report, his heavy lips drawn so tight in concentration that from time to time a soft, whistling sound came through them. Across from him, Idrissa was counting money, squinting over the coins and bits of paper brought in by the collectors appointed for that day.

'It's beginning to add up,' he announced happily. 'People are tired of contributing, but they do it just the same. There was even a *toubab* – I didn't dare to ask him, and he gave me a hundred francs . . . That makes eleven thousand francs for today. Enough to buy some sacks of rice.'

'Three sacks of rice exactly,' Deune laughed, 'and it's a damned good thing, because Arona made a bet that he could eat twenty pounds all by himself.'

Idrissa tried to focus his nearsighted eyes on Arona's belly. 'It's too bad that I don't have a sou,' he said. 'I would have taken that bet, and you would have lost.'

At this moment the door opened, and Beaugosse came in. He placed his hat carefully on top of the coat rack and greeted the others absent-mindedly, over his shoulder.

'I was beginning to be afraid you had been picked up by the police,' Alioune said. 'There has been another raid at M'Bott.'

'No, I was at home.'

'Have you had anything to eat?'

'Yes; and I saw Houdia M'Baye and N'Deye Touti. Everything is all right with them.'

'Everything is all right, except that there is no water, you mean. We've got to do something about that. I've written to Doudou, to Lahbib, and to Bakayoko, explaining the situation.'

A shadow seemed to fall across Beaugosse's face at the mention of Bakayoko's name. 'I've been wanting to tell you something, Alioune,' he said abruptly. 'I've been doing a lot of thinking in the past few days. You've been very good to me since I got out of the trade school, but

70

sometimes it hasn't been easy for me – with the other workmen, I mean. They know all about the how and the why of this strike, but I . . .'

'What do you mean, *this strike*?'

Abdoulaye, the director of the regional office of the French trade union federation – the C.G.T. – had just come into the room and interrupted Beaugosse. 'You always seem to be grumbling. I can never come into this place without hearing somebody talking about "this strike". Aren't you satisfied with the help you've been getting from the C.G.T. in France?'

'Yes,' Alioune said, 'we are very grateful to them. We have also received help from Dahomey, and a letter from Guinea, saying that they were going to do something.'

'Well, then – what's wrong?'

'We have still had absolutely nothing from here – and that's the important thing.'

'I've been thinking about it; I've been thinking about it . . . But it would require a meeting of all of the unions . . . Oh, while I think about it; Dejean and his people are probably going to consent to see you very soon. Did you know about it?'

'Yes, I did.'

Arona and Deune leaped to their feet at this news, and Idrissa squinted thoughtfully at Abdoulaye.

'I don't suppose you will be needing me at the meeting,' Abdoulaye said, but it was clear from his tone that he hoped to be asked to be a member of the delegation.

'I haven't heard anything from Thiès about that,' Alioune replied, 'but I do have a message for you, from your friend Bakayoko.' He drew a crumpled letter from his pocket. 'Wait a minute, here it is: 'Tell Abdoulaye that nothing is more damaging to our cause than a worker who plays at being an intellectual and patronizes his own comrades . . .'

In spite of the fact that his features were already so black that it would have been almost impossible for them to change color, Abdoulaye's face seemed to grow darker. Beaugosse bit his lip, as if Bakayoko's words had been meant for him, but the others understood little of what had been said or what was meant.

The telephone that hung on the wall of the corridor outside the office began to ring, and Abdoulaye hurriedly went out to answer it, relieved that the necessity for a reply had been removed. In just a moment, however, he thrust his head back around the door. 'It's N'Deye Touti on the line. She's saying something about Ramatoulaye, but I can't understand her very well. Do you want to talk to her?'

As soon as Alioune had left the room, Arona burst out joyfully, 'Did you hear that, Deune? Dejean is going to see the delegation at last!'

'*Eskaï Allah!*' Idrissa said. 'We'll have the pension plan, all of our back pay and a raise, the family allowances, and the four thousand auxiliaries!' He punctuated each item of the list by pounding happily on the table.

'I'd like to be in the delegation that goes to Thiès for the meeting,' Deune said, slapping Beaugosse on the shoulder. 'You'll probably go, Beaugosse – yes, you'll surely go, and then you will meet Bakayoko, my Bambara friend. It's been a damned hard fight, but now we have won!'

Beaugosse was standing by the window, looking out at the street. 'Oh, shut up!' he said, without turning around. 'Even if you get everything you asked for, I'm leaving!'

But before he could say anything else, or the others could recover from their surprise, Alioune came running back into the room.

'Idrissa, Beaugosse!' he cried. 'Get over to N'Diayène right away! Ramatoulaye has killed Vendredi, Mabigué's ram.'

'What?' Deune demanded, in bewilderment. 'How did she do that?'

'I don't know the details – that's not important. Beaugosse, take four or five men with you. Go by the Sandaga market and you'll probably find Dème, the taxi driver. Tell him I sent you and he'll take you there. But hurry!'

◆

From the four corners of the sky, an army of shadows invaded the city as the day drew to a close. In the small courtyard at N'Diayène, the women had brought out the great stewing pot that was used for feast days and celebrations and were filling it with chunks of meat. Whenever someone threw a fresh log into the embers beneath the pot there was a little explosion of sparks, and the flames, leaping high again, lighted the hungry faces of the children. For the moment, they had almost forgotten the gnawing pains in their stomachs, because they knew that soon the meat would be cooked and they would eat again.

It was then that the police arrived in the big central courtyard. The women had never really believed that there was any danger, and in their concern with the preparation of the food they had ceased to think about it, so that now the sudden appearance of armed men in their midst spread panic among them. Some, bewildered and frightened, ran out into the street, but even here there were men in uniform. Mame Sofi tightened the knot on her waistcloth and took up the two bottles, filled with hard sand, which she had prepared for an emergency. Bineta, Houdia M'Baye, and several of the others did the same.

The native policeman who acted as interpreter for the white officers came toward them. 'We want to see Ramatoulaye,' he announced, in the tone of a man who was accustomed to being obeyed, 'and we will take back the ram.'

The women repeated his words among themselves, as if they had no idea of what he meant. Those who were closest to the fire managed to stamp it out, and then they began taking pieces of the meat from the pot, wrapping them in leaves and throwing them over the wall into the courtyard of the Sow brothers' house. Some of the children imitated them, bawling loudly.

'Silence!' the interpreter shouted. 'Where is Ramatoulaye? We want to see her at once.'

'She doesn't live here, white gentleman,' one of the women said in French, speaking to the European officer who commanded the detachment of police.

'They're lying,' the interpreter said, and just at that moment Ramatoulaye appeared on the veranda. She was obviously still shaken by her encounter with the ram, and she came down the steps very slowly.

'That's her, chief,' the interpreter said, and six of the policemen moved toward Ramatoulaye. The eyes of everyone present were on the figure of the old woman.

'You must give us back the ram, and come with us to the police station,' the interpreter told her.

'Where is N'Deye Touti?' Ramatoulaye asked the women nearest her.

'She went to telephone the union office and hasn't come back yet,' Houdia M'Baye answered.

The interpreter had heard her and understood what she said. He went back to the white officer and murmured something to him in French. The officer called one of the policemen, gave him an order, and the man left the courtyard, running.

'We want the ram,' the interpreter repeated to Ramatoulaye.

'Tell him that the ram will stay here. If you want me, here I am, but the ram ate all of our rice . . .'

'He says that you must come – and with the ram!'

'Tell him that we are eating the meat of the ram, tonight!'

The interpreter changed his tactics. He had translated only part of what Ramatoulaye said, in an effort to soften its tone, and now he tried to persuade her. 'Come with us, and bring the ram – or the meat of the ram, in any case. They won't keep you there – you'll just have to sign a paper. I know the chief; he's a good man. He isn't like the other *toubabs* . . .'

'What others? I don't know any others – they are all alike! The only good ones were born dead. The meat will stay here!'

'What is she saying?' the officer demanded.

'This is a bad woman. She doesn't want to come with us.'

'Tell her that we'll just take the meat now, and that she can come tomorrow. Tell her that I mean her no harm . . .'

'Harm, no harm?' Ramatoulaye interrupted, in halting French. 'I don't know about harm. I know Vendredi does not leave here. He ate our rice; I killed him. The children were hungry; Vendredi ate the children's rice. I'll come with you, but Vendredi does not come. Vendredi will be eaten.'

Then, turning to the women who had gathered behind her, she said, 'Be quiet, all of you. What are you weeping about, Houdia M'Baye? You act as if there had been a death in the house.'

In the silence that ensued, a confused rumbling could be heard in the streets. The officer, sensing Ramatoulaye's defiance, looking into the hatred that flamed in her eyes, began to grow angry himself. The women were on the verge of panic. They scarcely recognized the woman beside them as the Ramatoulaye they had always known, and they asked themselves where she had found this new strength. She had always been quiet and unassuming and gentle with the children; at the street fountain she never took part in the arguments, and she never spoke badly of her neighbors. Where, then, had this violence been born? What was the source of this energy so suddenly unleashed? It was not the war; Ramatoulaye was not a man and knew nothing of the rancors that well up in soldiers on the march. It was not the factory; she had never been subject to the inhuman dictatorship of machines. It was not even in the too frequent association of men; she had known only those of her own family. Where, then? The answer was as simple as the woman herself. It had been born beside a cold fireplace, in an empty kitchen.

She took a step toward the white officer.

'Go away now,' she said in French. 'This is a house for us, not a house for white men. Vendredi ate the children's rice. I killed Vendredi, and now the children can eat again. We are even.'

On all sides of her the other women began brandishing bottles filled with sand, flatirons, and clubs of all shapes and sizes. In a few minutes the group of policemen was completely encircled.

The interpreter tried to say something, but Ramatoulaye would not let him speak. 'I have nothing more to say to you. It's only because of the *toubab* that you haven't yet been struck down.'

In the street, however, the reinforcements the officer had sent for had arrived – more policemen, and soldiers with them. And it was in the street that the battle between the women and the police began, though no one knew exactly how.

'For a piece of mutton!' the woman with the toothpick said. 'Well, if they want him they will have to pay! We'll sell him dearly.'

From the street, the commotion spread instantly to the courtyard. Mame Sofi, Bineta, and Houdia M'Baye led the attack, and the rest of the women followed, seizing upon anything that could be used as a weapon. Even the cat put out its claws and spat.

◆

Along the whole length of the Dakar-Niger line – almost a thousand miles of steel, linking together a million square miles of the African continent – the men were beginning to have enough of talking about the strike. They were still determined not to return to work, but they had to find some means of killing the time, and of cheating their hunger. In some way they had to use up all of these Sundays which followed each other relentlessly, week after week; they had to occupy all of these hours of idleness, which at first they had tasted with delight and now had drunk to their bitter dregs.

For a time they played at being on holiday. Clothed in whatever was left to them after all the trips to the moneylenders, they left their homes in the early morning and descended on the markets and all of the big and little squares and meeting places of the city, forming noisy, celebrating groups and wandering from shop to shop, from stall to stall, picking up anything that did not require payment. God himself seemed to have joined the party. He had swept His anterooms clean, and His sky contained not a single cloud. Above the trees and the mountains there was just an immense blue void, unsoiled by even the slender columns of smoke which normally waved from the rooftops.

Ceremonies that went back to time immemorial were revived, and pageants that had long been forgotten. Men armed with staffs or cudgels performed the saber duels whose ritual dated from the reign of El Mami Samori Touré. Women dyed their hands and their feet with henna enriched with the black of burnt rubber and colored their lips with antimony. The young girls wore incredibly complicated hairdos of elaborately combed and braided tresses and strolled gracefully through the streets, abandoning themselves to the rhythms of the Bambara dances that were playing on every corner.

But such revels could not go on indefinitely. An intangible sense of loss weighed on everyone: the loss of the machine. In the beginning the men had announced pridefully that they had 'put an end to the smoke of the savanna', but now they remembered the time when not a day had passed without the sight of that smoke, rising above the fields, the houses, and the trees of the brush. They remembered when not a night had run its course without the sight of the flickering colored lanterns of the teams at work in the marshaling yards, or the sounds of steel against steel, of the shock of buffer against buffer as the cars came together, and of the far-off whistling of the locomotives. All that had been their life. They thought of it constantly now, but they kept their thoughts jealously to themselves, even as they spied on each other, as if they were afraid that their secret thoughts might somehow become known. Even in the midst of their confusion, however, they were conscious that the machine was the source of their common welfare, and they sensed that the frustration they felt in these dark days was also common to them all.

Like rejected lovers returning to a trysting place, they kept coming back to the areas surrounding the stations. Then they would just stand there, motionless, their eyes fixed on the horizon, scarcely speaking to each other. Sometimes a little block of five or six men would detach itself from the larger mass and drift off in the direction of the tracks. For a few minutes they would wander along the rails and then, suddenly, as though seized with panic, they would hasten back to the safety of the group they had left. Then again they would just stand there, or squat down in the shade of a sand hill, their eyes fixed on the two endless parallels, following them out until they joined and lost themselves in the brush. Something was being born inside them, as if the past and the future were coupling to breed a new kind of man, and it seemed to them that the wind was whispering a phrase they had often heard from Bakayoko: 'The kind of man we were is dead, and our only hope for a new life lies in the machine, which knows neither a language nor a race.' They said nothing, though, and only their eyes betrayed an inner torment brought on by the mounting terror of famine and an inconsolable loneliness for the machine.

Sometimes, as they watched, a storm came up, and in the distance they could see the tops of great trees bending before the wind. Then, when the rains came down, little rivers formed in the cracks the sun had made in the cement slabs of the station roofs, and water poured over the verandas.

Beneath the force of the wind, the doors of the deserted railway cars flew open, grinding and clashing on their unoiled hinges, revealing a yawning emptiness. And the trespass by the forces of nature into the land of the machine tore at the men's hearts and left them humbled.

Only once each week did the 'smoke of the savanna' rise above the brush, from the trains run by the Europeans. On those days the strikers would stop whatever they were doing and turn their heads to listen, like hunted animals startled by an unwonted sound. For a moment, the passage of the locomotive would calm the torment in their hearts, because their fellowship with the machine was deep and strong; stronger than the barriers which separated them from their employers, stronger even than the obstacle which until now had been insurmountable – the color of their skin.

Then the smoke would disappear, and there would be only silence again, or the sighing of the wind.

BAMAKO

Tiémoko

Among the strikers there were some few who secretly went back to work. They rose very early and did not return to their homes until after nightfall. Tiémoko had recruited a group of commandos to take care of such men, and the 'renegades', as he referred to them at meetings, were dealt with harshly. This collective action made the strike-breakers more wary and discouraged others from joining them, but there was, nonetheless, one case which caused considerable commotion and provoked extremely varied reactions, depending largely on the age, the sex, or the particular situation of those who were involved. It was the case of Diara, the ticket collector.

When Diara's trial was held in the union building, the meeting hall was filled to overflowing and had lost its customary aspect – there were several women present, and this was something entirely new. Diara himself was seated at the center of the stage, alone, and without even a table before him. His head was bowed so deeply that all that could be seen was his forehead. He seemed to have shrunk – actually to have shriveled up somehow – giving the appearance of a piece of meat that had been set out here to dry. His back was bent beneath the weight of his humiliation, and his arms hung limply at his sides, grafted to his shoulders like lifeless stumps.

Seated at a table to his right were Konaté, the secretary of the Bamako local, and the regional director from Koulikoro. With them was Sadio, Diara's son, and facing them, aligned on a bench, were the eight jurors. The hall itself was so crowded that those who had been unable to find a place were jammed into the door and the windows, as they had been on the night the strike was called. But the atmosphere this night was frigid, and not a sound disturbed the silence.

Diara, the ticket collector, was accused of *dynfa* – a Bambara word that was seldom used any longer, but which meant nothing less than treason: betrayal of one's own people. This was serious enough in itself, but in addition there was the fact that this was the first time that anyone there –

in the hall or up on the stage – had taken part in a trial. Subconsciously they were torn between the feeling of brotherhood that each of them had for the others – including the accused – and a vague memory of what was meant by the law, which they knew only from fragments of stories they had heard. Because of this conflict of emotions, they had a curious feeling of having been removed from their natural element, but the very newness of being forced to make a decision of this kind for themselves had sharpened their interest and their curiosity. There were some of them who realized that, for the first time, they were being called upon to play the role of a man – of their own man.

It was Tiémoko, who was the official record-keeper for the local strike committee, who had insisted on holding the trial, and everyone knew that the idea for it, and even the manner in which it was being handled, had come from a book in Ibrahim Bakayoko's library. Konaté was presiding, and he began by exhorting everyone who would have something to say to do so without hatred or malice toward Diara.

Standing up, with one hand still resting on the table, he said sorrowfully, 'I have no need to tell you that this affair is disagreeable for all of us.' Over his shoulder, he glanced at Sadio, the son of the accused, who seemed as broken and unhappy as his father, and then he continued. 'Until this moment, we have punished strike-breakers simply by beating them, and, as you know, there are two who are still laid up as a result. I went to see them before coming here. That is a sorry business, because we all have wives, and mothers and fathers, and children.

'But now there is the case of Diara. Diara voted for the strike, and like ourselves he received his proper share of relief, but then he moved over to the side of our enemies. Now it is up to you to speak. Everything you say will be carefully noted, and then your judgment will be carried out by men who will be appointed for that purpose.'

Normally, when Konaté had finished speaking, he was always loudly applauded, but this time everyone was so conscious of the gravity of the matter that no one moved. For a moment there was utter silence in the hall, and even among the crowd at the door and the windows, and then a voice called out, 'Why don't we ask Tiémoko to begin?'

'If Tiémoko wishes to begin, I am willing,' Konaté said.

Tiémoko was seated in his customary place in the third row. He rose heavily, his bull neck seeming even more massive than usual. The sweating in his palms bothered him, and he folded his arms across his chest. Before speaking, he flicked his tongue over his lips, and his strong, white teeth bit down on them, hard. He knew very well what he must do, but his tongue rebelled against it. 'Ah,' he thought, 'if Bakayoko was here in my place, he could make them understand, right away!'

The eyes of everyone there went from Tiémoko to Diara, and from Diara back to Tiémoko. Diara's appearance troubled them. Where was his normal dignity, his splendid bearing? Deep lines, like scars, ran down from the bridge of his nose and circled the corners of his mouth, his eyes were glassy, and the tight skin around his nostrils was gray. Their hearts constricted at the sight of him, as if they were in the presence of a dying man. And Sadio, watching his father, felt that he, too, was dying, slowly and painfully. There was no hatred or bitterness in him, toward anyone, but just a sort of dazed incomprehension. He would gladly have taken his father's place and had even asked to be allowed to do so. Now he had a feeling of being lost, and like the sacred dancers of some parts of Central Africa he 'buried his countenance in his soul'.

In the silence which followed the moment when Tiémoko rose to his feet, the same voice which had called for him to begin was heard again. 'Well, Tié,' it said, 'we are listening,' and another voice said, 'Yes, go ahead, speak.'

And at last Tiémoko was able to open his mouth. 'I promised you,' he said, 'that we would take care of any renegades, and we have done it. But, is beating people really a proper way to convince them of anything?'

It was a big question he had asked, and since no one ventured an answer he went on. 'I know that some men are like mules, and sometimes you have to hit them just to make them move, but this kind of beating is no real solution, especially when we are all together in this thing, when we are all sharing the same hardships. Why, then, must we judge Diara, and why should I be here to judge him, when you all know that Diara is my uncle? If I asked why to this, then I must also ask why to the whole question of the strike, and the white men, and the machines.'

The words came to him with such difficulty that he seemed to be moaning rather than speaking.

'What I have to say is very difficult for me. If Bakayoko were here, he would have understood me and helped me to make you understand. As it is, I will have to go back to the beginning of this story of the renegades . . .'

This is the story Tiémoko told of what had happened.

◆

About ten o'clock one morning, when the strike had been going on for several weeks, the strikers had all come to the union office in a state of

80

great confusion. Every one of them had received an order drafting him back to work on the railroad. It seemed like an actual mobilization order, and they had no idea of what to do. Konaté had done his best to calm their fear and told them to leave the draft orders with him. Two days later, Tiémoko, recording the orders, discovered that five of them were missing. It could mean only one thing – the five men who had received those orders had deserted their comrades. The idea of a punitive expedition came to him at once and was readily accepted by the strike committee; all the more readily because, at that particular time, about twenty of the strikers had just been jailed.

The first two strike-breakers were trapped in the Place Maginot, almost in front of the police station. There was a brief scuffle, and then the men of Tiémoko's commando group had taken them to their own homes and administered their rough form of justice.

Two of the others were caught later, but Tiémoko decided that their punishment should not take place in the relative privacy of their homes; he wanted to make a public example of them. He chose a dead-end street between the statue of Borgnies-Desborde and the church for the purpose, and when his men had done their work the two deserters were forced to keep to their beds for several days. But from that time on the battle lines were drawn between Tiémoko's commando group and the authorities.

Since that day, Diara had been escorted everywhere he went by five policemen. His two wives lived at some distance from each other, and whenever he stayed with one of them both the commandos and the police were on guard outside. Tiémoko had placed men all around the station, and he scarcely slept himself, but he was forced to watch helplessly as Diara came and went. Returning to the union office empty-handed after one such vigil, he had been enraged to learn that Diara had begun forcing the wives of the strikers to leave the train whenever they attempted to visit one of the neighboring towns.

Tiémoko began reinforcing his group of volunteers. Konaté, who had other things on his mind, was of no use to him in this, but he did enroll his young cousin Sadio, Diara's own son, who joined the commando group out of a spirit of adventure and without knowing much about what it was doing.

A short time after this, the one train that ran every week was forbidden to the wives of the strikers, but the European employees and the soldiers who were functioning as mechanics and station masters were careful not to molest or annoy anyone. As for Diara, he was still the only Sudanese who was working on the line. When Tiémoko thought about it he became

81

so furious that, if he had been face to face with his uncle, he might have killed him. Sadio still played his part in the commando group and did as he was ordered, but without much conviction. He was well aware that his father was behaving badly toward his comrades, but he thought that they would never go so far as to beat him.

At last Tiémoko could stand it no longer and decided to risk pursuing his quarry into the station itself. He told his cousin to wait for him in front of the Chamber of Commerce and started off by himself. The streets that led to the station were swarming with people. Automobiles and carts were parked at every corner, and a long line of women was waiting patiently in front of the big general store owned by the Lebanese. Some children were playing in the shade of a huge flame tree, and emaciated dogs ran in and out of the crowds, growling angrily at everyone.

To reach the station, it was necessary to pass through a barbed-wire fence guarded by infantrymen and sailors. There was just one opening, scarcely wide enough for two people to walk abreast. In the courtyard behind the fence a group of legionnaires lounged about, laughing and joking. As Tiémoko went through the entrance he put his hand up to his face, as if he had something in his eye. He had no wish to be recognized by the militiamen.

Covered with sweat, he came at last to the central hall of the station, where a vast crush of people was gathered, waiting hopefully for a train that might never come. Every corner of the hall was crowded with men, women, and children, seated on the ground or resting on whatever baggage they were carrying – boxes and cases of every size, rolls of clothing, animal skins or matting, sacks of dried grass and herbs. A fearful stench filled the air and flowed out of the waiting room, on to the covered porches and the tracks, where still more people waited. The walls and floors were covered with dripping, spreading stains of spit, dyed red from the chewing of cola nuts, or black from plugs of tobacco. Clouds of flies swarmed over gourds which still held some remnant of food and clustered around the sandals which were scattered everywhere, as if waiting for their owners to return. The station looked like the camp of a conquered army, carrying with it its plunder, its wounded, its dead, and its limitless vermin.

Tiémoko was too preoccupied with the angry mission which had brought him here to pay much attention to the spectacle. He glanced briefly at the closed and barred service doors and the deserted ticket booths and then went over to a woman who was bouncing a baby on her knees.

'Woman,' he said, 'do you know if the train from Kati has arrived?'

'Yes, it has, and it left again a few minutes ago.'

As she was speaking, he heard someone call, '*Hé*, Tié!' and saw a man he knew leaning against one of the ticket booths. The man straightened up and said to the people who were standing around him, 'He's one of the strikers.'

When they heard this, a little circle of curious people formed around Tiémoko.

'Brother,' the man went on, smiling, 'when is this strike going to end?'

'I don't know,' Tiémoko answered. 'Perhaps tonight, perhaps tomorrow.' He knew very well that there was no chance of the strike ending, either that night or the next day, but he was beginning to be a little alarmed at seeing himself surrounded like this. He tried to slip away from the crowd, but to no avail.

'Do you work here?' one of the men asked. He was a big fellow, tall and straight as the trunk of a tree.

'Yes,' Tiémoko replied.

'Well, then, tell us what this strike is all about. Don't you ever think about people like us, who have to stay here and wait a week or more for a train? Look here – this is my daughter . . .' He took a pretty girl of sixteen or seventeen by the hand and pushed her forward. 'She was supposed to join her husband at Tamba-Counda, and now she is just waiting, like all the rest of us . . .' His arm made a sweeping gesture toward the throng in the hall. 'Everyone says that you don't want to go back to work. Do you think the trains belong to you? They don't – no more than they did to your fathers – but you decide to stop working, just like that, without thinking about other people. And yet you workmen, of all people, should be satisfied with what you have. You don't have to worry about drought or rain or taxes, and you don't have any expenses. Why should you prevent these farmers from going where they want to go?'

The man had seized Tiémoko by the shoulder, like a father reprimanding a child. He had the air of someone who was accustomed to giving orders. A little skull cap of cotton, set on the back of his head, left his enormous forehead free of any shadow, and his eyes were clear. For a moment he was silent, and then he said, 'Look at all of these poor people! One train a week, and that one is like a jungle! And on top of that, most of them have had nothing to eat for days.'

'Neither have we,' Tiémoko said. 'We have had nothing . . .'

'If you have nothing, it's your own fault,' the man said. 'and it's as it should be. Some of you are in prison, and that is as it should be, too.' He lowered his voice. 'You should tell your comrades to go back to work.'

'I will tell them – but let me go now please. The "soldiers" don't like to see us here.' By 'soldiers' Tiémoko meant the militiamen, because he had recognized that this man must be a retired watchman. He was beginning to feel very uneasy and had even forgotten why he had come to the station. 'If they should spot me, I'll be good for a trip to jail myself.'

The woman to whom he had first spoken rose to her feet, holding the baby in her arms. 'Let him go,' she said. 'He's not the only one who has stopped working, and he can't make the trains run again all by himself.'

'You don't know anything about men like him. In my day we used to throw them all in prison. I probably should call a watchman now.'

'Don't do that, Uncle,' the woman implored.

Tiémoko felt the hand on his shoulder relax its grip, and without waiting for any further discussion he made his way hurriedly through the crowd. But he didn't breathe freely again until he was past the barbed-wire fence and out of reach of the soldiers.

Lost in his thoughts, he walked right by Sadio at the corner where he had told him to wait.

'Tié!' Diara's son called. 'I was beginning to get worried.'

Tiémoko gestured to the young man to follow him and walked on silently, his head bowed. A horde of conflicting sentiments and confused ideas seemed to be doing battle in his mind. At Bakayoko's urging, he had done a great deal of reading, and he had not always understood what he read, but now a single phrase came back to him, and he murmured it half aloud, as if he were intoning a prayer.

'It is not necessary to be right to argue, but to win it is necessary both to be right and never to falter.'

'Are you reciting the Koran?' Sadio asked, in astonishment.

Tiémoko seemed not to have heard him and went on repeating the phrase like a litany. He could not remember clearly where he had read it, but he did remember what Bakayoko had said about it.

They crossed the park in silence, and then Tiémoko said suddenly, 'Let's go to Bakayoko's house.'

'What for?' Sadio asked. 'The others are waiting for us.'

'You don't want them to beat your father, do you?'

'That's a hell of a question!'

'Well, then, come with me, before it's too late.'

Tiémoko had remembered where he read the phrase that had come to him like a ray of light in the darkness, and now he was in a hurry. As they walked he explained briefly why he had been delayed in the station.

'I don't see the connection between that and going to Bakayoko's now,' Sadio said.

'You will see. This strike is like a school, for all of us. We have punished some people for what they have done, but is that a good thing?'

'I don't know, but in any case they haven't gone back to work.'

'Right; they haven't gone back. But is that enough, for the future?'

'Are you asking me that?' Sadio said, completely baffled.

Tiémoko himself was tormented by his inability to explain this phrase which resounded so clearly in his ears and seemed so true to his mind.

'Look, Sadio, your father is my father's brother; you are my cousin. Your honor is also mine; your family's shame is my family's, and the shame of our whole country, the dishonor of all of our families together. That is why we cannot beat your father.'

'I knew that you were a friend, and not just a relative.'

'Don't speak too soon. We won't punish my uncle as we have punished the others, but suppose we should decide to try him, before all of the workers?'

'What! Have you lost your mind? Do you know what you are saying? My father – there, in front of everyone – and everyone insulting him, disgracing him! I'd rather die than . . .?'

'It's not a question of dying, cousin. It's a question of learning, and of winning. It's a question of doing what is right, and of doing it as men should.'

They had arrived at the compound of the Bakayokos as they spoke, and after the customary greetings had been exchanged Tiémoko addressed himself to Fa Keïta, who had been talking quietly with old Niakoro.

'I came to borrow a book,' he said. 'Ibrahim told me that I might use them when I needed them.'

'What my son has is yours,' Niakora said.

'I will ask his daughter to help you,' Fa Keïta added, and called, 'Ad'jibid'ji, Ad'jibid'ji!'

Then, speaking to Sadio, he asked, 'And your father, is he well?'

'God be thanked,' Sadio answered, frowning. 'God be thanked, he is well, Fa Keïta.'

'Hé,' Niakoro said, 'you are Diara's son? Hé, how the children grow up! To think that I knew your grandparents. The Diaras are people of a good line. Come closer, and let me look at you.'

Sadio bent over a little, and the old woman put her hand up to touch his cheeks and his forehead, and the contact of her fingers against his skin made him realize again how old she was.

Ad'jibid'ji came out to the veranda where they were gathered, and Fa Keïta said, 'Tiémoko has come for some books.'

'Only one, Fa Keïta; there is just one that I need.'

The child showed no pleasure at the sight of Tiémoko. She had seen him only three times since the beginning of the strike, but on each of these occasions she had been aware of a surge of anger she could not explain, even to herself.

'Yes, Grandfather,' she said. 'Father told me he might. Follow me, Tiémoko.'

Sadio remained with the two old people and, as Ab'jibid'ji watched, Tiémoko rummaged through the shelves in the main room of the house. He had to search for a good ten minutes, but at last he pulled out a volume wrapped in blue paper.

'May I see what you are taking?' Ad'jibid'ji asked.

He showed her the title, and she read it aloud, '*La Condition Humaine*.'

She had read the book, without understanding it, and she couldn't help wondering if Tiémoko would understand. She took an index card from a little cardboard box and studied it carefully. 'Every time you take a book you don't bring it back until five or six months later. I hope you won't keep that one forever.'

'What?' Tiémoko demanded. 'Does your father keep a record of everyone who borrows his books?'

'Books are rare, and expensive, and *petit père* spends all his money buying them. But if it makes you feel any better, Konaté has six of them, including one he borrowed twelve months ago.'

'He's the person I want to see about this book.'

'Well, perhaps if you read it together it will go faster.' There was a note of sarcasm in Ad'jibid'ji's voice, but Tiémoko seemed not to notice.

When he went out to the veranda again, Assitan approached him. 'We haven't seen you in a long time, Tiémoko. Since Ibrahim left we never seem to see anyone.'

'Ah, woman, we have a lot to do . . .'

'What?' Fa Keïta asked. 'Chasing after your own uncle?'

'We are doing it for the good of everyone, Fa Keïta; and we will have need of you in the days to come.'

'Of me? After the way you treated me at the union hall the last time? And you, especially! What will you need me for?'

'For this matter of my uncle. When he is taken, which will be soon, we are going to try him.'

Keïta's eyes opened very wide, and the ritual scars seemed to bite deeper into his face. Old Niakoro looked terrified. For a moment she remained openmouthed in astonishment, and then she said, 'You are not a bearer of good news, Tiémoko. Sadio, what do you think of this?'

'What can I think?' the young man answered, close to tears. 'I don't agree, but it isn't up to me.'

'Tiémoko,' the old woman said, 'have you thought about this? You are not *toubabs*! How can you judge a man who is respected by everyone?'

'Everything we need is in this book,' Tiémoko said.

'That book was written by the *toubabs*,' Fa Keïta said scornfully.

'And the machines were built by the *toubabs*! The book belongs to Ibrahim Bakayoko, and right here, in front of you, I have heard him say that neither the laws nor the machines belong to any one race!'

'The *toubabs* do all kinds of things that humiliate and debase us, and now you want to do the same.'

'There is no law in this book that you would refuse to admit. It's not an unbreakable set of rules, it's . . . it's a way of thinking.'

Tiémoko was unable to explain what he really meant. His face twitched with the effort of concentration, and little streaks of red appeared in his eyes.

'In any case, don't count on me,' Fa Keïta said. 'And when it is really a case of your uncle, and not of a character in a book, you will not do it.'

'If it was my own father, I would do it, Fa Keïta; I swear it on the tomb of my ancestors! And if it were you, Ibrahim Bakayoko would do the same thing.'

All of the contradictory emotions he felt were still revolving in Tiémoko's head, like the humming of a motor he could not stop. He succeeded in controlling himself, however, and cut short the conversation.

'I hope that you will pass the night in peace,' he said. 'Come, cousin.'

And he went out, followed by the dazed, unhappy Sadio.

'I am going to put all of those books in the fire,' Old Niakoro said, as soon as they were out of hearing.

'No, Grandmother!' Ad'jibid'ji cried. '*Petit père* would not like that!'

'There would be no point to it,' Fa Keïta said. 'It would change nothing.'

'But think of it! To allow the honor of such a good man to be dragged through the mud – a man of such a good family! It is the *toubabs* who are to blame for this. These children will never have white hairs – our world is falling apart.'

'No, woman; it was your son who said, "Our world is opening up."'

'Wait until that one comes back . . . I may be old, but I will know what to say to him. Who would have thought that we should live to see such things?'

Niakoro's hands were trembling, and she was forced to cling to the old man's arm as she rose, but then she pulled herself erect, turned, and went into the house. Behind the door there was a staircase of hard clay which led up to the terrace. Ad'jibid'ji was already climbing the steps, skipping up lightly, two at a time.

◆

Still followed by Sadio, and cloaked in his new resolve as if by a protective armor, Tiémoko went directly to Konaté's house. Konaté had a diploma from the school and was the best educated of all the men on the committee, out at first he did not understand what Tiémoko meant and could only think of the necessity for avoiding arguments among themselves.

'No,' said Tiémoko, who was sitting on a strip of matting. 'We cannot be held back by that. After the trial is held, everyone will understand, and they will know that they must not go back.'

Konaté was afraid that such a move would destroy the unity of the strikers, which thus far had been very well maintained. He was perplexed, and to gain time he said, 'Why don't you leave the book with me, and tomorrow I will tell you what I think we should do.'

'No, Konaté, no! You won't find in this book what you think you are going to find. It's up to me to convince you, and if I don't succeed . . .'

The secretary of the union was growing more and more uneasy. He tried another argument. 'I'm not the only one to be consulted, you know. We would have to have a meeting of the local committee. There is one scheduled for the day after tomorrow.'

'No!' Tiémoko was risking everything now, in the hope of gaining everything. 'We must have the meeting tonight. We can call it for seven o'clock.'

And so the meeting had been held that same night, with everyone on the committee present, and only one question before them – the case of Diara. But Tiémoko found himself alone with his conviction, faced with eleven worried and hesitant men. To judge another man this way was not a part of their prerogatives, and the strangeness of the idea made them uncomfortable and uncertain. Tiémoko spared no effort to convince them. He had eaten nothing since early morning, but the intensity of his emotion had put his hunger to sleep.

'It is not because I ask it that you must decide,' he said, 'but because this case of Diara must be made to serve as an example.'

'It may be that you are right,' Konaté said, 'but suppose the others do not support us? What do we do then? The whole success or failure of the strike may hang on this decision. The risk is great, and I ask all of you to think about it very carefully.'

The twelve men broke up into little groups to discuss the matter, speaking sometimes almost in whispers, and sometimes in vehement exclamations. The primary obstacle to any decision was their fear of not being upheld by the rest of the strikers. Tiémoko went from one group to another, repeating his arguments, trying to communicate his own conviction to them, and although his phrases were broken and often confused there was no mistaking the depth of his feeling.

At last one of the men said, 'Tell me, Tié, why do you attach so much importance to this trial? Is it to prove that you are a leader, or just because you have said that it must take place?'

'Neither,' Tiémoko replied. His face was dripping with sweat, and his nerves were stretched to the breaking point. 'Neither the one nor the other. I don't have to look for a motive for something that is a motive itself. I want us to move forward to a point where it will no longer be necessary to punish men as we have in the past.'

'That is all very well,' Konaté said, 'but right now we couldn't try Diara if we wanted to. He is constantly guarded by the police.'

'I know, Konaté – he is protected as well as the governor in his residence. But if you leave it to me, you will have him here before you, very soon.'

And in the end Tiémoko had won, through simple obstinacy and the fatigue of the others. One of them spoke for all the rest. 'Very well, Tié,' he said. 'You have convinced us. We will go along with your idea.'

A few minutes after this, Tiémoko set out for his own house. The ground beneath his feet was still warm, although it was three o'clock in the morning.

As he walked, he considered all of the points of the plan he had in mind, and a sense of exultation swept through him. For the first time in his life, an idea of his was going to play a part in the lives of thousands of others. It was not pride or vanity he was experiencing, but the astonishing discovery of his worth as a human being. Walking very straight in the deserted street, he began singing aloud an ancient Bambara hymn to the founder of the empire of Mali, the *Soundiata*.

All the next day he didn't leave his house. His wife, a pretty little woman with high cheekbones and slender features, told everyone who came to the door, 'He spent the night with a book.'

Toward evening, Konaté came to see him.

'Are you ill, brother?' he asked.

'No, I have been studying. You know, when this strike is over we must organize courses in reading. This book is very complicated, and I am not sure that I agree with everything the author says.'

'After what you told me yesterday? Are you going crazy, Tiémoko?'

'Crazy? Oh no, don't worry about that! By the way, can you get me three policemen's uniforms for tomorrow?'

'Policemen's uniforms? What for?'

'To catch my uncle!'

'*Hé*, Tiémoko, you are a surprising man!' Konaté said.

When he received the uniforms, Tiémoko gave two of them to men he had chosen carefully and kept the third for himself.

The next morning, very early, they had gone to Diara's house, arriving there well before the real policemen.

BAMAKO

The Trial

The audience in the union hall had listened to Tiémoko's story in total silence, and in telling it he had recovered some of his normal self-assurance. Before sitting down, he summed up the case against his uncle.

'Diara is a worker, like all the rest of us, and like the rest of us he voted for the strike – for an unlimited strike, until we won what we were asking for – but he has not kept his word. He got help from the union, enough to live on, as we all did, and he has used it, but he has not repaid any of it since he went back to work. But more than this, he has informed on the women who are supporting us so valiantly, and he has forced them to get off trains whenever they have tried to use them. That is why I wanted some of the women to be here today, although there were a lot of people who didn't agree with that idea.

'That is all I have to say, and now it is up to others to say what they think. But let no one forget that while we are talking here, many of our comrades are in prison.'

When Tiémoko sat down, the silence was so profound that it seemed almost as if the big meeting hall had suddenly emptied. Diara had drawn his legs back under his chair and sat so stiffly he might have been made of stone. Looking at his father, Sadio saw that his eyes were empty of all feeling, lost in a faraway past where there was no strike, no place of judgment, and no accused.

Suddenly a woman's voice was heard. 'I would like to say . . .'

Several irritated voices called, 'Quiet!'

'Who spoke down there at the back?' Konaté demanded.

'It's one of these silly women!' someone said.

'But I told the women to come,' Tiémoko said. 'They have important things to say. Come forward, Hadi Dia.'

A woman with heavily tattooed lips and a face crisscrossed with scars rose and walked to the front of the hall. For an occasion such as this, she had obviously thought it a good idea to put on all of the best clothes she owned. Tiémoko made a place for her beside him on the bench.

'Hadi Dia,' he said, 'tell everyone now what you have already told your neighbors. You can speak here without fear and without shame.'

The woman had a hare lip, and when she opened her mouth to speak the people nearest her could see the gaps between her teeth. 'It was the other day ... that is, it was about two weeks ago ... I was with Coumba, her sister Dienka, and the third wife of ... of ...'

'The names are not important. Go on.'

'We took the "smoke of the savanna" to go to Kati. Diara asked us to show our tickets, and when we got to Kati he came back to us with a *toubab* soldier. He said something to him in the *toubab* language, and the soldier took away the tickets we had to come back, but he didn't give us back the money for them. I told the whole story to my husband when we got home.'

'Hadi Dia, is all of what you have said true?' Konaté asked.

'Ask Diara.'

'All right, Hadi Dia, you may return to your seat. And you, Diara, have you anything to say?'

The accused remained motionless and silent, while the woman went back to her own place. It was the first time she had ever spoken at a meeting of the men, and she was filled with pride. Another, older woman went up to speak, going this time directly to the stage. Her name was Sira, and she spoke rapidly and confidently.

'With us, it was on the way to Koulikoro – you all know the place where the train goes up a little rise between here and Koulikoro – he stopped the train and made us get off. Eight women alone, right in the middle of the brush! I tell you, he is nothing but a slave of the *toubabs*! Tiémoko is right – he should be crucified in the market place!'

'Thank you. Sira,' Konaté said, 'but you should tell only what you have seen. Go back to your seat.'

Two more women came forward and told of happenings that were more or less similar to the first ones, and after that there was a heavy silence in the hall. The idea of women addressing a meeting as important as this was still unfamiliar and disturbing. The men gazed absently at the stage, waiting for something to happen, their glances wandering from Konaté to Diara, and then to the unhappy figure of Sadio.

Suddenly a masculine voice said, 'I would like to speak,' and a towering, muscular workman got to his feet. His head was curiously shaved so that his hair formed a ring around his skull, and he seemed uncomfortable in his feast-day clothing. Everyone recognized him immediately as the first man who stopped work after the strike was called, and there was a murmur of approval from the audience. He was sure to have something to say, and it was right that he should speak.

He began by giving an account of his own actions during the strike, and of those of the men in his group, and only when he had completed this did he come to the case of Diara.

'Diara has behaved badly toward all of us,' he said. 'Yes, as God is my witness, he has done wrong. I am as sure of that as I am that some day I will be alone in my grave. When I told the men who worked with me to put down their tools, they did it as if we were all one man; and here today we are all still agreed to go on with the strike. But you, Diara – you are one of our elders; you should have guided us and helped us. Instead, you took the side of our enemies, and after you had betrayed us you spied on our women. We are not ashamed to admit that it is the women who are supporting us now, and you have betrayed them, too. For my part, I say that we should put Diara in prison – yes, that is just what we should do – put him in prison.'

'Brother,' someone in the hall said, 'you know that the prison belongs to the white men.'

'I know that, but we can build one!'

'And where would we get the money? We don't even have enough to feed a prisoner – not to mention that the *toubabs* would never let us do it anyway.'

'Everything you say is true, man – I know as well as you that the *toubabs* have stolen all of our rights, even the right to have a prison of our own and punish our own; but that is no reason to defend a traitor! If we can't put Diara in prison, we can at least do what the Koran teaches us to do – we can have him scourged!'

The man had begun to shout, and the muscles of his face and neck were contorted with anger. 'We should decide right now how many lashes he will receive and who'll be appointed to carry out the judgment!'

He sat down again, still muttering aloud, 'You are a traitor, Diara, a traitor, a traitor!'

There was a turbulence of voices in the hall; everyone seemed to want to speak at once. Some were in favor of flogging, while others still thought that a means of imprisonment should be found, and one man said that Diara should be made to turn in all the money he had earned to the strike committee. Theories and ideas went from bench to bench, and all sorts of advice was hurled at the members of the jury. In the midst of the uproar, only the accused remained motionless, as if he were not even present in the room. Once or twice, as the hearing went on, he had asked himself, 'Why *did* I do it?' and the question disturbed him, because he could not provide an answer. Surely it had not been because he wanted money or jewels or fine. clothes, richly embroidered and starched? Had his pride made him seek the stimulant that comes from holding power over others? He saw himself again, giving orders to the women, with the policemen at his side. Had it been the taste of flattery that had separated him from the others, or the sense of well-being that comes with a full stomach? Or had it been simply the cold emptiness of his own kitchen? The questions mingled and blurred in Diara's mind and then disappeared completely, leaving him alone again before the crowd in the hall, his eyes wide open but unseeing, his lower lip trembling.

Fa Keïta, the Old One, had been present throughout the trial, with Ad'jibid'ji sitting quietly beside him. He had been asked to be a member of the jury, but he had refused because he had not believed, until the last minute, that the young people would actually carry out such a plan. Now he rose slowly to his feet.

'I have a few grains of salt to contribute to the pot,' he said, and then added, glancing in Tiémoko's direction, 'if, that is, you are willing to accept my salt.'

Konaté said, 'Whatever you have to say, Old One, will be listened to with both ears.'

'A long time ago,' Fa Keïta said, 'before any of you were born, everything that happened happened within a framework, an order that was our own, and the existence of that order was of great importance in our lives. Today, no such framework exists. There are no castes among people, no difference in the quality of grain or of the bread that is made from the grain; there are no weavers, no artisans in metal, no makers of fine shoes.

'I think it is the machine which has ground everything together this way and brought everything to a single level. Ibrahim Bakayoko said to me, not long ago: "When we have succeeded in stirring up the people of this country, and making them one, we will go on and do the same thing between ourselves and the people on the other side of the ocean." How all this will come about I do not know, but we can see it happening already, before our eyes. Now, for instance, Tiémoko has had this idea, which he took from a book written in the white man's language. I have seen more suns rise than any of you, but this is the first time in my life that I have seen a ... a ... What is it called, child?' he asked, leaning toward Ad'jibid'ji.

'Tribunal, Grandfather.'

'A tribunal,' Fa Keïta repeated tonelessly. 'And I think that Tiémoko has done well. We all wanted the strike; we voted for it, and Diara voted with us. But then Diara went back to work. You say that he is a traitor, and perhaps you are right. If we are all to win, then we should live as brothers, and no one should go back unless his brothers do.

'I have heard you calling for punishment, but I know that you will not kill Diara. Not because some of you would not have the courage or the will, but because others would not let you do it, and I would be the first of them. If you imitate the hirelings of your masters, you will become like them, hirelings and barbarians. For godly men, it is a sacrilege to kill, and I pray that God will forbid such a thought to take root in your minds.

'You have spoken also of flogging, of beating Diara. The child who is seated beside me is punished that way very seldom, although my father beat me often, and the same thing is probably true of most of you. But blows correct nothing. As for Diara, you have already beaten him – you have struck him where every human worthy of the name is most vulnerable. You have shamed him before his friends, and before the world, and in doing that you have hurt him far more than you could by any bodily punishment. I cannot know what tomorrow will bring, but in seeing this man before me I do not think that there is one among us who will be tempted to follow in his footsteps.'

In the stillness, some of the women could be heard sniffing, trying to hold back tears.

'And now,' Fa Keïta said, 'I apologize for having abused your kindness. Diara, lift up your head. You have been the instrument of destiny here – it was not you who was on trial; it was the owners of the machines. Thanks to you, no one of us now will give up the fight.'

The old man looked around him for a moment and then left the hall in silence. Ad'jibid'ji remained seated on the bench.

Tiémoko had listened avidly to Fa Keïta's words, but even as he told himself, 'This is what I should have said,' he was angry with the Old One. He had moved the crowd with his gentle words and the calmness of his voice. 'I should have struck harder,' Tiémoko thought, 'and answered him firmly. He has beaten me now, because I don't know enough about these things, but it will be different next time. I must write to Bakayoko tonight.'

All of the earlier heat of argument seemed to have vanished from the hall. Men and women looked at each other furtively, and then one by one they began to walk silently toward the door.

While all of this was taking place, the eight members of the jury had not said a word. Now one of them rose and put on his cap, and two others followed his example. Konaté took the director of the Koulikoro committee by the arm, and the two men walked off together, conversing in lowered voices. Tiémoko himself started toward the door, and, as he passed the bench where Ad'jibid'ji sat, regarding him with a mixture of curiosity and dislike, he thought, 'There is more in that child's head than in all the rest of this hall.' His irritation with Fa Keïta had turned against himself, and the line of his jawbone hardened. 'It isn't a question of being right,' he muttered furiously, 'it's a question of winning!'

Soon after he had gone, there were just three people still in the meeting hall: Diara, his son Sadio, and Ad'jibid'ji, sitting quietly on her bench. Diara was unable to rid his mind of the thought of the woman Hadi Dia. He had held the votive lamb at her christening, and today she had denounced him; she had insulted him in public, and he knew that a wound like this would never heal. Sadio was still slumped in his chair. His fingers toyed mechanically with the papers scattered on the table, and tears ran down his cheeks. He was conscious that, from this day forward, his father could be reviled and insulted by anyone, perhaps even beaten, and he would have no defense. And he knew that wherever he himself went, people would look at him and say, 'Your father is a traitor.' Not one of the men in the hall, not one of his friends, had even spoken to him before he left. He was alone, desperately alone. He looked up toward the door and saw Ad'jibid'ji, who seemed to be following the silent drama on the stage with a kind of sadistic pleasure. Her eyes remained fixed on Sadio for a moment, and then turned to Diara, as if she were engraving the scene on her mind and wanted to be sure she missed nothing. From the intensity with which she regarded Diara, she might have been listening for the sound of his tears.

At last, Sadio got up and moved across the stage toward his father. A feverish trembling racked his slender body, and he seemed unnaturally tall beside the broken figure in the chair. He opened his lips to gulp in air, wanting to speak, and then he just fell to his knees at his father's side. Diara bent over the figure of his son and cried aloud, like a child who has just been punished.

◆

Fa Keïta had resolved, even before the trial was held, that he would make a retreat and address his troubled thought to the Almighty. He was angry with himself for what he considered a lack of resolution. He had firmly decided that he would not join with those who were going to the union building to try Diara, but he had allowed himself to be swayed by Ad'jibid'ji's artful insistence. He could recall the scene even now. He had been seated in his own room, while the child knelt on a sheepskin at his feet. Her long, slender fingers had been imitating the rhythmic march of camels across the desert formed by the shaggy hide.

'Grandfather,' she had said, 'please, let's go. I promise to be quiet, and after this I will never go again.'

'Never again?'

'Not until *petit père* comes back.'

'Are you afraid to go alone?'

'No, but when I do, Grandmother scolds me, and I don't like that.'

'Why do you always want to go to these meetings?'

'I have to start learning what it means to be a man.'

The Old One had laughed until the tears came, shaking his head at the child. 'But you are not a man!'

'*Petit père* says that men and women will be equal some day.'

'And what will you do then, if you are to be the equal of a man?'

'Drive one of the fast trains, just as *petit père* does. He says it's the most wonderful trade there is, and I believe him.'

Mamadou Keïta had looked deep into the almond-shaped eyes which were studying him so intently. 'Very well,' he said. 'We will go, but after that you will not go again until your father returns.'

'I promise, Grandfather.'

It was because of this that Fa Keïta had been present when the trial was held, and he regretted now that he had gone. As soon as he entered the house he had water brought to him, so that he might purify himself.

'I am beginning my retreat,' he told old Niakoro.

'What happened with Diara?' she asked.

'God knows. I left him with the others. Ad'jibid'ji was still there.'

He went into his room, closing the door behind him, so that everyone would know that, for the week to come, he had withdrawn from the world of the living. Niakoro sat alone in the little courtyard, staring at the empty mortar where the grain had always been ground, and her mind went back to its interrupted wandering.

In the old days, the singing of the pestles had begun even before the morning star disappeared in the first light of dawn. From courtyard to courtyard the women had exchanged their unceasing, pounding rhythms, and the sounds had seemed to cascade through the smoky air like the song of a brook rushing through a deep ravine. To the sharp rap of one pestle against the rim of a mortar, another rapping had answered. The women at work in their homes in the early morning greeted each other thus, in a dialogue only they understood; and the same echoes which announced the birth of the day presaged a peaceful day. They had both a function and a meaning.

The old mortar in Niakoro's courtyard had been a tree; its roots were still sunk deep in the earth. When the tree was cut down, the stump had been hollowed out to form the mortar, and pestles had been made from the branches. Mills, whether they be turned by wind or by water, have a language of their own; and the mortar has another. It vibrates beneath the blows of the woman who holds the pestle, causing the earth around it to tremble, and in neighboring houses the tremor is felt and runs through the bodies of others. But now the mortar was silent, and the only sound to be heard was the whispering of the trees, announcing a sorrowful day. Deprived of the oils from the pounded grain, the mortar and the neatly aligned pestles lay baking in the sun, from time to time emitting a little crackling sound, as a split appeared in the dry wood. And the women could only watch helplessly, as fissures ran up from the base of the stump and zigzagged toward the rim.

Niakoro was pondering on her unaccustomed solitude. All of the other women, led by Assitan, had left the house early that morning, going to the market at Goumé. Niakoro had been unable to conceal her apprehension at being left virtually alone in the compound.

'But, Mother,' Assitan had explained, 'there is nothing left here to eat, and the nearest place where we can hope to buy anything is the market at Goumé.'

'It's a long way, you know.'

'I know that, and we must go on foot. But if we leave at dawn we will be back in three or four days. There is enough food in the house for you, and Ad'jibid'ji will prepare it for you.'

'Have you told Fa Keïta?'

'No. He told me that he was planning to make a retreat. We will be back before he has completed it.'

'If God is willing. And if He brings you safely to Goumé, do not forget to go and see the Soumaré family. He married one of our cousins, and they are people of a good house. They will be helpful to you. I shall entrust you to the keeping of the Almighty.'

'We have confidence in His care,' Assitan had said.

And after the women had gone, the children had left the house. Led by the oldest, they had come to ask her permission as she sat in the courtyard grating a cola nut in her lap.

'Grandmother, we want to go to the river for water and to try to catch some fish.'

'Very well, but be careful,' she said, and the noisy group had gone off, laden down with old pots and jugs and makeshift fishing lines.

Now there was only Ad'jibid'ji to look after her, and she had gone up to the terrace.

Niakoro called out to her. 'Ad'jibid'ji, what are you doing up there?'

'I am cleaning *petit père*'s pipes, Grandmother.'

'Bring them here, and I will help you – even if I do dislike the odor of tobacco.'

'I'm almost finished, Grandmother. There is nothing left except the lighter.'

But Niakoro had had enough of being alone. With some difficulty, she managed to get to her feet and began climbing the stairway to the terrace. One hand, stretched out to the clay wall, steadied her on that side while she used the other in the painful process of bending her old knees to the rise of the steps. She was forced to pause for rest after every movement, and when at last she reached the top of the stairway, breathing heavily, she drew herself very carefully erect, her hands clasped to the small of her back. It was as if she were afraid that any sudden movement now might bring a total collapse of the fragile structure of her body.

'Here I am, Grandmother,' Ad'jibid'ji said. 'I was just getting ready to come down.' The child had sensed how much the old woman needed company and regretted her thoughtlessness of a moment before.

Niakoro had not been out on the terrace in a long time, and she looked around her curiously, but her weakening vision could take in only dimly the vista of rooftops, the slender spires of the minarets, the tower of the church, and the masses of flame trees and deodars. A fine mist of down from the silk-cotton trees floated in the air.

'Where are the pipes?' she asked.

'Here, Grandmother.' Ad'jibid'ji handed her a wooden bowl containing a dozen or more pipes of all shapes, made of ebony, of ivory, of clay, and of a rich red wood.

'Does your father smoke all of those?'

'Yes,' Ad'jibid'ji answered, seating herself astride the low wall that ran around the terrace.

99

'His throat must be as black as the bottom of a pot!'

'He cleans them all the time, and when I wrote to him I asked if it would be all right if I did them for him.'

'Did he give you his permission?'

'No. He hasn't answered yet. It was in the letter I wrote the day before yesterday, but I'm sure he will say yes.'

'Ad'jibid'ji, why doesn't your father ever address his letters to me?'

The child stopped swinging her legs back and forth against the wall and turned to look at her grandmother, seated at the top of the staircase sucking thoughtfully at her cheeks.

'I don't know, Grandmother,' she said aloud, but to herself she answered, 'Because you don't know how to read. Except for a little Arabic, I'm the only one in this house who knows how to read.'

'Your father told you in one of his letters that you should look after me, but you don't do it. You haven't written him that!'

'Yes, Grandmother. I did tell him that you had said I didn't look after you properly.'

'I don't believe you.'

'You can ask him when he comes back.'

The old woman sighed. 'If God is willing,' she murmured.

'If God is willing,' Ad'jibid'ji repeated, without much conviction.

'*Hé!*' Niakoro said irritably. 'You were born only yesterday, and you think you can take care of me! I took care of your grandfather, your father, and your "little father", too!'

Ad'jibid'ji could see where this discussion would lead. She jumped down from her perch on the wall, settled herself beside Niakoro on the steps, and began plucking away the little threads of silk-cotton that had lighted on her shoulder and her headcloth.

'Grandmother,' she said, 'why do we say, in Bambara, *M'bé sira ming* – I drink tobacco? *Ming* means to swallow, but in Ouolof *nane* means to swallow water, but *touhe* means to inhale smoke; so there are two different words, like there are in French. Why doesn't Bambara have two words, too?'

At first old Niakoro thought the question was senseless, but then she decided that it was impudent, and she said so sharply. This child upset her. Knowledge should not belong to children, but to their elders.

'Have you asked your father that?' she demanded.

'No, I just thought about it yesterday. I asked Mother, but she doesn't understand either Ouolof or French. She only speaks Bambara and her own family's language, Foulah.'

'And you, do you speak Ouolof?' the old woman asked, in that language.

'Just a little. You and *petit père* speak it better, but after all I am a Bambara, not an Ouolof.'

Niakoro's jaw dropped in astonishment. 'Where did you learn to speak Ouolof?'

'*Petit père* taught me.'

'*Hé!* You mean that you can understand everything I say to your father?'

Ad'jibid'ji laughed delightedly. 'Of course!'

'Well then, since you are such a little miss-know-it-all, tell me this – what is it that washes the water?'

'Why, it's the water, of course.'

'No, my child, it may be true that water washes everything else, but the water must itself be washed.'

'Grandmother, that is impossible.'

'No, child, it is not. The water is washed.'

'Then it must be water that washes the water.'

'*N'té, n'té,*' the old woman said, shaking her head.

'I will find out then,' Ad'jibid'ji said stubbornly. 'I will find out, and I will tell you.' Mechanically, her mind occupied with this new problem, she began arranging her father's pipes.

In this manner, sometimes explaining things to each other and sometimes arguing, Niakoro and Ad'jibid'ji passed the first three days after the women left the house. Mamadou Keïta remained behind the closed door of his room, lost in his meditations.

On the morning of the fourth day, Ad'jibid'ji, scarcely awake and still stretched naked on her bed, heard an angry knocking which seemed to shake the entire house. She leaped up and went out of the room, pausing in front of her grandmother's door.

'They have been knocking for quite a while,' Niakoro said. 'It must be your mother and the others coming back. Providence has been good to them. I will be there in a minute.'

In the meantime the knocking had become even louder. Ad'jibid'ji lifted the bar which secured the iron panel of the gate and found herself confronted by a policeman and three militiamen. She had been trying to shield her eyes from the glare of the sun, and before she realized what was happening they had pushed her aside and forced their way into the courtyard.

'Where is Mamadou Keïta?' one of the militiamen demanded angrily.

'Ask her quietly,' the policeman said.

Ad'jibid'ji had recovered her wits. 'I don't know where he is,' she said in French, before the interpreter had had a chance to open his mouth.

'Oh, so you speak French! Well then, child, tell us where the Old One is.'

Ad'jibid'ji was suddenly conscious of her nakedness and lowered her eyes. When she raised them again to look at the policeman, they held a flicker of hatred.

'I don't know where Grandfather is,' she repeated.

'Would you like some candy?'

'It's too early for that – and policemen don't usually walk around with pockets full of candy!'

At this moment Niakoro called out, 'Ad'jibid'ji, who are you talking to?'

'Some militiamen, Grandmother. They are looking for Fa Keïta.'

Niakoro came out to the door of her room. 'Sons of dogs!' she muttered. But the policeman had given his men an order to search the house, and the three militiamen simply knocked the old woman out of their way. She fell heavily to the floor, and Ad'jibid'ji ran to her side, trying to help her up.

'Miserable dogs!' Niakoro raged. 'Have you no shame?'

The policeman, one hand resting on the holster of his revolver, his legs spread wide, barred the door while the others searched. In just a few moments they reappeared, dragging Fa Keïta. He was wearing only a waistcloth, and his arms were held behind him, apparently causing pain in his back and shoulders, since he was moaning feebly, but he made no attempt to struggle. He opened his mouth to speak to Niakoro, but one of the militiamen slapped him hard across the back of the neck.

'Be silent!' he ordered.

Old Niakoro hurled herself at the man, but a violent blow of his elbow directly over her heart left her stunned and breathless. She fell back against the wall, gasping, her eyes opened wide in terror. Ad'jibid'ji then threw herself at the policeman, her little hands stretched out like a cat's, ready to scratch, but before she had moved more than a few steps his heavy boot caught her in the pit of the stomach. She turned slowly around, clutching at her middle, doubled over with pain, and fell at her grandmother's feet. Mamadou Keïta tried to free himself to help them, but he was rapidly subdued and carried off. There remained in the gloomy corridor only the prostrate figure of Ad'jibid'ji and the old body of Niakoro, still held up by the wall, but sliding gently to the ground, like an emptying balloon. When at last she fell, the light of morning from the open door lay coldly across the wrinkled, half-lifeless face.

She was groaning, 'Ad'jibid'ji, Ad'jibid'ji,' but it was no more than a breath, a sighing of the wind in the leaves.

The child was lying on the hard ground, with her legs bent up beneath her. Niakoro tried to reach the motionless form with her hand, but she no longer had sufficient strength.

'Ad'jibid'ji . . . Ad'jibid'ji . . .'

Finally the sound of her voice spanned the gap of consciousness and reached the ears of the little girl. In spite of the pain in her back and the fiery girdle which seemed to circle her waist, she tried to pull herself up.

'Grandmother,' she whispered, 'are you dead, Grandmother?'

'No, no, I am not dead . . . but try to find someone to help . . .'

Niakoro knew that her end was approaching rapidly. A final spasm of pain racked her body. 'Ad'jibid'ji . . . go look for someone . . .'

'I can't get up, Grandmother . . . I can't walk . . .' She managed to push herself up on one elbow and lifted her eyes, wide and frightened as those of a wounded doe. When she saw the old woman's face she said, 'They have killed her. The dogs have killed her . . .'

'Ad'jibid'ji . . . Ad'jibid'ji!' Niakoro said again, and this time it was a cry of anguish. Beneath the faded cloth, the old legs grew suddenly rigid, and her forehead cracked against the beaten earth.

◆

Returning from the river, where he had been bathing, Tiémoko was thinking about the letter he had written to Bakayoko. He had told him about the recent developments, but he could not tell him about his own disquiet. Since the trial he had remained almost constantly alone, prey to a disagreeable sense of constraint, almost of anguish. No one had attempted to return to work since Diara had been accused and judged, so in that sense he had achieved the goal for which he was fighting, but he knew that this was not enough. His physical strength and his brutal manner of dealing with the renegades had served him well in the past, but for the future he must read, study, and educate himself. The knowledge of his own ignorance gave him no rest, and for four days now he had closed himself up at home, surrounded by piles of books, while his wife, like all the wives of the strikers, roamed the countryside in search of food.

He stopped by the union office and found Konaté and a handful of the other men.

'Tié!' Konaté said. 'You are beginning to behave like the serpents, hiding away in the rocks some place, until you decide to come out and strike!'

Tiémoko shook hands with everyone, but made no reply.

'In any case,' Konaté went on, 'your idea about Diara was successful – there have been no more strike-breakers. But Diara is ill. I went to see him last night.'

'I'll go and see him later, but I have to go to Bakayoko's first.'

'Have you heard the news?'

'What news?'

'You can tell Fa Keïta that the management has agreed to a meeting for negotiations, and we must begin preparing for a return to work.'

Almost without realizing what he was doing, Tiémoko began to draw up a plan of action and outline it for the others. 'At least half of the workers have left the city and gone out looking for food,' he said. 'We'll have to get them together again quickly. All the rest of you, start right now; go to all the houses in Bamako and send the children to look for their fathers. I'll go to see the Old One.'

He left immediately, and as he walked he tried to think of what he would say to Fa Keïta. With the others he could bluff his way through, but he knew that these tactics would have no chance of success with the old man. Since the beginning of the strike he had thought of him almost as a personal opponent, and during Diara's trial he had been unable to rid himself of the consciousness of how widely their views were separated.

The door of the Bakayoko house was open, and as soon as he went in he saw the two bodies stretched on the ground.

'Assitan! Assitan!' he called, and when no one answered he cried out, 'Fa Keïta! Fa Keïta!'

Two or three frightened children followed him in from the courtyard and, seeing the bodies, began crying loudly. Stepping over Ad'jibid'ji, Tiémoko opened the door at the end of the corridor and ran through the rest of the house, calling for Fa Keïta and Assitan. When he was sure that no one was there, he went back to the courtyard.

'Go to the union hall,' he shouted to the children, 'and tell Konaté to come here at once!' Then he bent over and lifted the bird-like weight of Niakoro's body in his giant arms.

A quarter of an hour later the house resembled an ant hill crushed beneath a careless heel. In little compact groups people came and went through the doors and moved from one room to another. An old crippled woman told Tiémoko that the women of the household had departed some days before, but no one knew anything of the whereabouts of Fa Keïta. Two of the neighbors had carried Ad'jibid'ji to her bed and were gently massaging her bruised body. The child wept and moaned and called constantly for her father, but she had not yet been able to tell them what had happened.

At about noon the women returned from Goumé, and, as soon as they saw the crowd of people in the courtyard and recognized the anger and fear on their faces, they knew that misfortune had descended on the house. With Assitan and Fatoumata in the lead, they dropped their baskets and jugs at the gate and ran down the corridor to the central room, where the old women who had been her neighbors had already taken up their death watch around the body of Niakoro.

Fatoumata uttered a shriek which seemed to mount to the heavens and fell backward as if she had been struck by a hammer. She pounded her head against the ground and her body writhed convulsively, but her wailings went on. From the courtyard and from all the other rooms of the house the voices of the other women were heard, lifted in ritual lamentation.

In the meantime, Ad'jibid'ji had recovered consciousness sufficiently to tell her mother about the circumstances of her grandmother's death and the arrest of Mamadou Keïta. Cries of rage from the men and the cursing of women calling down the wrath of heaven on the authors of this outrage mingled then with the tears for the dead.

Old Niakoro was buried that same afternoon, with the men accompanying her body, and the women, as ancient Bambara custom decreed, remaining at home to observe the rituals of lament.

After the burial ceremonies, the strikers returned to the union office to await news of the preliminary negotiations with the company. Very late in the evening a telegram arrived from Dakar: 'Uncle refuses. Treatment must continue.'

On the following morning there was a mass exodus from Bamako. Men, women, and children departed for the surrounding fields and the brush; the men because there was nothing for them to do in the city and they ran a constant risk of being rounded up by the police, the women in the hope of finding food in some of the near-by villages.

As the days passed, the union hall was silent and empty. A chalky dust powdered the benches, a window with a broken hinge slammed against the clay wall at every gust of wind, and lizards basked in the sun on the steps of the porch. Only Konaté and Tiémoko came by occasionally, and sometimes then, scarcely speaking to each other, they took long walks beside the river or around the station and the freight yards.

One day they decided to go to see Assitan, and when they arrived at the Bakayoko house they found that Fatoumata and the two other wives of

105

Mamadou Keïta had entered on a period of forty days of mourning. The elders among the women of the neighborhood were keeping watch over their room to insure against any temptation to succumb to the weaknesses of flesh.

From behind a protective screen Fatoumata spoke to Tiémoko. 'Tié! Don't lie to us. You know as well as I that Fa Keïta is dead. The *toubabs* have taken him into the brush and killed him.'

'No,' Tiémoko said. 'That is not true. He is in prison with the others. There is no reason for you to be in mourning. There are other men in the same place where Fa Keïta is, and their wives are not in mourning.'

'But the elders have already purified us.'

'This is stupid, Fatoumata,' Tiémoko said angrily. 'Who is going to feed your children? Everyone has gone out to the brush. We all sympathize with your grief, but you and the children still must eat.'

He was interrupted by one of the old guardians. 'Mourning cannot be abandoned,' she said sternly. 'The time must be fulfilled.'

'It is a sacrilege to speak like this to women afflicted,' said another, and all of the old women began murmuring among themselves.

Tiémoko shrugged irritably and motioned to Konaté to follow him. 'It's idiotic!' he said. 'We'll have to starve them to get them out of there. Let's go and see Assitan. Maybe she can do something.'

They walked across the courtyard to where Assitan was kneeling in the shade of the drying room, crushing herbs for the evening meal in a little stone mortar. Beneath the handkerchief knotted around her head, beads of sweat stood out on her forehead.

By the ancient standards of Africa, Assitan was a perfect wife: docile, submissive, and hard-working, she never spoke one word louder than another. She knew nothing whatever of her husband's activities, or, if she did, she gave no appearance of knowing. Nine years before, she had been married to the eldest of the Bakayoko sons. Her parents, of course, had arranged everything, without even consulting her. One night her father had told her that her husband was named Sadibou Bakayoko, and two months later she had been turned over to a man whom she had never before seen. The marriage had taken place with all of the ceremony required in a family of ancient lineage, but Assitan had lived only eleven months with her husband when he was killed in the first strike at Thiès. Three weeks later she had given birth to a daughter, and once again the old customs had taken control of her life; she had been married to the younger Bakayoko, Ibrahim. He, in turn, had adopted the baby and gave her her curious name, Ad'jibid'ji. Assitan continued to obey. With the child, and the child's grandmother, Niakoro, she had left Thiès to follow her husband to Bamako. She was as submissive to Ibrahim as she had been to his brother. He might leave her for days at a time, he might even be absent for months, he faced dangers she knew nothing of, but that was his lot as a man, as the master. Her own lot as a woman was to accept things as they were and to remain silent, as she had been taught to do.

'*Hé*, woman, what are you preparing for tonight?' Tiémoko asked, with the easy familiarity of an old friend.

'*Hé*, man, it is just what is left from yesterday. You will stay, of course?'

'Whenever I see you at work I can see also that there is no danger that Bakayoko will ever take a second wife.'

'Ah, man, I would ask for nothing better than to have a "rival". At least I might be able to rest a little then . . . and, besides, I am getting old. Every time he goes away I wish that he might return with a second wife, someone younger . . .' Assitan plunged both hands into the mortar, withdrew the greenish herb paste she had been mixing, and put it into a cooking vessel.

'Assitan,' Tiémoko said, 'you must tell the other women to give up their mourning. Fa Keïta is not dead.'

'I don't know if there is anything that I can do. If my husband were here it would be different . . . but I am only a woman, and no one listens to women, particularly now.'

Assitan rose and walked over to the main house, and the two men followed her. Ad'jibid'ji was seated on the bed in the big central room, alone.

'We never see you at the union hall any more, Ad'jibid'ji,' Konaté said. 'Are you on strike?'

'I promised Grandfather not to go there again . . .'

'It is a good thing to keep to your promises.'

'. . . until *petit père* comes back.'

'Ah,' Konaté said, seating himself on the edge of the bed. 'And how are you feeling?'

'I'm much better now.'

'Good. Remember that you are our *soungoutou* – our little daughter.'

Ad'jibid'ji was silent for a moment and then, speaking to her mother, she said suddenly, 'Mother, what is it that washes the water?'

'Washes the water? What put that idea in your head?'

'It was Grandmother who asked me, and I promised to find out, so that I could tell her. Now I want to know for myself.'

'For yourself?' Her daughter never ceased to astonish Assitan. She shook her head and turned to the men. 'Do you know the answer to that?'

'I don't,' Tiémoko said.

'I may have known once,' Konaté said, 'but I have forgotten.'

'I'll ask *petit père*, or Grandfather. Grandfather is not dead, is he?'

There was a silence in the room, and then Tiémoko said, 'Woman, we must leave you now. It's too bad that Fatoumata will not listen to reason. It just makes more work for you.'

'That is the way of things. Pass the night in peace.'

When the two men had gone, Assitan sat down beside the child. 'Ad'jibid'ji,' she said, 'you must not ask older people about things they do not know. It isn't polite.'

'But it was Grandmother who asked me, and Grandmother was an older person.'

'But you must not ask visitors about it again.'

'Very well, Mother.' Ad'jibid'ji wiped away a tear, and Assitan looked at her in astonishment. Ad'jibid'ji never cried.

'Come with me; we'll go and prepare the evening meal. We have eaten nothing since yesterday.'

The child rose obediently and followed her mother out of the room.

DAKAR

Mame Sofi

The battle between the women and the policemen in the courtyard of
N'Diayène was of short duration. Overcome by sheer weight of numbers,
the police beat a hasty retreat, and after they had gone the crowd that had
gathered in the compound also began to disperse. Some of the women,
however, formed into little groups and began patrolling the streets of the
neighborhood, armed with bottles filled with sand. Still caught up in the
excitement of the fight, and a little drunk with victory, they accosted every
man who appeared in their path.

'Are you a soldier?'

'Me? No!'

'Are you from the police?'

'Of course not!'

'Well then, what are you doing here?'

And if the man's reply was slow in coming, a dozen bottles would be
brandished in front of his face, while the women shouted, laughed, and
hurled insults at him.

Night had fallen, and Mame Sofi took advantage of the darkness to
direct her group toward the house of El Hadji Mabigué. The general
disorder that prevailed in the area delighted her, and she had an old grudge
against Ramatoulaye's mercenary brother. Two servants were on guard
before the door of the house and barred the entrance to the women.
'Mame Sofi,' one of them said, 'you have no right to force your way into
other people's homes. El Hadji is not here now – he is ill. This afternoon
N'Deye Touti insulted his second wife, then Ramatoulaye cut the throat
of his ram, and now you are here, looking for an argument. Are you all
just trying to cause trouble?'

'Listen to the slave talk!' Mame Sofi cried. 'Don't you know that it's
because of his precious Vendredi that the slaves of the *toubabs* came and
attacked us? Well, you can tell that old she-goat that Ramatoulaye is still

safely at her house, and Vendredi is safely stowed away in the children's bellies!'

The man tried to calm her and placed a hand on her shoulder. 'Very well, I have heard, and I will tell him. But now, good wives, return to your homes in peace,'

'Don't touch me!' Mame Sofi screamed, and then, turning to the women, 'Come with me – we'll see what's in the kitchen!'

A heavy bottle hit the servant squarely in the forehead. He clasped his hands to his face and fell back against the wall, shouting for help, while the women raced through the courtyard and fanned out through the room on the ground floor of the house. Mame Sofi, paying no attention to three men who were seated on the steps praying, stationed herself in the middle of the courtyard.

'Mabigué!' she cried. 'Come out! Come out if you are a man! You only have courage when you're hiding behind the *toubabs*! You made them close down the fountains; now come out here and see if you are man enough to make me close my mouth!'

'There is nothing here but some millet,' a woman called from the kitchen.

'That's all right – take everything that can be eaten!'

◆

In the meantime, Ramatoulaye, Bineta, Houdia M'Baye, and a half dozen other women who were too old or too exhausted from the battle with the police to join the groups in the streets gathered in the courtyard at N'Diayène.

'The sons of dogs!' one of them said, seating herself on the rim of the old mortar. 'They tossed me around as if I were a sack of flour.'

'They did the same thing to me, but I still can't help laughing when I think of that one with the neck of a bottle sticking out of his mouth!'

'And, Bineta, that Mame Sofi is really something! Your husband must have his hands full with her! Do you know what she did? When one of them fell down, she grabbed him by his ... you know what I mean ... you could hear him yelling even with all the other noise. Then Mame Sofi said to me, "Piss in this pig's mouth!" I tried, too, but I couldn't do it – I was too embarrassed. I got out of there, but I had to knock Mame Sofi out of the way to do it. He got away after that, but I still have his cap!'

Proudly the woman held up a red military fez, and it was passed around like a trophy of war.

Ramatoulaye sat by herself, saying nothing. This vulgar gossiping irritated her, and although she was not in the habit of brooding over her thoughts or her actions the things she had done that day astonished her. The reasoning behind it all was still vague in her mind, and the unaccustomed effort of seeking for reasons tired her.

Without knowing really to whom she was speaking, she asked suddenly, 'What about the children?'

'They have eaten.'

'And the baby, Strike?'

'He's sleeping – I took care of him.'

It was N'Deye Touti who answered. She came out of the main house and walked over to the circle of women clustered around the mortar like a gathering of witches in the darkness of the courtyard. She had taken no part in the fighting and disapproved strongly of what her aunt Ramatoulaye and the other women had done. She had learned at school about the workings of the law, and she had been taught that no one had the right to take the law in his own hands. And for N'Deye there was no questioning the truth of anything she learned at the school.

One of the women rose, pressing her hands against the aching muscles of her back. 'I think I'll go to bed,' she said, 'and dream of how those black policemen are going to remember what happened tonight.'

'They'll be back though . . .'

'How do you know they will come back, N'Deye?'

'I just know it.'

'But how?'

'Because . . .'

'Because of what?'

'Because you have no right to do what you did. When the policemen came, they wanted Ramatoulaye, and you attacked them while they were doing their duty. That's an offense against the law.'

'And what about Mabigué's ram? Didn't he commit an offense against the law?'

'Yes, he did, and this wasn't the first time he had done it, but you should have put in a complaint against him with the police. Now, after what you did today, they have two things against you – Mabigué's complaint because you killed the ram, and the fact that you attacked the policeman. They'll come back, all right, because the person who is responsible for all that is Ramatoulaye.'

'Is what you say true?'

'Yes, Aunt, it is true.'

Ramatoulaye remained silent for a moment. She could not argue with the words of N'Deye Touti, who had studied and learned at the great school, and she was disturbed. At last she got to her feet. 'If they come back and want me, I will go with them. That will prevent any more trouble.'

'You are mad, Ramatoulaye!' Houdia M'Baye cried. 'You will not go! Who knows if what N'Deye Touti says is true? To listen to her, anyone would think that she would be happy to see the police come back! Is this what they teach you at school, N'Deye – to turn your back on your own people?'

'Don't get so excited, Houdia,' Ramatoulaye said. 'The children have eaten, and that is the important thing. I can go down there, and perhaps if I explain to them they will understand . . .'

She was interrupted by the sound of footsteps at the main gate of the compound. It was Mame Sofi and the group of women with her, returning from their expedition.

'Ramatoulaye,' she said, 'no one in this house is going to the police station. I heard what you said, and I heard what N'Deye Touti said. I don't know how to read myself, and it is true that she is the only one here who can tell us what the white men write in their language, but I am sure it is not written in the mother of all books of the law that honest people should be deprived of water and starved and killed. And if you think that when you go down there they are going to reward you for it and say, "Here is a hundred pounds of rice, because your men are on strike", then you are mistaken; and so is N'Deye Touti, in spite of all her learning.

'But we have more important things to do than to stand around arguing. Here is what we brought back from El Hadji Mabigué's It's only millet, but it will help.'

The women who accompanied her set the jugs and gourds they were carrying on the ground; and Mame Sofi had begun distributing the millet when a terrified voice was heard, calling to them from the street. 'Ramatoulaye! Mame Sofi! There are *spahis* coming!'

'Well,' Mame Sofi said calmly, 'we'll give them the same kind of reception we gave the policemen!'

'Are you crazy?' Bineta said. 'How are you going to fight against men on horses?'

'Don't worry, I have an idea. Horses are afraid of fire, aren't they? All of you run and get some live coals and embers from your houses. Carry them in anything you can, but we'll have to have them – there isn't a match left here. We'll need some straw, too. Now hurry!'

In less than a minute the women had spread out through the cabins in the courtyard and into the neighboring houses. Ramatoulaye herself, forgetting her earlier doubts, reappeared shortly carrying an armload of straw.

'Now go out,' Mame Sofi ordered, 'and line up on both sides of the street. Don't light any of the straw yet – wait until I give the signal.'

In the blackness of the night a file of slightly blacker forms slipped out of the courtyard and took up their positions beside the fences and the mud walls of the houses. The sound of hoofs on the hard-packed ground of the street, and the metallic jingle of bridles and stirrups, could be heard clearly now. It was a platoon of horse soldiers, coming to reinforce the police. No one had told the white sergeant who led them that the police had been routed a long time before.

From the moment they turned the corner in front of Mabigué's house and started down the long alley that led to the compound of N'Diayène, the men of the platoon were forced to hold their horses to a walk. They leaned forward in their saddles, trying to see through the darkness, surprised and uneasy at glimpsing here and there a little pinkish glow or the sudden flash of a spark. When the whole length of the column was between the double row of women, Mame Sofi shouted, 'All right! Now!'

In an instant there was pandemonium. Sheaves of flaming straw and pots of coals were flung at the horsemen from every corner of the darkness, while the women shouted at the top of their lungs and beat on tins, trying to frighten the horses with the noise. The animals reared and plunged, whinnying frantically, and the men swore. The *spahis* were veterans of a thousand parades, but they could do nothing to control their horses now. A fiery bundle of straw struck one of them full in the face and chest and he screamed in terror, trying to tear off his heavy jacket, which had already begun to burn. The men clung desperately to the necks of their terrified mounts, trying to calm them. One, then two fell to the ground and were instantly seized on by a dozen hands. The women had been joined by men from the near-by streets, and two of these succeeded in cornering one of the *spahis* against a fence, and a woman thrust a torch between the legs of his horse. The soldier managed to draw his sword. The blade flashed wickedly in the light of the flames, and a shout of 'He has killed me!' could be heard above the din, but no one paid any attention. Mame Sofi and her group of women had pulled the leader of the platoon from his horse, and when they had him on the ground they dragged him

113

by his boots to a little ditch where the people of the neighborhood relieved themselves at night and thrust his head in the accumulated filth.

It was at approximately this same moment that a frightened voice cried, 'Fire! Fire!'

Some of the flaming sheaves must have fallen too close to one of the wooden hovels across the street from N'Diayène, and the greedy fire had found a willing victim. A pall of foul-smelling smoke spread rapidly over the scene, and flames began to leap up everywhere, wrapping the straw huts in crimson arms. One after another the wooden cabins and the mud-walled houses went up like hayracks. Blinded by the smoke, and burned by flying sparks and balls of fire, the terrified rioters ran off in all directions, trying to escape from the inferno, which was gaining ground with every second that passed.

Voices could be heard calling, 'Water! Bring some water!' but most of the crowd seemed to have been struck dumb as soon as they reached a place of safety and simply stared at the spectacle, fascinated. In the dancing light of the flames, their faces looked like the masks of witch doctors.

The sheets of tarpaper and the oil-soaked timbers from the railway yards burned like match sticks; the white-hot zinc of the roofs and the flattened tin cans that had been used for fences gave off a wave of heat that made the bravest and the most curious recoil. The rumor spread that a woman whose clothes were in flames had been seen to vanish into a courtyard surrounded by fire. There was no water in the neighboring districts, and the nearest street fountains were still closed.

'Sand!' someone shouted. 'Get some sand!'

Men brought out shovels and wheelbarrows of sand, but they were just laughable toys. The conflagration went joyously on, devouring hovel after hovel and fence after fence, rumbling and leaping with pleasure. It had reached Mabigué's house, and was beginning to mix the greens and ochers of the painted walls with its own reds and yellows, when the firemen, whose barracks were on the other side of the European quarter, arrived at last. The hoses were unstrung and put to work, but with only two water trucks there was little they could do. A few yards from the steaming skeleton of a gutted house the fire licked at another roof and started off again with renewed vigor.

At last, directed by the firemen, all of the men took up axes and picks and began to cut down whole rows of houses surrounding an entire section of the miserable buildings that formed the district. Within the vast trench they cut out, the fire was left to rage. Just before dawn, having devoured every stick of wood and scrap of cloth within its reach, it died of starvation. A thick cloud of oily smoke rose from the ashes and the charred debris.

◆

Mame Sofi and Ramatoulaye returned to N'Diayène with the first light of the sun. They were weeping, coughing, and overcome by spasms of nausea. By some miracle, the wind had carried the flames away from the house, and the entire compound had been spared.

They found N'Deye Touti sitting on the bed in the central room, cradling Strike in her arms. Beaugosse, his face almost unrecognizable beneath a film of ashes, was sleeping on a strip of matting at her feet. Dazed and exhausted after hours of fighting the fire, he had come to N'Diayène to rest.

Some of the other women came into the room, and one of them lifted the cover of the big water jar. 'There is none,' Ramatoulaye said, and at the same moment three of the men came in: Alioune, Mame Sofi and Bineta's husband, Deune, and the squint-eyed Idrissa. Their eyes were red with fatigue, and their clothing was in shreds.

Alioune went over to Beaugosse and grasped him by the shoulder. 'Get up,' he said, 'I must talk to you.'

The young man sat up and rubbed his eyes with filthy hands. 'Well, at least give me a little water so I can clean up,' he said wearily.

'There is no water,' Ramatoulaye repeated. 'We couldn't even bathe the dead.'

'Beaugosse, you have to go to Thiès, right away. There is to be a meeting with the management down there, and we have to send a delegate. I can't possibly go now, so I am sending you in my place. Come to the union office with me, and I'll give you some money for the trip. You'll have to take the first bus.'

As the men started toward the door, Ramatoulaye left the group of women and came over to speak to them. 'Alioune, something has got to be done. If today is anything like yesterday, it will be the end of all of us. You must tell them, Alioune, that the women can do no more. You are not strong enough for this thing. We haven't given up the fight, but it is no dishonor to be conquered when the enemy is stronger. Look at that baby Strike – no one has any more milk for him. We have no more rice, and even if we did we have no water to cook it in.'

'Be patient, woman, for just a little longer. There is a meeting with the

115

management at Thiès tomorrow, and after that everything will be normal again, and . . . well, we can try to forget . . .'

After the four men had left, N'Deye Touti decided to go out herself. She was sure that the policemen would come back soon, and she had no wish to be present at still another battle. Her feet carried her, almost automatically, to the burned-out area across from N'Diayène, and she found that she was walking in a black dust littered with charred and shapeless refuse. N'Deye Touti had grown up in this very spot; she had played in these tortuous alleyways, these vermin-ridden courtyards and gloomy cabins. The memory was as sharp as the pain of an open wound, and she was almost ready to bless the fire which had destroyed the witnesses to her childhood and her shame. She had a vision of houses painted in clear, fresh colors, of gardens filled with flowers, and children in European clothes playing in tidy courtyards.

But what she saw around her was something else again. Men and women were already prowling busily through the ruins. Stakes had been set out here and there, marking the limits of what had been a house or a court, and boxes and trunks and empty cans were piled everywhere. In the midst of clouds of black dust, the women and the men were sweeping and digging at the wreckage, pulling out an old kettle or the framework of a bed, while naked children whose skin was the same color as the ashes ran about as if it were a holiday.

N'Deye Touti turned away from the scene and tried to conjure up another, happier vision. Titles of books and names unrolled before her eyes and stopped for a moment at that of Bakayoko. She was curiously drawn to this hard man who seemed sometimes to live in another world, but who was he, after all? A workman. Was she to be the wife of a workman, a workman who was no longer young? What, then, was the purpose of having gone to school? A lawyer, or a doctor perhaps, and love – a love that would carry her far from this cemetery of the living, far away, to the other side of the European quarter, where there were pleasant villas surrounded by gardens, not huts of wood and zinc shut up behind rotting fences or meager hedges of bamboo stalks.

Suddenly N'Deye Touti stopped, disconcerted. Just a few paces from her, three white men were standing with their backs to her, talking animatedly, and she recognized them at once. There was the director of the public health services, an officer of the native constabulary, and the chief of police of the district – the same man whose troops had fled before the bottles of Mame Sofi and her band of harpies. They had climbed up on a little hillock to get a better view of the area, where their men were working with the victims of the disaster. N'Deye Touti hesitated for a moment. She would have liked to go over and speak to them, to show them that she understood their language, but she was much too timid. She moved into the shelter of a section of wall and listened.

'It will be finished by tonight,' the public health man was saying. 'They can sleep in their own holes. It wasn't as bad as the last one. I don't even think there was anyone killed.'

'Yes, one,' the chief of police said.

'Well, it's their own fault,' the officer said. 'They started the fire themselves when they attacked the troops with those torches. Why doesn't the public health service move them all out of the city and settle them in the outskirts, the way they do in South Africa and the Belgian Congo?'

'There was a plan for something like that, but it would take time, money, and patience. They're as proud as the devil, you know – and, after all, we're not in South Africa.'

'They're nothing but savages,' the officer said. 'Good God! Look at the woman over there! Look what she's doing – in plain view of everybody! Savages! We ought to arrest her and slap a fine on her, just as an example to the others.'

'And what would she use to pay the fine?'

N'Deye Touti's eyes had followed the officer's gesture. Not more than a dozen yards from where she stood, a woman was squatting on the ground, with her skirt drawn up around her buttocks. This lack of modesty in front of white men seemed like another wound to the girl's pride, and she felt ashamed and ill, but suddenly her attention was caught by the sound of a familiar name.

It was the chief of police who was speaking. 'Well, I'll leave you now,' he said. 'I have to go and arrest this Ramatoulaye.'

'You're going to pick her up?' the public health man asked. 'I wouldn't advise it. I've known this district for ten years, and if you push the women around too much there's liable to be trouble. I don't think they know very much about the strike, but if they get involved in it and join forces with the strikers God knows where it will end.'

'Shit! I know all that as well as you, but I have a complaint against her, and on top of that there was the riot. I have to go. You come with me, captain – my men are probably already there.'

As the three men came down from their vantage point they saw N'Deye Touti, who had been too startled to move.

'What the devil are you doing there?' the chief of police demanded. Even if the girl couldn't understand him, she would know what he meant from his tone of voice. 'Go on, get out of here!'

N'Deye was so humiliated and frightened she could think of nothing to say, but she could still hear the white men talking as they walked away.

'Did you see those eyes?' the officer said. 'And those breasts? A real little filly – just the way I like them!'

'Bah! Tell one of your men to find out where she comes from, and send her a couple of pounds of rice. Right now they'll go to bed with you for less than that.' It was the chief of police who had spoken. He turned around and, seeing that N'Deye Touti had not budged, he shouted, 'Are you still there? Do you want my boot up your ass?'

Tears of rage and shame flooded the girl's eyes. She had a feeling that the earth was trembling beneath her feet, and she was forced to lean against the wall for support. She heard the public health inspector say, 'I'll let you go on alone from here. I'm not about to have a bunch of wild women throwing stones at me!' Then she turned and ran, not even seeing where she was going.

Once again Mame Sofi had assembled all of the neighbors before the gate of N'Diayène. She had realized that N'Deye Touti was not mistaken as soon as she saw the policemen forming a cordon around the compound. This time they were supported by constabulary troops, and their ranks stretched far back down the street. She hurled an insult at the interpreter who was walking toward the group of women, and the man stopped and said uneasily, 'We've come for Ramatoulaye.'

'You didn't have enough yesterday?' Mame Sofi shouted. 'You want to taste the bottle again?'

The man stepped hastily backward and almost collided with the chief of police and the constabulary officer, who had just arrived. The chief of police took him by the arm and stepped forward with him.

'Tell them that we don't mean her any harm – we just want her to sign a paper and after that she will be free.'

The interpreter translated this, adding some comments of his own to the effect that Ramatoulaye would be treated with all the respect due to a person of her age, but the announcement was greeted with jeers and laughter from the crowd of women. The man turned back to the chief of police.

'There is nothing to do,' he said, glancing about for a possible escape route. 'They say they won't let us in. They are going to kill us all.'

It was as he was saying this that N'Deye Touti came back and joined the other women at the gate of her home. To anyone who knew how careful she was of her appearance, she was a strange sight. Her normally well-combed and braided hair was in wild disorder, her eyes glittered angrily, and her clothing was disarranged and covered with dust.

'Ah, there you are at last,' Mame Sofi said. 'Well, tell these *toubabs* that we are not going to let them take Ramatoulaye. We'll die here if we have to, but she is not going to the police! If they want to talk to her, they can bring their whole station house down here.'

Still breathless from running, the girl translated what Mame Sofi had said. The chief of police stared at her in astonishment.

'I didn't know you spoke French,' he stammered.

'Ha! A little while ago that one said that I was a real little filly – just the way he liked them – and you told him he could sleep with me for a handful of rice! What about your women? They'll sleep with the zouaves for nothing!'

'What? What?' The chief of police was finding it hard to believe his ears.

N'Deye Touti, still caught up in the first flush of her anger, told the other women the story of her meeting with the three white men in the middle of the burned-out district, and the effect of her words could be seen immediately on the drawn and hungry faces around her. This time the women had gathered together everything they could find in the area that might serve as a weapon, and now their fists clenched around the handles of wrenches and knives as well as the necks of the inevitable bottles. For a moment it seemed that the battle might start again then and there, but suddenly there was a sound of voices at the rear and the crowd began to part, reluctantly making a path for Ramatoulaye. She was followed by Houdia M'Baye, who was carrying Strike in her arms. The child Anta was clinging to her mother's skirt.

'We must have no more of this,' Ramatoulaye said. 'Since yesterday we have been tossed about like grain in a winnow, and we cannot let it start again. There have been people killed, and there has been a terrible fire, and we have gained nothing from it – not even a few crumbs to eat. I will go with them. I heard what he said . . .' She motioned to the interpreter. 'They just want me to sign a paper, and that is not hard. I'll take N'Deye Touti with me, and she can tell me what is written on the paper. In that way we can have peace again. I don't want to see widows and orphans and mourning brought to the homes of my neighbors, just because of me. It would not be right.'

Then, addressing the chief of police, she said in her halting French, 'All right, white gentleman . . . we go.' She walked over to stand beside him, followed by N'Deye Touti.

'Anta,' Houdia M'Baye said. 'Take care of your brother. I am going with her.'

'So am I! So will all of us – we'll all go with her!' Mame Sofi cried. 'We can't believe what they tell us – we'll go with her and make sure!'

And so a curious kind of parade began to form. At its head were the two representatives of the authorities, one on either side of Ramatoulaye; behind them came N'Deye Touti, her fists still clenched with anger, and Houdia M'Baye, who had difficulty walking, as she had been badly bruised in the battle the night before; and behind them, flanked by lines of policemen and soldiers, came the long procession of women. At every corner along the way, new groups fell into line, swelling their ranks.

It took almost twenty minutes to reach the police station of the district. At the door, the constabulary officer gave some orders and the soldiers formed a guard around the building. He watched them for a moment to be sure his instructions were carried out, and then he and the chief of police walked up the staircase with the two women and the interpreter.

In the office of the chief of police, the two officials took their places behind the desk, and N'Deye Touti sat down on a bench beside the interpreter, but Ramatoulaye refused to be seated and remained standing defiantly in the middle of the room. The chief of police put one hand to his chin and began massaging the skin of his jawline reflectively. This was a nasty business. It was all very well for this hotheaded young soldier to announce what he would do if he were in the chief's place, but if the thing got out of hand he wouldn't be the one who had to pay for it! If he were to lock up the old woman now, it might touch off a riot that would run through the whole district. But if he were just to release her, it would be an admission of weakness that could cause other disorders. The chief of police lit a cigarette and waved his hand through the little cloud of blue smoke.

'How long have you been going to the school, *mademoiselle*?' he said, speaking to N'Deye Touti, and when she didn't answer immediately, he went on, 'I want you to understand one thing. It is your mother, or your aunt, whichever she is, who is responsible for what has happened. She is the one who killed Mabigué's ram, she is the one who prevented the law from being carried out, and she is the one who incited the women to riot.'

N'Deye Touti's thoughts were still on the shameful incident of the morning, and she made no reply. The chief of police grew angry. 'If you have nothing to say, *mademoiselle*, get out of here! I have an interpreter and don't need you.'

'What is he saying?' Ramatoulaye asked.

'He wants me to leave, but I'm afraid if I do they'll take you out by some other way.'

Ramatoulaye looked around the room. 'There isn't any other door,' she said.

The interpreter leaned over to N'Deye Touti. 'Go ahead and leave, my sister,' he said. 'I swear that I will tell you everything they say.'

Reluctantly the girl left the room and stood by a window in the lobby outside, looking out at the mass of people gathered in the square in front of the police station. The women were seated all along the sidewalks, and even in the square itself, holding up traffic and jibing at the soldiers on guard, mixing insults and vulgarities and laughing among themselves.

Houdia M'Baye saw N'Deye Touti at the window and called out to her. 'Where is she? What's happening?'

'They told me to leave. I don't know – I'm afraid they'll take her out by some other door and take her to prison.'

'Do you hear that?' It was Mame Sofi's piercing voice again. 'The *toubabs* are trying to trick us again! They're going to sneak Ramatoulaye out the back and put her in prison! Come on, get up, all of you! We'll surround the building!'

In the midst of a babel of voices and waving of arms and fists the women surged forward, pushing the soldiers out of their way and forming a vast circle around the police station. No one knew exactly what was going on, and questions and answers flew back and forth: 'Where are we going? – Have they taken the woman out? – No, she's still inside, but the *toubabs* are planning to take her out the back way – Ah, those stinking *toubabs*! – Are you coming with us? – Sure, that's why I came down here! – Do you know this Ramatoulaye? – No, I've never even seen her, but if there are this many women here just because of her, she must be someone . . .'

Houdia M'Baye came as close as she could to the building and called out again to N'Deye Touti, who was watching and listening to the spectacle, though her thoughts were still far away.

'You had better go back and see what's happening!'

The girl went back to the door of the office, and the two policemen on guard there, having seen her go in earlier with their chief, allowed her to pass.

Nothing seemed to have changed inside the office except that the chief of police and the constabulary officer had left their chairs behind the desk and were standing by a window, talking in lowered voices. Ramatoulaye still stood in the middle of the room, and the interpreter was still sitting motionless on the bench.

'Have they gone?' Ramatoulaye asked.

'No, they are all around the building now. What have they been saying, brother?'

The interpreter motioned to the girl to sit down beside him and whispered in her ear. 'He called for the firemen, to use their hoses on the women, and then he telephoned the Imam. He is coming over here right away.'

'The pigs!' N'Deye Touti cried, not realizing that she was speaking French.

The chief of police heard her and turned quickly back to the room. 'What did you say?' he demanded.

'The firemen! To turn their hoses on people! No wonder you wanted me to go out! I'm going to warn them . . .'

The chief of police came around his big desk, almost running, and seized her by the arm. 'You're going to stay right where you are!'

Ramatoulaye hurled herself at him angrily, trying to free N'Deye Touti. 'I don't understand,' she shouted. 'I can't understand what you're saying, but let the child alone. You wanted me, and here I am, but let her alone or I'll go home myself!'

The constabulary officer dragged her away and at last the two white men succeeded in pushing the old woman and the girl onto the bench beside the terrified interpreter.

'Now,' the officer thundered, 'the first person who moves will have to reckon with me!'

◆

In the square outside, the sirens could be heard long before the two water trucks from the fire department arrived and pulled up, with a violent screaming of brakes, midway between the police building and the ranks of the women. The firemen leaped to their tasks, and in a matter of seconds the hoses were unrolled, the nozzles screwed on, and two enormous jets of water sprayed over the crowd.

'Stay where you are!' Mame Sofi screamed. 'There is no water for fires, but there's plenty for us! Just stay sitting down and it can't hurt you!'

But in spite of her words the wet and frightened women in the first rows began trying to crawl away, slipping and falling in the streaming gutters. In a few minutes only Mame Sofi and Houdia M'Baye were left, and the hoses were turned directly on them. After receiving the initial shock full in the chest and almost being knocked over, Mame Sofi leaned far forward, putting her head between her knees and grasping her ankles with her hands, so that only her shoulders and the top of her skull were exposed to the spray. Houdia M'Baye, however, did not have the same presence of mind, and the powerful jet struck her squarely in the face, knocking her head back like a blow from a giant's fist. She opened her mouth to cry out, but no sound came forth, and the pitiful little snapping of the cartilage in her neck was lost in the roar of the hoses. For an instant she beat at the air with her arms, as drowning people do, then her hands seized convulsively at her blouse, tearing it open, and she fell on her side, her shriveled breasts drooping out from her body like gourds left too long in the sun.

The crowd had reassembled a few yards away, and when Houdia M'Baye fell the first ranks surged forward again. The powerful jets held them back for a minute or two, but the massed pressure of hundreds of bodies was stronger than any pumps, and they burst out of the clouds of water and raced across the square. The firemen fled in panic, while the policemen and soldiers, not daring to use their weapons, were pushed back against the walls of the police station and the neighboring houses.

Bineta and Mame Sofi knelt down beside Houdia M'Baye, staring in horror at the clay-colored face. Water still streamed down the cheeks, and a semblance of a smile contracted the lips above the naked gums.

'She is dead,' Bineta said.

Mame Sofi drew the soaking cloth over the wrinkled belly and thighs and stood up. 'We'll need a wagon,' she said hoarsely. 'Someone go get a wagon.'

A handful of men left the crowd in the square and came back a few minutes later with an old cart, on which they placed the body of Houdia M'Baye. As if the suddenness of death had calmed their anger, the women just stood where they were or gathered in little whispering groups. No one knew what to do next. Just five minutes before, all these arms and hands, united in a single force, had seized and overturned the water trucks, but now they seemed lost and helpless. The trucks lay on their sides in the middle of a little swamp, and the abandoned hoses still spurted little rivulets of water.

It was in the midst of this scene of silence and indecision that the Imam – the Sérigne N'Dakarou, they called him – made his appearance. His portly body was draped in a flowing white tunic, with a row of decorations across his chest, and his already imposing height was accented by an elaborate turban. He was an impressive figure, and the crowd parted automatically to make way for him. El Hadji Mabigué, also wearing a turban and a row of medals, was with him, and two of his followers walked behind them. He moved across the square with a stately, pontifical tread, his hands clasped behind his back under the tunic. When he came to the cart bearing Houdia M'Baye's body, he stopped and lifted one hand, with the index and second fingers extended.

'This is your work, women!' he said. 'You burn the homes of innocent people, and you obstruct the law – you are behaving like infidels! It is you who are responsible for the death of this mother, and you will answer for it before the Almighty. You are shameless and without pride in yourselves! What has happened, to make you abandon your homes and your children and roam the streets like this?'

In spite of the fact that the Imam's voice was cracked with age, it retained sufficient authority to impose silence on the crowd, and the men and women in the first rows lowered their heads. He glanced around him briefly, shaking his head in stern disapproval.

'I am going to see Ramatoulaye, and the white men, too, thank God. If I had not intervened for you, they would have put you all in prison. El Hadji Mabigué has withdrawn his complaint, at my request; now it is up to you to be reasonable. When I come out of this building I want you to be gone from here; and if you are not, there will be nothing further I can do.

'It is time you understood that your husbands are just the instruments of a band of infidels who are using them for their own purposes. It is the Communists who are really directing this strike, and if you knew and understood the things that happen in their country you would pray to God that he might forgive them. They speak to you of famine, but in their own country there is constant famine. Their laws are the laws of heretics who permit a brother to sleep with his sister – tell your husbands that.

'God has decided that we should live side by side with the French *toubabs*, and the French are teaching us things we have not known and showing us how to make the things we need. It is not up to us to rebel against the will of God, even when the reasons for that will are a mystery to us. It is always possible to fall into error, but I have done my best to help you with my little knowledge, and I tell you now to go back to your homes. I will tell the chief of police, as I have already told the mayor, that this will be the end of it. May the Almighty and His Prophet protect and keep you.'

With these words the Imam turned his back on them and walked slowly up the steps to the police station. The door had scarcely closed behind him when Mame Sofi broke the embarrassed silence which had fallen on the crowd.

'It isn't true!' she said. 'We're not the ones who killed Houdia M'Baye. I'm going to stay right here and wait for Ramatoulaye. Stay with me – all of you!'

She seized the bridle of the old horse that had been harnessed to the cart and forced the animal back until they stood directly in front of the door, facing the policemen and soldiers, who had reformed their ranks while the Imam was speaking.

◆

When the guard knocked on the door of the office, the chief of police and the constabulary officer glanced at each other in relief, and they both called, 'Come in,' at the same time.

Followed by El Hadji Mabigué and his two attendants, the Imam came into the room at the same slow and dignified pace he had used to cross the square. 'Assalamou aleïkoum,' he said, and then, holding out his hand to the two white men, he added in French, 'Good morning, gentlemen.'

'Ismaïla, draw up the chairs,' the chief of police ordered.

The Imam sat down. 'Ramatoulaye, sit down, too. I want to speak to you.' And since Ramatoulaye remained standing, her gaze fixed on the figure of her brother, he went on irritably. 'Woman, you are pigheaded and stubborn, and it is going to get you into trouble. You have drawn the anger of the toubabs down on you, which causes trouble for all of us, and you have even involved me and my position. You know that I was a friend of your father's, and that I am a friend of your brother. You come from a noble and honorable family – I have told the mayor that – but your conduct is unworthy of an honorable woman.' He had been speaking in Ouolof and switched abruptly to French, addressing the chief of police. 'She is not really wicked, but just a little simple-minded. Her brother has withdrawn his complaint, and I have had a talk with the mayor about it. The people who are really responsible for all this are the Communists who are behind the strike – white men, so I am told. You should do everything you can to hunt them out. For my part, I plan to preach a sermon on the subject to the entire community next Friday.'

The chief of police leaned back in his chair. 'If the complaint has been withdrawn, she is free to go,' he said.

'Not so quickly. I still want to teach her a lesson and make her ask her brother's pardon; so pretend that you are not satisfied yet. That will frighten her.'

The Imam turned back to Ramatoulaye and said in Ouolof, 'The chief of police has agreed that you may return home, but not until you have asked forgiveness of your brother, who has been kind enough to withdraw his complaint and promised that you will cause no more trouble.'

Ramatoulaye bit down hard on her tongue, in an effort to hold back the words that came to her lips, and remained motionless and silent. It was a direct affront to the Imam, in front of the white men, but in spite of his anger he tried to keep his voice on an easy level. 'We are waiting, Ramatoulaye. I am well aware of your pride, and I promise you before God, who sees and hears everything we do, that not a word of what you say will leave this room.'

The chief of police spoke to the interpreter. 'Tell her that as soon as she asks his pardon she can go.'

N'Deye Touti leaned forward on the bench. 'Aunt,' she whispered urgently, 'do as they say and . . .'

But she was unable to complete the sentence. With the back of her hand, and without even turning to look at her, Ramatoulaye slapped her across the face. The girl fell backward from the bench and began to weep, putting her fingers to a thread of blood that ran from the corner of her mouth. Ramatoulaye leaned over her. 'Get up, N'Deye Touti,' she said. 'I didn't want to do that but I told you to stay out of this. I would rather lose my eyes and be burned alive over a slow fire than ever speak a word again to that man. If I had to do what I did to Vendredi again, I would do it gladly. People like those two are neither relatives nor friends. They would kiss the behind of the *toubabs* for a string of medals, and everyone knows it. Now stop crying and get up; we are going. I have seen enough of their faces!'

And before any of the men had even thought of interfering, she took the girl by the arm and went out, slamming the door behind her.

The crowd in the square had dwindled to a handful of men and women gathered around the cart, the others having gradually wandered off, in a silence that was rooted in both fatigue and fear. Ramatoulaye saw the rigid body, starkly outlined by the folds of the wet cloth, and tears flooded up behind the dam of her eyelids and spilled over to her cheeks.

'She is dead,' she said, 'and I am living. And everything I did was done so that she and her baby would not die of hunger. What will her family say?'

'They will understand,' Mame Sofi said. 'They will know that it was the will of God. No one can live beyond his hour, and it is not you who are

126

responsible.' She had turned to the man who had brought the horse and cart. 'Do you know where the compound of N'Diayène is?' and when he nodded, she said, 'Take us there.'

As the little group formed to retrace the path the crowd had followed just an hour before, Ramatoulaye went over to Alioune, who was one of the men who had stayed with the cart.

'Alioune,' she said, 'it can't go on. If you won't put a stop to it for your own sake, then do it for us. We can do no more, and there are too many dead.'

Alioune lowered his head. 'We must wait for the results of the meeting at Thiès . . . Perhaps tomorrow . . .'

THIÈS

Sounkaré, the Watchman

When the soldiers had attacked the crowd in front of the workshops on the first day of the strike, Sounkaré, the chief watchman, had fled at the sound of the shots, and all that night he had been awake and watching. His infirmity and his loneliness had made him bitter, and in his innermost thoughts he was jubilant about what had happened to the workmen. When they came back to work he would be able to say, 'I told you so.'

He had a little store of rice, and for two weeks after the battle in the streets he never once ventured his crushed and battered nose beyond his own door. He lived alone in the midst of the complex of warehouses and workshops, in a cabin put together from scraps of steel sidings and leftover timbers. Its furnishings consisted of a bed, made of old shipping cartons and covered with the sacking from bags of coal, and another large carton, on which there were two books in Arabic, a tin basin for washing, and a string of prayer beads. Two long tunics hung from a nail in the wall at one corner. The door was a sheet of rough cloth from an unstitched bag.

Sounkaré was sitting on the bed, his useless leg stretched out before him, his torso listing awkwardly to one side, his cane within easy reach. The old watchman had aged so much in the past weeks that he was almost unrecognizable; his eyeballs had whitened into lifelessness, his heavily lined face had crumpled until it looked like a dried-out fig, his enormous ears stood out from the sides of his head as if they wanted to leave it altogether, and his skin had taken on a dirty gray color. He was accustomed to loneliness, but this absolute solitude was gnawing at his mind. For a long time the only people who had come to see him had been some of the old workmen, those of his own generation, and little by little time had weeded out most of these. But now no one came; he was entirely alone.

Supporting himself on the cane and the side of the bed, he got up and put his feet into a pair of slippers so old and worn that they no longer covered the cracked, whitish skin of his heels. Bent almost double, as though his head was too heavy to be supported by an empty belly, he made his way out of the cabin, moving with the jerky, awkward steps of a sleep-walker. When he paused for breath and straightened up a little, he saw that he was in the machine shop, a vast, hangar-like building with large windows, cluttered with lathes, planes, drill punches, soldering torches, and a dozen other tools whose names he didn't even know. The silence and the immobility were absolute, and an impression of enormous sadness seemed to spread through the room like a tangible thing. The only sound Sounkaré could hear was his own breathing. Looking slowly around him, from one to another of the dead machines, he saw that the spiders had already woven thick, gigantic webs from the driving belts to the flywheels, from the electric bulbs to the switches. He inhaled deeply, and nothing came to his nostrils but the cold scent of iron and steel; the human odor of sweat had vanished. And yet hundreds of men had worked here. As if in a dream, it seemed to him that he could still hear their shouts and laughter and singing, punctuated by the hammering of the tools and the roar of motors. The sounds brought life back to the building, and the strong, warm bodies again gave out their steamy, powerful smell. Then the vision disappeared, and the gears, the pistons, the axletrees, the connecting rods, and the open jaws of the vises were motionless again. The old watchman felt his heart shrink within him. There were too many bonds between him and this sleeping metal.

Four rays of sunlight filtered through the smoky windows, two of them slanting across the cement floor and breaking up in the pyramids of refuse and steel shavings, and the others resting on the workbenches. A flash of light caught Sounkaré's attention. Through a thousand motes of dust dancing in the sun's rays he saw a piece of copper tubing, still held between the teeth of a vise. He walked toward it, and on the sheet of greasy dust that covered the bench he saw the marks of tiny feet. 'There are rats,' he murmured. 'If I can catch one, I'll have something to eat.' Then he recognized this particular bench. 'It's Yoro's place ... the one who is always grumbling. I knew his father ...' He rested his tired body against the hard wood of the bench. 'I'm getting very old. I was here when all of these machines were installed ... They have a big advantage over us – they can be repaired, recast, made new again. I knew the ones that were here before these; in the days when the line from Dakar only came as far as this. People said that some day the "smoke of the savanna" would reach as far as Bamako, but no one really believed it. But you could never swear that a thing wouldn't happen, if those red-eared men wanted it to happen! I remember my father telling me the story of Mour Dial, the tribal chief everyone called Greed. He swore that the rails would never cross his lands and make him lose the tribute he collected from travelers, but the red-eared men weren't interested in anything he swore or anything he lost. Their chief – the one who wore a round cap with a flat crescent of black leather at the front to shield his eyes from the sun – just put some of his soldiers in the railway cars and took them to where Mour Dial's lands began. When they got there they fired a few shots and there were bodies stretched all over the ground, but they were on Mour Dial's side of the ground because the shots came from only one direction. Mour Dial was arrested and taken to Saint-Louis and then to Dakar, to the big council hall of the *toubabs*. People who saw that hall said that it was entirely red. After that, people never talked about Mour Dial any more, except with their mouths glued to their neighbor's ear, and no one ever knew what had become of him.'

The flood of memories dried up, and Sounkaré realized that he was cold, in spite of the hour and rays of the sun; an icy liquid seemed to flow through his veins and drip through the bones in his back. And the cold brought another memory. A few nights before, sleepless and a prey to the constant nagging of hunger, he had been huddled in his bed, and a kind of prayer had formed within him.

'Lord,' he had said, 'Oh Lord who loves me, I am alone on the only road I know. Having suffered as much as I have, I am still at the beginning of suffering. Does this mean that I am damned? Lord, what are You doing for me? You do not prevent the wicked from doing as they will, nor the good from being crushed beneath the weight of their misery, and by Your commandments You stay the arm of the just man when he would lift it to repair the evil. Do You really exist, or are You just an image? I don't see that You show Yourself anywhere. Lord, You are a God of goodness, and You have given me Your grace; is it I who have failed? Forgive me, and help me, Lord, for I am hungry, I am very hungry. Do something in my behalf, oh Lord who loves me, for I am worthy of Your help.'

At this point, Sounkaré's litany had ended, but all that night he had thought of nothing but death. He had trembled with fear at every breath of wind that moved through the old cloth across his door. How long that night had been, and how he had been haunted by the thought that soon he would die! The memory of it revived the icy trembling in his back and kidneys, and it seemed to him that the silence in the vast deserted shop was suddenly pervaded by a whispering from another world. He shivered again, but this time it was because he had been thinking of the first strike at Thiès, in September 1938.

He could still see the corpses strewn around the square, lying in the grotesque, obscene positions in which they had fallen; the little pools of blood, drying in the wind; the earth littered with sandals and sneakers and workmen's caps and fezzes. And now the men who were the sons of those corpses were on strike again. They were bullied, they were beaten, they were starved and even killed, but they would not give in. How strange it was! Sounkaré was one of the oldest employees of the company, but he no longer understood all this. The other men teased him constantly because he always made mistakes in the dates when someone asked him how long he had worked on the Dakar-Niger. Was it thirty-five years, or was it fifty? He had worked on the line all through his youth and middle age, and then a watchman in the shops had died and he had been offered the job. He had always been grateful to the company for this, because it was a good job for a man who was disabled and growing old, but what was to become of him now? He had never before worried about the future; at the school where he had learned the Koran he had been taught to live in the present and to leave tomorrow in the hands of God. The only thing that had been certain in this teaching was that he would live again after death, but the thought of death still frightened him.

Suddenly Sounkaré was startled out of his musing by the appearance of a rat at the other end of the bench where he was sitting; a rat as big as a man's forearm. He was as frightened as the watchman and sat stock-still, his nostrils twitching. Sounkaré could not take his eyes from the animal. He had never eaten a rat, but he was so hungry that he could already taste it. This one had a good solid rump, firm and fat. Boiled, he would surely be very tender, and it was said that the meat of rats had a flavor that was a little strong, but not at all disagreeable. Another one appeared now, on the floor between the bench and the shelves of tools. It must be the female; her coat was a lighter color than the male's. She didn't seem to notice Sounkaré and began cleaning her snout with her forefeet. Very slowly, moving only his hand and never turning his eyes from those of the male, the old man loosened the vise and seized the heavy copper tube. But the rats were quicker than he was, and at the same moment he hurled it they vanished. The piece of metal rolled across the floor, echoing noisily in the deserted shop.

Sounkaré sighed and got to his feet, leaning heavily on his cane. As he made his way back to the cabin he remembered how he used to go to the house of Dieynaba. For years he had taken his meals there and was almost a part of the family. Sometimes the young apprentices had brought food to him at his cabin, and then he had paid for it with bundles of firewood

131

he had made up during the night, and in which he occasionally hid a bottle of oil stolen from the shops. Since the strike he had prepared all of his meals himself – rice, nothing but rice, and now even that was gone. No one had come to bring him a morsel of anything to eat; no one had even come to see him. 'I am abandoned,' he thought, 'like an old dog who is no longer worth his keep.'

◆

In the shade of a freight car which was serving now as a house, three women were gathered, surrounded by children. At a little distance from them, Maïmouna, the blind woman, sat cross-legged on the ground, in the manner of camel drivers, intoning one of her endless ballads in a sorrowful voice. Dieynaba chewed on the stem of her pipe and listened absently to her neighbor, a big, very black-skinned woman whose ears were slashed in the old manner.

'There is only enough left to eat for one night – two pounds of rice for twelve of God's bits of wood, and eight of those children. What the strike committee gives out isn't enough.' She lifted a corner of the handkerchief on her head and scratched angrily at her hair. 'Oh, these lice!' Then she said, 'It seems that there are some merchants who have come in from Djourbel, and apparently they have rice to sell, but no one has any money to buy it. I wonder why the committee doesn't give a larger share to people who have more children. It isn't fair, Dieynaba.'

'I don't know any more what is fair and what isn't. That's as hard to decide as to separate cold water from hot in the same bowl. I saw Samba N'Doulougou, and he told me that for the moment there was nothing they could do. The money they got from France and from Dahomey and Guinea and some other country whose name I forgot is gone. Bakayoko sent the money for the last distribution of food from Kaolack. If nothing more comes in, I don't know what they'll do, but right now the treasury is empty. That's all I know.'

'I wish these lice would go on strike,' the big woman said, still scratching.

'Buy some of that powder from the Syrian – it's good.'

'Good or not good, I don't have the money.'

It was at this moment that the old watchman appeared. The three women stared at him in amazement. They had completely eliminated Sounkaré from their thoughts, they had even forgotten his existence, and at the sight of him now they hastily rearranged their clothing.

'Is this group at peace?' the old man asked.

'And only at peace,' the three women replied.

'*Alham Doulilah* – God be thanked,' Sounkaré said, and with some difficulty he seated himself on the ground, within their circle.

His presence made the women uneasy, and their conversation ceased abruptly. They glanced at each other awkwardly, and then the two younger ones got up and went into the freight car, leaving Sounkaré and Dieynaba alone.

'*Hé*, Uncle Sounkaré, things are going badly,' the woman said, on a note of timidity that was nothing like her normal voice.

Disconcerted by her attitude, the watchman just mumbled, 'It is the way of things – the will of God.' Then he belched.

Dieynaba looked him straight in the face, and Sounkaré lowered his eyes.

'Uncle Sounkaré,' she said, 'there is nothing here. Less than two pounds of rice for all of us, and you know that we are many.'

The watchman had understood. He was being sent away. His lips came together over his teeth and he murmured, 'I can wait, Dieynaba, and perhaps you could spare a little of the rice?'

The woman got up, and the shadow of her massive body blotted out the meager figure of Sounkaré. 'I don't have enough for everyone. You are still working; you have never left the shops. The men are on strike, but you aren't. What do you do with the money you earn? Go and ask Dejean to give you money for food!'

The last words, spoken loud and hard, brought the other women out of the wagon again, and they formed a silent group around the old man. Leaning on his cane, he got slowly to his feet.

'Go see the other men,' Dieynaba said. 'They are all at the union hall.'

Sounkaré tried to hurry, but it was hot and he was feeling very weak. There was an aching in his belly, and his legs would scarcely carry him. He crossed the market place, thinking that he had never seen so many beggars in Thiès. He seemed to pass one at every step – cripples, lepers, naked children. He would have liked to do as they did: sit in the shade at the foot of a tree and hold out his hand. But he was the oldest employee of the company, and he couldn't do a shaming thing like that.

At last he arrived at the shop of Aziz, the Syrian, behind the Place de France. But he had no more than opened the door when a voice called out, '*Yalla!* Enough beggars for today! No, no, don't even come in!'

Aziz was seated behind the counter of the store, with his father-in-law and his wife, who covered her face with a fine muslin veil when she saw the old man.

Since Sounkaré had not moved from the threshold, the Syrian cried out again, '*Yalla!* Have pity on me! I am not the only merchant in Thiès – go someplace else!'

The old watchman seemed not to have heard him. He could see nothing but the shopkeeper's father-in-law, a fat man who was literally stuffing himself, putting enormous morsels of a green, dough-like substance in his mouth and following it with a great chunk of bread. Sounkaré watched the movements of his hands and jaws, the swelling in his cheeks, like a dog waiting beside a table. When he had finished scraping his plate, the man thrust his little finger into his mouth and scratched at his teeth and gums. The woman, watching Sounkaré from the shelter of her veil, spoke a few words in Syrian, and the man stopped what he was doing and belched loudly. Aziz rose, came out from behind the counter, took the watchman by the shoulders, and thrust him back into the street.

Sounkaré was alone again. He was not far from the office of the strike committee, but he hesitated to go there, for fear of meeting with a third rebuff. A burning, tingling sensation seemed to be climbing up from his loins and running through his shoulders down the length of his arms to the tips of his fingers. Twice he almost lost his cane. 'That would be the end,' he thought. He paused for a moment in the shade of a mango tree and then started off again. Old memories and visions floated through his head like clouds of flies, and he was powerless to brush them away. His childhood, soft and gentle as a sheet of silk; the marriage arranged by his father, and the savings carefully put aside from his first earnings, in provision for the payment for his bride ... Then there had been that stupid accident – a sudden burst of flame from the firebox, which had made him jump from the locomotive. He had broken a hip. The bonesetters had worked over him for months, and all the money had gone – but worse than that, the accident had left him impotent. 'To die without leaving anyone behind, with no one to bear your name; to have your whole line die with you ...'

A shadow came between the sun and him. 'Ah,' he said surprised, 'it's you, Bakary?'

Bakary and he belonged to the same generation, but the meeting brought little comfort to the old watchman. 'He will make fun of me,' he thought. 'He is on the side of the strikers. They are the ones who have caused all of this, but they are eating.'

'Do you have peace?' Bakary asked, in the old fashion, and then added, in the idiom of his young friends, 'How are you?'

'God be thanked, I am well; thanks to His goodness,' Sounkaré replied, tapping nervously at the ground with his cane, 'But I no longer go out at all. With this affair . . .' He did not want to use the word 'strike', 'one cannot be sure of anything, and you need strong legs to run.'

Bakary tried to repress a fit of coughing. 'I have no need to avoid the soldiers,' he said, rubbing his sunken chest with the palm of his hand. 'With my lungs as they are, I haven't far to go in any case.'

Sounkaré was beginning to feel a trifle more calm. 'And our young warriors?' he said. 'How are things with them?'

'They are fighting like men. Seeing them, I almost envy them and find myself wishing that all of this had happened in our time. They are at the office, working day and night, and, you know, they have received money from all over the world and hundreds of letters. I am going to have to learn to read French!'

'The dog!' Sounkaré thought. 'Now he is singing the praises of these strikers – and he knows that I am hungry! The good Lord should sweep all of them away, along with me!'

But all he said, aloud, was, 'Learn French? At your age? For what little time is left, you would do better to put your soul at peace with the Lord.'

Bakary had opened his mouth to answer when another fit of coughing seized him, doubling him up with pain. He brought a bit of cloth from beneath his tunic and wiped his eyes and his forehead.

'The body,' he said at last, 'is the dwelling place of the soul. How can you expect to save the soul if you know nothing of the body – if you don't even know what causes its suffering? Right now, it is true that things are hard, but the only thing we can do is have confidence in these youngsters. I think we will get our pension as a result of what they are doing, and then our bodies, and our souls, too, will be at peace. You will receive it, of course, like everyone else, and you will have it longer than I. I am only good for the refuse heap – not even for the repair shop!'

This conversation disheartened Sounkaré strangely. He had had enough of it. Silently he cursed his friend and he cursed the strike.

'I must go back now,' he said. 'Pass your days in comfort and in peace.'

'God be thanked. And you. Come to see me the next time you come out. I am always at the union office . . . with the young men.'

Sounkaré's thoughts were bitter as he walked slowly back to the workshops. 'He might have said, "Come with me to the office – they will give you a little rice." But instead of that he was just making fun of me.'

135

He was still caught in the tangle of his memories when he went into the motor repair shop. Here, too, there was only silence. The massive diesels, their copper still gleaming, were formed in solid ranks, standing clean and powerful, and remote as gods. This building was their temple, and the acrid odor of hot oil their incense. Here they were ministered to and worshiped by the best mechanics in the land, working amid the thunder of the forges and the rolling whisper of the lathes. Pistons, wrenches, gears, and flywheels passed from hand to hand like votive offerings, and everything that was worn out was replaced. Not far from here, the locomotives stood idle, in a great circle in the yard, like monstrous children of cast iron and steel, frozen in a round of play.

Just a few feet from where Sounkaré stood, there was a grease pit, and suddenly he realized that the two rats were sitting on the other side of it, watching him. The female was preening the feeler hairs at either side of her sharp little face; the male was crouched beside a pile of greasy cloths. The old watchman was seized with dizziness, a violent cramp wrenched at his stomach, and his vision clouded. It seemed to him that the pit was moving toward him, then slowly drawing away. The icy liquid was running down his back again. The cane fell from his hand and clattered briefly on the ground; the two rats leaped away and then resumed their waiting.

Sounkaré bent over to retrieve his cane, but the effort to straighten up again was too much for him and he pitched forward into the pit. His skull struck against the gray cement, and his body twitched oddly; for an instant his arms beat at the air and slid across the greasy floor. One hand contracted around the cane; his legs seemed to fold up beside him, then slowly straightened and lay still.

The two rats descended cautiously into the pit, led by the female. She stopped before the naked soles of the feet, hesitated for a moment and sniffed, and then her sharp, white teeth bit into the cracked and grayish flesh.

As if the news had been carried to them by some mysterious telepathy, other rats began to appear, always in couples, and they, too, slipped down the walls of the pit. They circled the body in a curious kind of ceremony, and then two of the hardiest climbed up to the head and face. They began their work with the lips and the eyeballs.

THIÈS

Penda

Little by little, the women of Thiès had been forced to sell everything they owned of any value, and they were beginning to be disturbed by the lack of buyers. It was impossible now to find a market for their best headcloths, or for the waistcloths, of fine cotton from the most highly skilled weavers of the city, which had been the symbols of their virginity and were the pride of the entire family. The merchants were turning down even the rarest fetishes – those which protected their owner from the evil eye and turned away the *Jinn* and any other form of misfortune.

But the women had arrived at a degree of apathy where even such wounds to their pride as this no longer seemed of any great importance. They would turn away silently, with the rejected object clutched in their hands, and return to their homes, making a detour through the empty lots in the hope of finding something of value among the litter. It was a hope that they knew was vain, however; there was not an empty lot in Thiès that had not already been scoured by the bands of emaciated children.

Several of the wives of the strikers had fallen into the habit of meeting at Dieynaba's house. Dieynaba herself had nothing left of the supplies she had accumulated for her stall in the market place, and she passed her days sucking fruitlessly at the stem of an empty pipe but the other women were encouraged just by the strength of her presence. She listened quietly to their endless complaints and their cursing at the 'owners of the machines' and always urged them not to give up now.

After the evening meal – on the days when there was a meal – the women would gather in a circle around the elders, and then their talk would go on far into the night. Sometimes an uneasy silence would fall, broken only by a mournful sighing, and then, in an effort to avoid the dark shadow of hunger and the dejection about the future which weighed on all of them when they were together, someone would begin to sing. First one woman would sing a verse or two, then another would take up the theme, and soon everyone was adding a stanza of her own thoughts and feelings, and the song echoed through the darkness. And it was always a song which was a kind of vow by the women to their men.

◆

One day Mariame Sonko, the wife of Balla, the welder, came back from the market place where she had found a little hoard of old, but still edible, cassava roots. In the courtyard outside the house she saw Dieynaba, surrounded by women and a swarm of children who had just cut off the head of a vulture they had caught in a trap. Dieynaba held the bird up by the feet, and the blood dripping from its neck fell on her own feet, spotting them with red.

'Here is what we will have to eat today,' she announced. 'A vulture! Have any of you ever tasted a vulture? It lives on carrion and offal, but we can do the same thing! We'll eat it, and at least we won't starve.'

They seasoned the flesh of the bird as best they could and served it with the cassava roots, but even so it was tasteless; they could only bring themselves to swallow it by adding salt to every mouthful. Mariame hesitated after every bite, half expecting the spasm of pain in her stomach which would be the signal for a violent death, but nothing happened. Maïmouna, the blind woman, refused to touch the fetid meat. Her surviving twin was suffering from cramps in the stomach as it was, and she was afraid that it would taint her milk.

Later that same night, after everyone else had gone to bed, the girl Penda returned home; she had gone off with a man and stayed with him for several days. It was very late, and the sleeping earth was cool and fresh beneath her feet. Penda often went off like this, and for a long time no one had even tried to restrain her. From her earliest childhood she had demonstrated a resolute independence which only increased as she grew up. As a young girl she had seemed to develop a hatred for men and had turned away everyone who had wanted to marry her. When her mother died, she had been adopted by Dieynaba, her father's second wife, who had given her an unused cabin next to her own house. She had lived in it for several years now – or at least she had always come back to it after her periodic escapades.

When she went into the cabin that night she heard a frightened voice calling, 'Who's there?'

'Who do you think it is? It's me – the owner of this hut!' Penda's voice was rough – she had never been known to be overly gentle. 'Light a light,' she said, 'so I can see who you are, and you can tell me what you are doing in my house . . .'

'Dieynaba said that I could stay in your cabin while you were away,' Maïmouna said, clutching her baby against her breast.

Penda could see nothing in the darkness of the hut, but the creaking of the bed betrayed the other woman's smallest movement. 'Light a light,' she repeated. 'I can't see a thing in this hole.'

'I can't – I am blind.'

'Don't try that kind of story with me. I know you've got a man in here.'

'Except for Adama, who is my baby daughter, and myself, there is only God in this cabin.'

Penda groped her way across the hut, bumping against the walls and swearing. '*Vrai!* Light a light, you numbskull!'

'I tell you I can't; I am blind. But I don't think there are any matches here anyway. There have been none left anywhere for days.'

At last Penda located the bed and, feeling about with her hands, caught hold of Maïmouna's ankle. Her fingers traveled over the other woman's leg and felt the body of the wailing child.

'Lie down now,' Maïmouna said. 'You can see that I am alone, and the morning will soon be here. I'll lie down at the bottom of the bed, with the child between us . . . unless you want me to sleep on the floor?'

'Sleep wherever you please!' Penda snapped, and those were her last words that night. After hunting vainly for matches in all of her usual hiding places, she went back to the bed and lay down, but it was a long time before she closed her eyes. The baby was still moaning feebly.

Maïmouna slipped out of bed very early in the morning and cautiously made her way out of the cabin, with the sleeping child in her arms. For a moment she stood outside, listening, and when she heard the creaking of the pulley she knew that the women had already gone to the well. Dieynaba was there, crushing some leaves from a bush between her twisted fingers and stuffing them into her pipe in place of tobacco. When the blind woman had located her, she told her the story of Penda's return.

Mariame Sonko, who had been hunting for some live coals to rekindle the fires before they went out entirely, came over to them just as Maïmouna was completing her account.

'That foster daughter of yours isn't very friendly!' she said. And a few minutes later, when they returned from fetching the day's supply of water, all the other women heard the story, and Penda's return was the sole topic of conversation.

The sun was already high in the sky when the girl came out of her cabin.

She was wearing only a brief cloth, wrapped tightly around her firm young body and knotted on the left side.

'Has everyone passed the night in peace?' she asked.

'And only in peace,' Dieynaba replied. 'We return your greeting, Penda.'

Penda walked nonchalantly over to Mariame Sonko's house and picked up a jug of water which had been standing near the door. Without a word to anyone, she poured it into a basin and carefully washed her face and rinsed out her short-cut hair. As she was drying her hands she said casually to Maïmouna, 'You're the blind woman who is sleeping in my house?'

From the manner in which she spoke, it was impossible to tell whether she was simply stating a fact or whether she wanted Dieynaba to know that she disapproved of what she had done in her absence.

'Yes, I am,' Maïmouna said, her dead eyes seeming to be searching for her friend, Dieynaba. 'Is it so unpleasant to sleep in the same room with a blind woman, or are you one of those people who believe that the sight of someone like me when you wake up will bring you misfortune in the day?'

Penda had finished washing and was drying off her body with the cloth around her waist. For a moment she looked at the blind woman without answering and then said to Dieynaba, 'It seems to me, Mother, that you might have let me know . . . written to me . . .'

Dieynaba's lips were drawn tight around the stem of her pipe. 'And where would I have sent the letter,' she asked, 'even if I knew how to write?'

Penda lifted her shoulders and walked back across the courtyard. Some drops of water in her hair flashed in the sunlight. When she came to the door of her cabin, she turned back to the blind woman.

'You will stay here with me,' she said, 'but remember that I don't like beggars or people who are not clean . . . I won't call you "blind woman" any more.'

'My name is Maïmouna, and it is true that I prefer it to being called "blind woman". I thank you for your kindness.'

But Penda had gone into the house and closed the door, without waiting for an answer.

The walls of the cabin were covered with a material the color of red earth, printed with a design of palm trees in green. Photographs of movie stars and singers, and prints and drawings of white women from fashion magazines, were pinned to the material everywhere. Near the foot of the bed a trunk which was propped up on some old tin cans formed a kind of dressing table. Penda removed the toilet articles from its top and began transferring the contents of a battered straw suitcase into the trunk. When she had finished, she hung a mirror on the wall behind the dressing table and carefully combed her hair and studied her eyebrows to see if they needed plucking. Satisfied with her own appearance at last, she straightened up the room, stretched out on the bed again, and promptly went to sleep.

◆

The long days of the strike passed slowly. Penda and Maïmouna grew accustomed to each other's presence in the cabin, but they seldom spoke unless it was absolutely necessary. One night, however, Penda said suddenly, 'Who is the father of your twins?'

The blind woman did not answer. She was no longer very sure herself whether she wanted to remember that man. Her infirmity had deprived her forever of her normal status as a woman. What man would have wanted to sleep with a blind woman? But that was in the past, and her entire life was centered now on the child who remained to her. Her eyes may never have seen it, but her hands knew and loved every curve of the wasted little body.

Penda was leafing through the greasy pages of an old fashion catalogue. When Maïmouna did not reply to her question, she said, almost as if to herself, 'I'll find out for you!' and then she added angrily, 'Men are all dogs!'

Relieved that the subject had been changed, Maïmouna said, 'I don't think that they are all dogs.'

'If you could see their faces after they've had their fun with you, you would know better.'

'It's true that I can't see them, but when I hear one of them speak I can tell a lot about what kind of man he is.'

'*Hé!* Well, in that case perhaps you can tell me how you let yourself get in this fix?'

Maïmouna was silent again. Cradling the baby gently in her arms, she asked, 'Is she pretty – my little Adama?'

Penda looked at the sickly child, whose eyes exuded a yellowish pus.

'She is a beautiful girl,' she said. Then she hurled the old catalogue across the room and went out to the courtyard.

◆

141

It was a few days after this conversation that Lahbib asked Penda to take over the distribution of rations to the women.

'Why not give the rations to the men,' she asked, 'and let them take care of it themselves?'

'We tried it that way at first, but there were all kinds of arguments, and we were afraid that the trouble the wives were causing would make the men decide to go back to work. That's why we thought it would be better to give the rations directly to the women.'

'That's reasonable enough, but what about arguments between the women? Aren't you afraid of that?'

'Oh, we know that will happen, but it's not such a serious problem. They would argue, whether there was a strike or not.'

Penda laughed. 'That's true, too. All right, I'll do it for you.'

Twice each week, after that, Penda supervised the ration distribution, assisted by two other women, one of whom was older than she and the other very young and constantly laughing about something. The three women stood behind a table, set up in an open field not far from the union building. Each of them held a two-pound measuring scoop and transferred the rice in this from the big sacks behind them to the receptacles handed to them by the women. Before coming up to their table, the queue filed in front of Lahbib, who checked off their names on his list. He had two assistants also; Samba N'Doulougou and the herculean Boubacar. There were constant arguments among the women, and it required no less than three men to maintain a semblance of order.

As she measured out the rice, Penda studied the long line of housewives thoughtfully. The light of day in the field betrayed their misery far more clearly than the uncertain light of the evening fires and revealed to everyone the frayed and threadbare stuff of their blouses and waistcloths and the patches in the handkerchiefs around their heads. They always formed in the line in groups made up of the members of their own family, or the people of their own district, exchanging whatever news there was, consoling each other, quarreling, lamenting the present, and hoping for a day when at last they could satisfy the hunger of their children.

At a moment when her two assistants were busy, but there was no one in the line in front of her own station, Penda noticed Awa, the first wife of Séne Maséne, waiting a few paces away. She leaned across the table and called, 'Come forward, Awa.'

Awa was a large, square-jawed woman who seemed to take a perverse pride in her widespread reputation for maliciousness. She planted herself in front of Lahbib, her eyes glittering and her nostrils flaring like a cat preparing for battle, and repeated her husband's name loudly enough for everyone to hear, 'Séne Maséne, foreman carpenter.'

'Pass,' Lahbib said, without lifting his eyes from the list of names.

'Do you think I'm going to let myself be served by a whore?'

Lahbib looked up at her angrily. 'I might have known it,' he said. 'This is the third time in two weeks that you've tried to start a fight. Penda, give her her ration!'

Penda filled her scoop to the exact level, ready to empty it into Awa's container, but the woman just stood there with her hands on her hips, glaring at her. Then she turned to the crowd in the line behind her and said in broken French, 'I don't want that this whore should serve me!'

'Listen, Awa,' Boubacar said, 'take your ration and get out of here.'

Penda leaned forward. 'Awa, I don't speak French, but I don't have to to know what you said – and I'm going to give you your ration, and no one else. Lahbib, tell the others to go on ahead – she'll stay here.'

'I won't even speak to the likes of you!' Awa shouted, and then, before the men had had a chance to intervene, she was screaming like a sow in a slaughterhouse. Penda had reached across the table, seized her by the neck, and spat full in her face. It took both Lahbib and Boubacar to separate them.

'I don't want your rice,' Awa screamed, trying to adjust her disordered clothing, 'and my husband is going back to work!'

Samba N'Doulougou pulled at Boubacar's sleeve. 'So much the better,' he whispered. 'That will be one troublemaker less.'

The incident was quickly forgotten. Everyone was too hungry now, and there would be time to gossip about it later.

In the days that followed, Lahbib often congratulated himself on having enlisted Penda's help. She kept the women in line, and she forced even the men to respect her. She came to the union office frequently to help with the work, and one day, when one of the workmen had stupidly patted her on the behind, she gave him a resounding smack. A woman slapping a man in public was something no one had ever seen before.

In the evenings, Penda would usually remain in her cabin with Maï-mouna, looking through old magazines and saying nothing. But one night, recalling the promise she had made the blind woman, she said, 'I am still looking for the father of your twins.'

'And what good would it do you if you were to find him?'

'Me, personally? None at all – but I'd like to find him so I could spit in his face.'

'You don't seem to like men very much,' Maïmouna said, 'and yet you are helping them with the strike . . . I wonder why . . .'

Sometimes, before going to sleep, Penda had asked herself the same question. 'Why did I ever get myself involved in this business? I've got nothing to gain from it . . .'

But she always fell asleep before finding the answer.

THIÈS

Doudou

As secretary-general of the union, Doudou had been responsible for the conduct of the strike in Thiès, and the difficulties had been even greater than he feared. In the six weeks that had passed since the battle with the troops on the first day he had become more and more conscious of the burden of his new position. His shoulders were no longer broad and straight, his chest seemed to have shrunk into his body, and when he walked his head drooped toward the ground, like a fruit too heavy for its branch. The excitement and the agreeable sense of euphoria that had buoyed him up in the first days of the strike had long since passed. Now he could see only the hunger etched around the rim of the children's eyes; and when he looked at the men and women around him he asked himself constantly if he was right in urging them to stand firm and go on with the struggle. They had no food, no money, and no credit, and the help that came to them from the outside was far from enough even to fill their stomachs.

On the evening of the day he and Lahbib had made the decision to distribute what rations there were directly to the women, he returned home very late. The children were already asleep, but Oulaye, his wife, was sitting on the bed, waiting for him.

'You weren't sleeping?' Doudou asked.

'No. Dieynaba, Penda, and Maïmouna came by to see me. Have you eaten? There's still a little left, if you want something. Magatte never eats here any more – I don't know where he finds whatever it is that he puts in his stomach.'

'Oh,' Doudou said wearily, sitting down on the bed, 'boys always manage somehow.' He did not want to disturb his wife, so he added, 'I've already eaten. I stopped at your mother's and she gave me something.'

Oulaye had started for the kitchen, but she turned and came back to sit beside him, avoiding the center of the room where the five children and the apprentice Magatte were stretched on the floor. The single cloth which covered them had slipped down around their feet, and they were huddled together in a confused mass of arms and legs.

Oulaye lay down on the bed and pulled the patchwork cover up around her chin, so that only her eyes and the handkerchief she still wore on her head were visible. She studied her tired, motionless husband thoughtfully. He was no longer very handsome, and his forehead was heavily lined. Looking at the profile of this aging man beside her, she couldn't help thinking of the first years after they were married. They had been happy then. Bakayoko had taken them to see a motion picture one day – a story about some miners. There had been a scene of a cave-in in the mine, with men shouting and women weeping. Oulaye had not understood what was happening very well and was puzzled by the fact that the men on the screen looked like Negroes. But, at the end, the one who seemed to be the leader had been embraced by a pretty white woman who kissed him on the lips. Oulaye had been tempted to laugh, but now, looking at her husband, she suddenly wanted to put her arms around him that way and kiss him on the lips. She turned over in bed nervously, with the supple movement of a wild animal.

'Do you want something?' Doudou asked, trying to break the somber spell of his thoughts.

Oulaye pretended to be asleep. She was ashamed of herself, and of her abnormal and incomprehensible desire. Doudou had never embraced her like that, but she was still thinking about the kiss in that film when at last she fell asleep.

Doudou, however, was unable to shake off the problems that had weighed on him so heavily in the past weeks. He had volunteered to be secretary of the strike committee, and his offer had been accepted immediately, both because he knew how to read and because Bakayoko's and Lahbib's other responsibilities made it impossible for them to assume the position. From the very first he had thrown himself into the work, which was entirely new to him, with all the zeal and enthusiasm of a beginner. Holding meetings, traveling from one station to another, he had given everything he had to the task of bringing to the workers the realization that a new life was being born out of their present misery. He was completely convinced of the rightness of what they were doing, and he did his best to convince others, but he was an awkward speaker. Words came to him with difficulty, and his phrases crashed against each other like freight cars that had not been properly coupled. One day, after such a meeting, he had met Bakayoko, who had remonstrated with him.

'I'll give you books to read,' he had said. 'Take the time to study them carefully. We can't afford to risk defeat now, just because of our own ignorance. The way you were talking to those men you wouldn't even convince Ad'jibid'ji.'

But in spite of this warning Doudou had gone on in the same manner, carried away by his own fervor and by the enthusiasm of his audiences. Crowds of men always came to hear him, pressing around him and asking questions, and the thought that they looked up to him and respected him was a heady incense to the nostrils of the lathe operator. His heart had known the pleasurable sensation that stems from a gratified pride – even when Lahbib had added his voice to that of Bakayoko.

'You're weaving the wrong kind of cloth,' he had told him one day.

'What do you mean by that?' Doudou demanded. 'I'm talking to the men about the strike, that's all.'

'That isn't part of your job. Each one of us has his own work to do, and you should stick to yours.'

The watchfulness of Lahbib and Bakayoko might not have held Doudou back from the pursuit of a popularity which had made him better known than they – he had even envisaged the possibility of undertaking discussions with the management on his own authority – but at just about this time he had suddenly been overwhelmed by a sense of his personal responsibility for what was happening. The duties he had assumed so lightly became burdensome, and the wine of his new renown took on a bitter taste. Sometimes, in the course of the meetings, he would just sit silently by, like a man who has been thrust by destiny into a position of leadership and is bewildered by the suddenness of it all. He would have liked to recapture the spirit of the first days of the strike, but he could no longer do it. He knew that, from this point on, he would never be able to free himself from the thought of the thousands of men and women who had listened to him and trusted him, and to whom he no longer knew what to say. Bakayoko's patient and thorough preparation for just such a time as this was a thing he had never known.

The strike had lasted now for more than forty days, and the management had not even consented to talk with them, so there could be no hope of an early return to work. The men were growing restless and nervous from the constant spectacle of their hungry families. Quarrels broke out within the family, and particularly between the wives of the same man. When a striker received his portion of the ration of food or money, he gave it sometimes to one wife and sometimes to another, and this had been the cause not only of quarrels but of actual battles. It was because of this that they had decided at last to distribute the rations directly to the women, but they could not be sure that this would make things any better.

Doudou stretched out on the bed beside the sleeping Oulaye, but all of these things were still turning over in his mind, and it was a long time before he went to sleep.

◆

He went to the union office early the next morning and found the little room already crowded. In addition to Lahbib, there was Séne Maséne, the foreman from the carpenter shop, Bachirou, the 'bureaucrat', Samba N'Doulougou and his inseparable companion, the giant Boubacar, old Bakary, and several others. Doudou was in no mood to join in their ceaseless arguments and discussions, and since there was nothing that had to be done at the moment he left almost immediately.

His steps carried him instinctively in the direction of the station, and when he arrived in the square he stood there for some time, looking around him at the familiar scene – the warehouse and the workshops; the big, hangar-like sheds, whose doors were standing open; the pile of rails; and the silent mass of the locomotives. In the yards he could see some of the white workmen who had been brought in from France to perform the necessary work of maintenance and to operate the trains on the one day each week when they still ran.

Lost in his thoughts, Doudou turned around and started back to the office, but he had scarcely entered the labryinth of walls and courts surrounding the houses when he found himself face to face with a white man. It was Isnard, the supervisor of the repair shops. Like a man long accustomed to the heat of the tropics, he was wearing nothing on his head. His face was the color of red leather, and his powerful neck was as deeply ridged as the hide of an old buffalo. Although he had shaved that morning, a black stubble already covered his jaw and cheeks. His hairy arms bulged with muscle beneath the short sleeves of a carefully pressed work shirt.

He held out his hand to Doudou, who was so surprised by the gesture that he returned it automatically. It was the first time in the fifteen years he had worked for Isnard that they had ever shaken hands.

'Well, Doudou,' the supervisor said, 'I didn't expect to see you around here. But then I keep forgetting about your work with the strike committee. How does it feel to be the chief of the whole thing? You know, I can't help feeling proud that the men picked out someone from our group. At least I can tell myself that after fifteen years in the colony I've finally accomplished something! When I think of how you started out . . .'

Isnard launched into a highly imaginary biography of Doudou, but Doudou scarcely heard what he said. In all the years he had worked under Isnard's orders, the only words he had heard him speak before this were, 'Have you finished yet?' or 'See that this gets to section three.' Among the men in the shop, Isnard had been known as 'No Pay Today.' Whenever one of the workmen came in late, the supervisor would write down his name and number in a notebook and when evening came he would announce to the guilty party, 'No pay for you today.'

When he realized that anyone who saw he was going to be late simply stayed at home, rather than put in a day's work for nothing, he found another way to 'punish them', as he expressed it. To prepare their morning tea, the men had to go to the forge at the end of the building and leave their pots there to steep. And in some way Isnard always managed to overturn the pot of anyone who had been late that morning.

One day Doudou had had an argument with Dramé, the lynx-eyed deputy supervisor of the shop. 'Why should the white men have ten minutes off for their tea when we don't?' he had demanded. Dramé had reported the words to Isnard, who immediately summoned Doudou and told him, in front of all the other men, 'Go and make yourself white and you can have ten minutes, too!' Doudou had controlled his anger, but the humiliation had never left him. He had never again spoken a word to the supervisor except when it was absolutely necessary.

His meeting with Isnard now caused him considerable uneasiness. His old feelings about him were mingled with his fear of being seen talking to a white man, and he tried to pass it off by staring fixedly at the blackened tips of his sneakers.

'The strike is really annoying,' Isnard was saying. 'The appointments for the new positions on the staff have come in, and I saw your name on the list. Of course I knew it would be there because I proposed you for it a long time ago, but I wanted to keep it as a surprise.'

Isnard had prepared his speech carefully. He knew all of Doudou's weak points, and he knew that one of them was his love of flattery. He put a hairy hand on the other man's shoulder, and at the same time glanced rapidly around him, in the hope that someone would be there to see them together. Doudou had noticed Bachirou and Séne Maséne at the corner of the rue du Marché, and he bent over hastily, pretending to be tying a shoelace, but in reality just to escape the contact of the white man's hand.

Isnard understood the meaning of the trick perfectly and went back to his other arguments. 'The appointments are effective as of four months ago. That means you would get the pay rise for the whole time all at once – a nice little bundle. You could afford a new wife! I'm damned if there aren't times when I wish I was an African and could have four wives! But don't misunderstand me – you know me, and you know that I respect your customs.' He paused for a moment and then went on, seeming very serious. 'But that isn't all. I saw Monsieur Dejean, the director, the other day. You don't know him now, but you will. He knows you, and we talked about you. You know, I'm going to be retiring soon and -- well, it's you who are going to take my place. It should be Dramé, because of his seniority, but he doesn't know how to read. So you see, you will soon be taking my place, and then you can have three or four wives if you like, not just two. You're a damned lucky fellow.'

Isnard's hand was resting on Doudou's shoulder again, and his fingers were tapping gently against the collarbone, but Doudou still said nothing. He had scarcely looked at the other man, and when he raised his eyes from studying his shoes he seemed to be looking over his head at the faraway clouds.

'Ah,' Isnard said hastily, 'you almost made me forget the most important thing. Monsieur Dejean told me that I could put three million francs at your disposition right away. It's not a bribe – I know the African too well for that, and I know it would never work with you. It's just an advance. What do you think about that? Three million francs in the company's money – good for anything you want around here.'

This time Doudou looked him straight in the face. The supervisor's countenance was even redder than usual, and he ran his fingers nervously through his hair. Since Doudou had still said nothing, he was already reproaching himself for having gone too fast. The other man's silence annoyed him.

Doudou felt a warm glow flooding through his veins, and he flashed a triumphant smile at two astonished passers-by. 'Neither my grandfather, nor my father, nor myself, in our three lifetimes, could ever have had that much money at one time,' he thought, and then, aloud, he said, 'Are you trying to buy me?'

'No, of course not! I told you that already! It's just an advance against your seniority rights and your new job. Look, Doudou, you are going to be on the management staff – it's in your own interest to get the others to go back to work. This strike isn't doing anyone any good – you or me or the company or your comrades. You're the secretary of the strike committee, and as soon as the men go back to work it will be you who will work things out with the management.'

'Three million francs is a lot of money for a Negro lathe operator,' Doudou said, 'but even three million francs won't make me white. I would rather have the ten minutes for tea and remain a Negro.'

For a moment Isnard was silent, but when Doudou started to walk away he walked beside him. 'You'll get the ten minutes, and a lot of other things, but the main thing now is to get the men back to work. After that I'm sure that we can work things out. You know that you can trust my word, and I consider the Negro workers just as good as the whites. More than that, I like them.'

Doudou thought he saw his chance for revenge at last. 'Ibrahim Bakayoko, who is one of our leaders, says that anyone who says, "I like the Negroes", is a liar.'

'Ah, that one!' Isnard growled. 'He'll see, when the strike is over . . .' Then, as if Doudou had really upset him, he said, 'Are you saying that I don't like the Negroes?'

'Well, if you do, tell me why you do. A black man isn't an object to be liked or disliked like an orange or a pear or a piece of furniture. So why should you say, "I like them"?'

The simple question perplexed Isnard. He had never thought of Negroes as anything but children – often contrary children, but easily enough managed if you knew how. He sought for a subterfuge. 'Negroes are men, just like white men, and just as capable – sometimes more so.'

'Then why don't we have the same advantages?'

The discussion was beginning to irritate the supervisor, and his expression hardened. He was no longer even thinking about the fact that his three million francs had been turned down; he was too concerned with the whole nature of this astounding rebuff. The structure of ideas on which he had based his life and his conduct in all these years had been shaken, and a rage so great that he doubted his ability to control it surged through him. And then, as if he were to be spared nothing in this moment of humiliation, he saw Leblanc approaching them. He was staggering and waving his arms as he walked, and obviously very drunk. His khaki suit was stained and spotted, and his jacket was hanging open, revealing his naked chest. Isnard clenched his fists.

Leblanc halted when he came up to them and weaved back and forth unsteadily, his bloodshot eyes regarding the two men curiously.

'Well, well,' he said. 'If it isn't our hero. Just the man we need to make

151

these backward slobs knuckle under. And you, black man, don't listen to a word he says – he's a bloody liar.'

'That's enough, Leblanc – go home to bed!' Isnard's voice sounded as if he were strangling.

'I'm going – don't worry, I'm going. But you, black man, tell me something – you know I don't like you, but that doesn't mean I don't think you're right – do you know anything about Greece?'

'No,' Doudou said. 'I don't.'

'There – you see! You're nothing but an ignorant slob!'

'That's enough, Leblanc,' Isnard repeated.

Leblanc ignored him. 'I tell you, you are ignorant – but you're not alone in that either. No one has ever been able to tell me why the Greeks knuckled under to the Romans. When you find the answer to that, black man, come and see me!'

Isnard's anger was now centered entirely on his drunken colleague. He seized him by the shoulders, turned him around, and pushed him violently toward the corner of the nearest street. Doudou turned his back on them and started to walk in the direction of the market place, but had taken only a few steps when Isnard rejoined him.

'Doudou,' he said urgently, 'listen to me! You're a smart man – you should be with us in this thing, do you understand? . . . If you don't want to stay here, in Thiès, we can have you transferred . . . make you the supervisor in some other town on the line . . .'

Doudou turned to face him. 'Do you remember the day you told me that if I wanted the ten minutes all I had to do was to make myself white? And now you're offering me three million francs . . . Well, you can keep them; and tell Dejean that whenever he wants to talk about the men going back to work the committee will be at his disposition.'

Then he walked off abruptly, leaving Isnard standing in the middle of the street, muttering angrily to himself, 'You pig . . . you dirty son of a bitch . . . you'll pay for that!'

◆

On his way back to the union office, Doudou passed Bachirou and Séne Maséne, who had been watching his encounter with the supervisor from a distance. He held out his hand to them.

'It's not so bad, what I just did,' he announced cheerfully. 'I turned down an offer of three million francs. Maybe I should have taken it and turned it over to the committee! Are you coming to the office?'

'I don't know what you're talking about,' Bachirou said, 'but we're not going to the office. We have an errand we have to do. We'll see you later.'

A little bewildered by this reaction to his news, Doudou continued on his way. Several of the strikers were seated on the steps outside the union office, and in the little room he found Lahbib, sorting mail, and Boubacar, Samba N'Doulougou, and Balla, the welder, sitting about waiting for something to happen.

'Oh Doudou,' Lahbib said, 'I'm glad to see you – there is some news from Bakayoko. He's on his way here, going to Touba and Djourbel first. There's also a letter that was mailed here in Thiès, with a ten-thousand-franc note in it. It's the second time that has happened.'

'It's hard to believe that it was a white man who sent it,' Boubacar said.

'But they're the only ones who have that much money right now . . .'

Lahbib had noticed the smile on Doudou's face and the gleam of pleasure in his eyes immediately. 'What happened?' he asked. 'Do you have some news?'

Doudou told them in detail about his meeting with Isnard, and, when he had finished, Samba began leaping with joy. He hurled his old cap at the ceiling and caught it again repeatedly, laughing like a child.

'Hurrah for Doudou!' he shouted. 'We'll have to put this in the newspaper!'

'I didn't know you had a newspaper,' Boubacar said, in his stolid fashion.

'We don't, but that doesn't make any difference. We'll make up a pamphlet.'

'And with the money we get for the pamphlet we can go and see the Syrian.'

'Ha! Listen to him! Listen to my father, Boubacar!' Samba cried.

'What did I say now?' Boubacar demanded.

'Nothing wrong, brother; nothing at all. Listen, all of you – we'll take up a subscription for the pamphlet, and then we'll use the money to buy rice.'

'But that isn't honest . . .'

'Honest! And Doudou isn't honest? If the men don't subscribe for the pamphlet, he'll have to sell himself for three million francs!'

The room had filled up rapidly, as the news was already being spread through the city, and Doudou was forced to retell his story a dozen times. Suddenly Lahbib, who had been listening thoughtfully, lifted his head.

'For weeks now,' he said, 'I have been wondering where the first crack in their armour would appear. And now we know – this is the first time they have tried anything like this. Now we can beat them!'

Doudou was still talking. '. . . and then Leblanc came up. He was loaded from the bottom and started asking me questions about Greece.'

'He has been drunk ever since the strike began,' Balla said.

'Excuse me, Balla,' Samba interrupted. 'Brother Lahbib, you should think about this business of the pamphlet and the rice.'

'We'll hold a meeting about it tomorrow, and you can take charge of it, Samba.'

'Hurrah!' Samba cried. 'Hurrah for Doudou! Hurrah for Lahbib! Hurrah for everybody! I'm going to look for Bachirou and Séne Maséne.'

'No!' Doudou said. 'Leave them out of it!'

He wasn't sure why he had said it, but he didn't want anyone there who might spoil the pleasure of this moment of rediscovered acclaim. For the first time in weeks he was happy again.

THIÈS

The Apprentices

In all this period, there was one group in Thiès that lived entirely apart, separated from both the workers and their wives and the closed circle of the company itself. It was the group of the apprentices, and because of them a series of momentous events was building up at the very moment when the deceptively calm city seemed just to be sinking deeper into the apathy caused by the strike.

Magatte, Doudou's apprentice, had rapidly become the unquestioned leader of the little band. There were twelve of them, of whom the youngest was fourteen and the oldest seventeen. In the beginning, the strike seemed to them to be just a sort of prolonged holiday; the older people appeared to have forgotten them completely, and they savoured their freedom as if it were a new and exciting game. Then, as money ran out and the days grew harsh, it occurred to their families that they could be useful, and they were sent out to search for chickens that had wandered off or to pick the 'monkey bread' of the baobab trees, the only fruit available at that season of the year. For a time it amused their elders to see them running and jumping from one compound to another, ferreting out anything that was edible and happy with the task; but soon there were no more chickens to be recaptured, and even in the ravine which led to the airfield the baobab trees had been stripped of their fruit. Every morning then their shouting and running through the courtyards was broken up with cries of, 'Go and amuse yourselves somewhere else!'

On the outskirts of N'Ginth, the largest suburb of Thiès, there was an old baobab tree standing by a path that led into the fields. Its enormous trunk was completely hollow, and its leafless branches made it look like some gigantic old woman waving her arms in the air. No one knew exactly how old it was, but it was certainly the oldest tree in the district. The moment the apprentices discovered it they knew that this would be their future home. They scraped out the inside of the trunk to form a secret hiding place and built an elaborate ladder of huge nails up the side of the tree. They would sit in there for hours, talking or sleeping, but one of them was always on guard, astride a great branch just outside the entrance. Their discussions were invariably concerned with the same subject – the films they had seen in the days before the strike. They told the stories of every one of them over and over again, but never without feverish interruptions: 'You're forgetting the part where . . .' or, 'No, that's not the way he killed the Indian!' Next to Western films, war films were their favorites. Sometimes, as a change from their enforced inactivity, they played war games themselves. The old baobab became the enemy, and they bombarded it with stones, but after a time this became too simple and they turned their attention to the swarms of little snakes and lizards in the fields around them. Occasionally they had killed as many as a hundred of them in a single day. They would gather the dead animals together in one place, shouting to each other with each new addition to the pile, 'That one didn't say his prayers today!' for they had always been taught that any serpent who neglected his daily prayers would die before the night.

One day, when they were playing idly with a hedgehog in the field beside the baobab tree, Souley came and sat down beside Magatte.

'We ought to have some slingshots,' he said.

Magatte chewed thoughtfully on a blade of grass. 'Where would we get the rubber to make them?'

Séne, the son of Séne Maséne, joined them, carrying the hedgehog, which had curled itself into a spiny little ball. 'It's a good idea,' he said. 'We should have some slingshots.'

'I saw some inner tubes for bicycles at Salif's,' Gorgui said, scratching his egg-shaped head. He still had a bad case of ringworm, and his forehead and the back of his neck were painted blue again.

'Automobile inner tubes would be better,' Magatte said.

'Maybe we could find some at Aziz's shop. He has a truck.'

'That's true – I saw it last week in the court behind his shop.'

'But how could we get in it?' Séne asked, rolling the hedgehog about in the palm of his hand.

'Put that animal down,' Magatte said, chopping at his wrist. 'We have to make a plan.'

The hedgehog fell to the ground and vanished almost instantly, and the apprentices gathered in a circle around Magatte. Their conference went on all through the afternoon.

◆

The next morning they set to work on the execution of their plan. The shop of Aziz the Syrian was located on one of the corners of the Place de France, and behind the shop was a large courtyard surrounded by a bamboo fence. Magatte opened a small gap between some of the stalks and peered through. The truck was standing in the center of the yard.

'I'll go in, with Souley and Séne,' he said. 'Gorgui, you stay in front of the shop and watch out for Aziz. If you see him coming this way, you whistle to warn us. The rest of you keep an eye on the square.'

'Look out,' one of the boys said suddenly, 'there's a policeman now.'

The group promptly improvised a noisy game to distract attention from Magatte and his two assistants, who were cutting a space in the bamboo wall large enough to pass through. The policeman, however, was watching the passers-by in the square. His red tarboosh was set precisely above his ears and he carried his heavy night stick with military precision. A band of noisy children was of no interest to him. At last he walked off, and the game subsided as quickly as it had begun.

Magatte finally succeeded in cutting through the wires that held the bamboo stalks together and crawled into the courtyard, motioning to his two lieutenants to follow him.

'There's no one here,' he whispered hoarsely.

'I'm scared,' Séne said.

They made their way slowly across the courtyard, walking on their toes and holding their arms tautly at their sides, like tightrope walkers. The wheels of the truck, an ancient Chevrolet, had been dismounted, and the chassis rested on some large wooden cases, serving as blocks. They had almost reached it when the sound of an opening door made them hurl themselves to the ground. They scrambled on their stomachs into the shelter of the cases.

Aziz's wife had come out on the porch at the back of the house. She was wearing no veil, and in the shelter of a flimsy mosquito net she began to take off her clothes. When she was completely naked she began to bathe her body with a glove of toweling material. The color of her skin, which was as white as chalk, was not the least of the surprises to the frightened boys. They were observing her every movement, in silent astonishment, when they heard a warning whistle, followed almost immediately by the sound of Aziz's voice, talking to his wife from the interior of the house. The conversation seemed to last for an eternity, but finally the woman put on her robe and went back inside.

Gorgui breathed a sigh of relief. 'There's an inner tube in there,' he said, gesturing to the driver's compartment of the truck.

Magatte opened the door of their side of the truck, seized the rubber tube, and dropped back beside the others. 'Let's get out of here,' he said.

The three lithe little bodies never stood up from the dust of the ground until they reached the fence. Séne, who was the last, kept glancing fearfully over his shoulder, but the porch was empty.

A half hour later the whole group was gathered again beside the baobab tree. They set to work in an atmosphere of lazy triumph, and that day the anatomy of the Syrian woman replaced the films as the topic of discussion.

The following morning a band of lighthearted apprentices went hunting, armed with brand-new slingshots and little balls of lead. Hummingbirds were the targets of their first expedition, and then it was the turn of the lizards again. Anything that showed itself in the grass of moved in the wind was fair game. At the slightest movement or sound, a dozen projectiles were zeroed in on the suspected enemy. By noon they had collected several crows, two magpies, and a bird none of them could identify.

'We have to learn to shoot these things properly,' Magatte said.

'Yes, general,' replied the eleven soldiers of an army whose lowest ranking member was a lieutenant.

The dead birds were hung from the branches of the baobab, and stones and lead pellets began whistling through the air in an organized drill. Each time a goal was scored, the victor marked a stripe on his naked arm with the point of a charred stick.

At night they would return to their homes tired but happy. Their parents, preoccupied with their own troubles, paid no attention to their wandering, and since they got their own meals out at their tree no one even bothered about feeding them. Sometimes they would be seen with the groups of the other children, but they rarely took part in their games any more. They wore the slings around their necks as though they were strings of prayer beads and behaved like guardians of a secret which had set them apart from ordinary humans.

One day, however, Dieynaba, who had noticed their constant absences, stopped her son as he was on his way to join the others.

'Where are you going, Gorgui?' she demanded.

'I'm going to look for Magatte, Mother.'

'What do you do all day, you and the others?'

'Nothing much – we usually go walking in the fields.'

'Well, instead of wandering around doing nothing, like a bunch of dumb animals, why don't you do your wandering in the *toubab*'s district? Some of them have chickens running around loose . . .'

It took Gorgui a minute to realize what his mother meant, but then he went off like a shot and didn't stop running until he reached the baobob tree. The idea of raiding the chicken coops of the white men took their breath away at first, but the more they thought about it the more exciting it became.

'Do we go, general?'

'We go, soldiers!'

The first expedition was so successful that they didn't even have to use their slingshots. They were back at home before noon, and each one of them was carrying at least one or two chickens. They were overwhelmed with praise for their daring, and their chests swelled proudly above the sharp-boned cage of their ribs. From that moment on they had found a new reason for their existence.

Each morning one of them would go out on a scouting trip, and that night the whole band would pay a visit to the selected spot. On their return, the women would be waiting and sometimes would even come out to meet them, crying, 'Our men are back!' Thus exonerated from any feelings of guilt, they redoubled their zeal in the hunt and only the failure of a mission caused them any misgiving.

Following their success with Dieynaba's idea, Penda conceived another one. She summoned the apprentices to her cabin, and, when they came out after a long conference, their faces were marked with the expression of men who have embarked on a serious venture. Penda herself was carrying two large cloth bags. Dieynaba was sitting alone in the courtyard at the time, puffing at a new mixture of leaves in her pipe. She couldn't help smiling as she watched the little band walk off in the direction of the shop of Aziz, the Syrian.

The shopkeeper's father-in-law was stretched out on a chaise longue, sleeping, and Aziz himself was dozing behind the counter, occasionally inhaling deeply from a Turkish water pipe. The early afternoon heat seemed to have overcome him completely. Penda had chosen her time well. She went into the shop with her 'crew', as she called the apprentices, close on her heels.

Without moving an inch, Aziz said, 'What do you want?'

Acting as if she had already made her choice, Penda indicated a pile of cloth on the shelf behind the counter.

'The print?' Aziz said, turning his head, but without removing the tube of the water pipe from his mouth.

'No, the one next to it.'

'The muslin?'

'Is that really muslin?'

'You can see for yourself, woman!'

While this dialogue was taking place, the 'crew' had wasted no time. Three of them stood behind Penda, forming a screen, and behind them Magatte had pierced a hole in one of the two enormous sacks of rice that stood between the glass doors of the shop. Into the opening he thrust a long tube whose other end he had placed in one of the bags Penda had been carrying.

'Well?' the Syrian said.

'No – don't bother getting up – but, tell me, is the muslin really good quality?' Penda glanced over her shoulder in time to see one of the boys dash off, with a well-filled bag on his shoulder.

The shopkeeper looked at her irritably, and the water in the bowl of his pipe gurgled as he inhaled again. 'Look, if you don't want anything, at least don't bother me.'

Séne had noticed that the shrinking sack of rice was beginning to fall off balance, and he gestured frantically. Penda took a few steps backward.

'Well, never mind about it. I just wanted to know how much it cost.'

'I don't sell anything at this hour. Come back at two o'clock,' Aziz said.

Penda had reached the door safely. 'He doesn't want to sell anything now,' she said. 'Let's go, children.'

It was high time. Just as she spoke, the sack of rice collapsed completely and fell over on its side. The band scattered through the alleys like a flight of quail.

The rice lasted for two days of a feasting and gaiety they had almost forgotten, but the exploit of Penda and her 'crew' was talked about for a week, and the Syrian shopkeeper was the butt of all kinds of jokes. After that, however, Penda seemed to lose interest in the apprentices; she had other ideas in her head now and was working to create a 'committee of women'. So the boys went back to the baobab tree, the hedgehogs, and marksmanship drills and boredom.

They had tasted the bitter fruits of danger and now nothing else had any flavor.

But one night, destiny, which has an infallible sense of timing, called out to them again.

The shadows were lengthening on the ground as the sun went down. From somewhere in the distance the mournful notes of a bugle could be heard, signaling the changing of the guard. The apprentices were walking across the field of the watchmen's camp in the twilight. No one paid any attention to them, and at the end of the field they came to the district administrator's house, standing in the center of a well-tended garden. Not far from them some automobiles were parked beside the gateway.

Souley, the smallest of the group, was swinging his slingshot back and forth in his hand. Suddenly he stopped, picked up a stone, and placed it carefully in the leather sling. The rubber strips on either side stretched taut, the stone whistled through the air, and a headlight on one of the cars shattered noisily. For an instant the other boys were dumbfounded, but only for an instant. Then they began searching through their pockets, and the air was filled with the whistling of stones and pellets of lead, and the explosion of headlights, windshields, and windows. The watchmen came running out of their tents to see what was happening, but the band had already scattered. An hour later the windows, the showcases, and even the electric light bulbs of the station were serving as targets.

They had found a game to replace all the others. They waited until darkness had enlisted on their side, and then, moving in little groups to throw the guards and the soldiers off their track, they invaded the European quarter. Hidden behind the trunk of a tree, flattened against a wall or crouched in a ditch, they adjusted their slings, fired, and vanished into the shadows. Everything that shone in the night was a target, from windows to lamp posts. At daybreak the bulbs and the glass might be replaced, but it was a wasted effort. The following night the ground would again be littered with sparkling splinters.

They even pushed their luck so far as to attack the police station. Some of the older people did not approve of this latest manifestation of the 'crew's' activities, and there were even parents who forbade their sons to go out on the expeditions, with the result that General Magatte's army was reduced to seven soldiers. Others, however, could not help thinking that every window that broke, every light that went out, helped to establish a kind of balance: they were no longer alone in carrying the burden of the strike.

As for the Europeans, the feeling of constraint and uneasiness they had known for weeks gave place to panic. The patrols on the streets were reinforced, but, in spite of this, fear was an unwelcome guest in every house in the quarter. It was not so much the stones or the little balls of lead themselves as the thought of those black bodies slipping through the shadows that transformed every home into a fortress as soon as darkness came. Native servants were sent home, and men and women went to bed with weapons at their sides. At the slightest sound, nervous fingers reached out for the trigger of a pistol or the stock of a rifle. And, in the meantime, the members of the 'crew', exhausted from their work, slept the sleep of the just.

In-between their nocturnal expeditions, they had acquired the habit of practicing their marksmanship constantly, since they were determined to remain masters of their craft. Anything, living or dead, that could serve as a target was put to use. It was as a result of this that one evening, as they were wandering along the siding which connected with the main line from Saint-Louis, little Kâ, the youngest of the group, happened to notice a lizard basking in the last rays of the sun. His sling was already in his hand, and the child pulled back slowly on the rubber bands, sighted through the branches of the stick, and fired. The lizard leaped slightly and fell over on its back. They saw its little white belly twitch for a second against the crushed stones between the rails and then lie motionless. A second lizard thrust his nose from behind the wheel of a car and arrowed in the direction of a near-by-wall. Seven projectiles instantly smashed into the dust around him or clattered against the rail he had leaped.

It was at this moment that Isnard appeared from behind the same car that had sheltered the lizard. His hand went to his pocket, and three shots rang out. Little Kâ received the first bullet and dropped without uttering a sound. Séne fell while he was still in the act of turning around, and the other children fled, screaming. Isnard's arm was trembling, but he continued firing until the magazine of the revolver was empty. One of the last bullets struck Gorgui in the leg, and he collapsed in the middle of the tracks.

For a moment Isnard just stood there, dazed, his arm still stretched out in front of him, holding the smoking gun. Then, with a mechanical gesture, he put it back in his pocket and began to run toward the European quarter, muttering breathlessly to himself, 'They were shooting at me! They were shooting at me!'

Magatte ran straight to the union office to tell the men what had happened. Breathless, his lips trembling, his eyes swimming with tears of shock, he tried to explain how he and his comrades had been hunting lizards when Isnard had suddenly appeared with a revolver, fired on them, and killed them all. At his first words everyone in the office moved out to the street, where there would be room for the others to join them. Lahbib and Boubacar, Doudou and Séne Maséne, the father of one of the dead boys, were there already. They were joined almost immediately by Penda, who had taken to wearing a soldier's cartridge belt around her waist since she had been made a member of the strike committee.

The news spread like fire through the courtyards of the district, traveling from compound to compound and from main house to neighboring cabins. Men, women, and children flowed into the streets by the hundreds, marching toward the railroad yards. The crowd swelled at every step and became a mass of running legs and shouting mouths, opened on gleaming white teeth or blackened stumps. The headcloths of the women fluttered convulsively, and a few lost scarves floated above the crowd for a moment before falling and being trampled in the dust. The women carried children in their arms or slung across their backs, and as they walked they gathered up weapons – heavy pestles, iron bars, and pick handles – and waved them at the sky like the standards of an army. On their faces, hunger, sleeplessness, pain, and fear had been graven into the single image of anger.

At last the crowd arrived at the siding, and the bodies of the two dead children were wrapped in white cloths, which were rapidly stained with blood. Gorgui was carried away, weeping and moaning, and the long cortège turned in the direction of home. This time the women were at its head, led by Penda, Dieynaba, and Mariame Sonko. As they passed before the houses of the European employees, their fury reached a screaming peak; fists were waved and a torrent of oaths and insults burst from their throats like water through a shattered dam.

In front of the residence of the district administrator the two corpses were laid out on the ground, and the women began to intone a funeral dirge. Watchmen, soldiers, and mounted policemen were hastily summoned and formed a protective cordon around the house. When the last mournful notes of the dirge no longer hung in the air, the entire crowd simply stood there silently. But the silence was heavier with meaning than the oaths or the clamor: it was a witness to the unlit fires, the empty cooking pots, and the decaying mortars, and to the machines in the shops where the spiders were spinning their webs. For more than an hour they stood there, and the soldiers themselves remained silent before these silent people.

At last the cortège formed up again, but the ceremony was repeated, and the bodies of the children laid out, four times again – in front of the station, in the suburbs of N'Ginth and Randoulène, and in the market square in the heart of Thiès.

It was not until almost nightfall, when the mass of this human river was already indistinguishable from the shadows, that the funeral procession ended and the remains of the two children returned at last to their homes.

Three days later, the directors of the company notified the strikers that their representatives would be received.

THIÈS

'The Vatican'

The villas of the European employees of the company stood in a district, well outside the city proper, which Lahbib – without knowing quite why – had once christened 'the Vatican'.

The houses themselves were all alike, with prefabricated roofs, well-kept lawns, graveled walks, and porches surrounded by a low cement railing. In spite of the nearness of the railroad yards and the constant pall of smoke that hung over them, they had been painted in clear, light colors. Ivy and flowering vines climbed up the posts supporting the porch roofs, and flowers in pots or boxes ornamented the railings. In the gardens at the rear, rose bushes and borders of daisies and snapdragons made vivid areas of color, shaded from the tropical sun by giant bougainvilleas.

Life was easy in 'the Vatican' – so easy that it became extremely monotonous, and the adults all seemed to have taken on that scowling, sullen appearance which is the hallmark of boredom. The strike, however, had changed the atmosphere considerably; a constant nervous tension hung in the air, and fear was mingled with normal irritability. The men had secretly organized vigilante committees.

The Isnards lived at No. 7, between the villas of Victor and Leblanc, and the 'old hands', as they liked to call themselves, met frequently at the supervisor's house. They came, usually, just to gossip about the general situation, to speculate on the chances for promotions or transfers, and to give out or learn whatever news there was; and in the course of their meetings they formed petty alliances and conspiracies and spread a good deal of slander. A large part of the time it was the mistress of the house who led them on.

Beatrice Isnard was well past forty, but she was fighting a desperate rear-guard action against the advance of the years. Each night she covered her face with a thick coating of fatty cream, and before the strike she had always slept on the veranda, in the belief that the freshness of the night air would keep her skin firm and youthful. She was not at all satisfied with her face; her nose was too long, and despite her creams and depilatories a fine black down persisted in reappearing on the line above her upper lip.

On the evening of the day the company had notified the strikers of the prospective meeting, she had invited Victor, Leblanc, and a newly arrived young man, whom everyone already called Pierrot, for dinner. In the spotlessly clean and well-ordered kitchen she was grumbling irritably at the Negro cook and kitchen boy.

'You haven't even beaten the eggs yet? Well, for heaven's sake, get a move on! The dinner will be ruined.'

The second boy was setting out the silver and arranging the bottles of wine on the gleaming white cloth of the dining-room table. Through the open door the voices of the men could be heard from the living room. They were seated around a coffee table whose highly polished wood reflected the varied colors of apéritif bottles, glasses, and packages of cigarettes.

'I don't know what happened to me – I fired without knowing what I was doing!'

For the hundredth time, Isnard was repeating the same phrase, in a nasal, almost childlike voice, as if he were trying to remember a passage from some schoolday lesson he had long since forgotten. He had been living in a sort of suspended animation ever since the night of the shooting. For twenty-four hours he had not spoken a word to his wife, and several times he had gone in search of his children, holding them close to him for a moment and staring absently into the distance. He had forbidden them to go any farther from the house than their own garden.

When he had at last told Beatrice what happened, she had simply said, 'After all, one or two children more or less won't make much difference to them. The number of children running around over there is incredible anyway ... The women don't wait to have one before they're pregnant with another ...'

But Isnard just went on muttering. 'I don't know what happened to me ... I don't know ...'

'Look here,' Victor said. 'You've got to stop thinking about that. We're all living on our nerves right now. There are times when I find myself talking to myself and saying stupid things like, "All right, go ahead – go out and get yourself killed!" The way they have of just looking at you all the time is enough to set anyone crazy. Don't think about it anymore. No one saw you – it will all be forgotten.'

Pierrot, the newcomer, listened to them silently, his lips clasped firmly around a cigarette. Since his arrival he had found himself unable to avoid

165

a kind of admiration for these 'old hands' in the colony and for the hard and thankless, but fascinating, life that must have been theirs.

Victor uncrossed his legs, leaned across the table, and poured himself an apéritif. 'You'll see,' he said to his young neighbor, 'you have to learn how to forget. Twenty years ago there was nothing here but an arid wilderness. We built this city. Now they have hospitals, schools, and trains, but if we ever leave they're finished – the brush will take it all back. There wouldn't be anything left.'

Pierrot leaned back in his chair and lit another cigarette. 'I'd like to know something about how they live,' he said uncertainly. 'I've wandered around a little in the past few days, but I haven't seen very much. In the district around the airfield the houses are nothing but rats' nests. They were swarming with vermin, and, my God, the smell . . .! I wanted to take some pictures of a child, but his mother came out and cursed me to my face, so I didn't bother with it. I never thought Africa would be like that.'

'It's their own fault if they live in places like that. You can always take pictures of the boys or the beggars, but don't give them more than twenty francs. This part of Africa is pretty ugly anyway, though – aside from two or three cities there isn't anything of any interest in the whole of Sénégal. Now you take French Equatorial Africa – that's something else again. You'll find all the real animal life of Africa there – and the natives are a lot more peaceable, too!'

The young man refused to be discouraged. 'You could give me some tips, though. For one thing, I'd like to get to know a real African family.'

'You must have read too many books! The best thing you can do is forget that nonsense. I've been out here longer than almost anyone else, and I don't know any of them except for my servants and the men in the shop. They keep their distance, and so do we. Ask Isnard.'

But Isnard had left them, although he still sat across the table from them, his eyes half closed, staring at the wall. He had fled from everything around him, escaped from it completely, and taken shelter in a dream. It was winter, and snow lay deep on the gabled roofs of the houses and on the pine trees climbing the slope of the hills. Isnard was home again, in a little village in the Vosges. Spring came suddenly, with burgeoning flowers everywhere and the clear mountain streams running fresh again. Soon it was summer and the Bastille Day festival in the village square. The owner of the hotel brought out tables and chairs, and at night there was dancing in the open air. There were young girls – there was one young girl who left the dancing and walked off alone, toward the viaduct. He followed her, and when he joined her she pretended to be angry and pouted a little, but her eyes gave her away ... And then the summer had passed. The leaves from the trees covered the ground, only the pines were still green, it was the time for gathering in the honey ...

Beatrice came into the room, untying her neatly pressed white apron. 'Well, gentlemen,' she said. 'We're not very talkative tonight.'

'Oh, good evening, madame,' Pierrot said, rising politely. 'I've just been asking Monsieur Victor and your husband how I could get to know one of the native families.'

'Well, I don't advise you to do it.' The tone of Beatrice's voice indicated clearly her intention of organizing the newcomer's life in her own fashion. 'You have absolutely nothing to gain from it except lice or one of their diseases ... When you think of these half-savages going on strike! Honestly, I think I've seen everything now.'

'That's exactly what I would like to understand, madame.'

'There nothing to understand. They are children, that's all. Somebody has put some wild ideas in their heads, but they'll see sooner or later – this strike is going to cost them a lot more than they can possibly gain from it. Just imagine – they're all polygamous, and yet they're asking for family allowances. With the number of children they have! It's incredible!'

His wife's diatribe had brought Isnard out of his trance. He swallowed a mouthful of his apéritif and turned to Pierrot. 'I've done everything I could for them. I've given my youth and health to this country of theirs, trying to do something for them; and now they are treating us as oppressors!'

'Tell him the story about your Negress,' Beatrice said, seating herself on the arm of the couch.

Isnard put down his glass and brought his eyebrows together quizzically, as though he had difficulty in remembering. 'It was one night a long time ago,' he said at last. 'I had just gone to sleep. In fifteen years in the colonies I've never seen a night like that – black as a pit and a wind that you thought would carry the huts away. In those days we didn't have these bungalows yet. Well, I had gone to bed and finally gotten to sleep when suddenly I heard someone calling, "*Missé! Missé!*" At first, I'll tell you I was scared, but as soon as I was really awake I started laughing, thinking it was just some girl for the night – they used to come around like that – and what a fool she was to be out. Well, I got up and went to the door and lit my flashlight, and what do you think I saw? A Negress, all right, but a gigantic one. I took a closer look at her and saw that she had a belly as big as a wine barrel. Then she started bellowing, "Doctor! Doctor!" in English, and for a minute I didn't know what she meant. All of a sudden she fell down on her hands and knees, screaming like a wild woman, and started to have her baby – yes, to have a baby, right there on the ground in front of me! The baby came out all right, but I had nothing to separate it from the woman's body, nothing at all. Do you know what I did?'

Pierrot, who was feeling slightly ill at the thought of the big black body opening up, and blood flowing across the ground, shook his head.

'Well, I did it with my teeth. That was the only thing I had, so I did it with my teeth.'

'Good God,' the young man murmured.

'You see what I meant?' Beatrice demanded. 'That's the sort of thing that happens in the colonies.'

At this moment they all heard a thick, slurring voice from the veranda. 'Don't believe a word of what that liar says!' It was Leblanc. He was already very drunk and almost fell as he came up the steps.

'He's told that story a hundred times, and it's the stupidest thing I've ever heard.' He pointed an unsteady finger at Isnard. 'Take a look at him. With his teeth, he says! With those store-bought teeth of his he couldn't bite into a rum baba! As for you, my young friend, you seem to have all the right ideas, but just wait a little while and you'll see what happens to them. And as for me, I'll tell you frankly that I don't like these blacks. They not only despise us but now they're trying to pretend we aren't even here. Do you know what we are, in this place, my young friend? We're nothing but an advance guard in an enemy country!'

Isnard, Beatrice, and Victor stared at Leblanc in disgust. They called him 'our intellectual' sneeringly, and although they continued to receive him in their homes because he belonged to their race they had nothing but contempt for him. He was an ex-student who had arrived in Africa one day 'to study anthropology'. After wandering about the continent for some time with a Haitian Negro companion, he had accepted a minor position with the company and remained in Africa ever since, dividing his time between work and drinking.

There were very few people who recognized that Leblanc's present condition was more the result of unrealized hope than of any thwarted ambition. He had tried in vain to establish some sort of friendly relationship with the Africans, but his knowledge intimidated them and his natural shyness made it difficult for them to approach him. This hostility – or rather, this lack of any response to his efforts – had gradually discouraged him, and his drinking had completed the work. He had become a narrow, bitter person, laughed at by the blacks and mistrusted by the whites.

Pierrot could not take his eyes from Leblanc's flabby, rumpled face. The yellowish, unshaven skin made him look like a plucked fowl, his eyelids drooped, and the scars of climate and alcohol had deformed and pitted his features. A heavy odor of sweat steamed from his open shirt.

The young man rose to say good night, but Beatrice stopped him. 'No, no, Monsieur Pierre – you must stay and have dinner with us. We're waiting for Edouard.'

'By all means stay then, young man,' Leblanc said, pouring himself another drink. 'Edouard is a very important man – it's a good idea to have him on your side. Believe me, in the colonies a few friends in high places are worth a lot more than twenty years of work. And tomorrow it will be Edouard who is going to represent the gangsters against the Negroes.'

Beatrice turned to him abruptly. 'Aren't you ashamed of yourself, Leblanc, acting like this? What will Monsieur Pierre think of us?'

'Ah, but that isn't the question. The question is, what do the Negroes think of us?'

'Oh, shut up about your Negroes,' Victor interrupted angrily. 'You get damned boring after a while.'

'But I'm not really the one who bores you – it's "my Negroes", as you call them. But you haven't seen anything yet. Now that those two kids have been murdered, we're going to see the hour of truth.'

'What truth, Leblanc?' asked a jovial voice from the veranda. 'Good evening, everyone.'

Edouard came into the room, carrying a large briefcase. 'Good evening, madame – Isnard, your wife is just as beautiful as ever – the heat doesn't seem to affect her at all.'

Beatrice laughed. 'And you don't change either – always the flatterer. How is your wife?'

'Still fighting with the boys, as usual, but, aside from that, everything is fine.'

'They are really becoming impossible. I . . .'

'. . . should be damned glad to have them,' Leblanc said. 'Another one of our privileges that will be hard to give up – four black servants for the price of one in Europe.'

'Be careful what you say, Leblanc – you could get yourself in trouble. It might be a good idea if you went to see Doctor Michel.'

'Oh, I know all about your Doctor Michel, and I know exactly what would happen. I wouldn't have turned my back before his telephone was ringing. "Hello, is that you, doctor? Leblanc is coming over to see you. He isn't well, and he really should be sent home . . . you understand, don't you? Of course, thank you, doctor."' Leblanc acted out the scene as he spoke, holding his glass in one hand and an imaginary telephone in the other. When he had finished, he tossed off the drink in a single swallow and collapsed against the back of his chair, as if he had been knocked unconscious. No one except Pierrot paid any attention to him.

'What news is there from Dakar?' Victor asked Edouard.

'Nothing; but they have heard the news from Thiès. They know the story of the apprentices ... and I'm to meet with the fellows tomorrow and see what they have on their chests, that's all.'

'Are you supposed to satisfy their demands or try to work out a compromise?'

'Satisfying their demands isn't possible – but we have to talk to them. They are children who want to learn to walk by themselves, and it is up to us to give them a hand.'

'You know that if they get everything they are asking for we are finished here?'

'Look, Victor, I came from Dakar with very clear instructions, and I saw Dejean before coming here tonight. We're going to try to do everything we can about the matter of salaries; for the rest, I'll see what they want and make a report, but you have to realize that the bastards have got us over a barrel. Do you know that at Bamako they picked up a man who had gone back to work, by disguising themselves as policemen? And then they held a trial, right under our noses! They're talking about it everywhere, and since it happened we haven't been able to get one of them to go back. At Dakar and Saint-Louis some of the women have been battling with the police in the streets. Then there is that story about the three million francs ... Did you know that Bakayoko, their leader, raised more than fifty thousand francs when he spoke at a meeting in Saint-Louis?'

'I thought he was at Kayes,' Victor said.

'He was, but then he came back this way. We thought he was coming here, but he stopped at Djoubel and then went to Saint-Louis. He'll be back here soon, though.'

'He's a dangerous man,' Isnard said.

'For once, you are right,' Leblanc said, opening a bloodshot eye. 'Very dangerous. But be careful – he'll be more dangerous dead than alive.'

'There's nothing more disgusting than a drunken failure,' Victor said, looking at Leblanc angrily.

'That's true; I am a failure,' Leblanc said. 'I've failed at everything, even treachery. I like the Negroes, or I used to like them – but they shut their doors in my face. I'll tell you something, though. I sent them twenty thousand francs to help out with their strike. Yes, that's right; you don't have to look at me like a bunch of dead fish – I did it. Twice, I sent them a ten-thousand-franc note.'

He got up and bumped heavily against the coffee table, causing the glasses to jump. He filled his and emptied it again with a single gulp.

'That took you by surprise, didn't it? Why, you . . . I think I'll go and tell them what you are planning now. I may be a failure, but when I'm around you . . . Victor, do you know why Greece couldn't defend herself against the Romans? No, of course you don't, you're much too stupid for that. All right, it's true enough that the Negroes don't like me, but it's because of you and people like you that they don't. It doesn't mean that I don't understand Africa – this trollop of a continent! Do you hear me, my young friend? If you really love Africa, she will still give herself to you – she is so generous that she never ceases to give; and so greedy that she will never stop devouring you.'

He had started toward Pierrot, but he stumbled against a chair and would have fallen if the young man had not caught him.

'Just understand that,' he mumbled. 'The Negroes hate you; that's one thing we're all agreed on. I think I'll go and see what I can do to make sure they hate you more.'

'Someone had better go with him,' Victor said.

'Right,' Isnard said. 'We'll take him home.'

They caught up with Leblanc, who was weaving uncertainly around the veranda, looking for the steps.

'I don't need you – I know what you're going to do. Let me go!'

They each took him by the arm and almost carried him away. Some children had come out to the sidewalk to see what was happening, and windows were being opened in the neighboring houses.

Pierrot was still standing beside the coffee table, embarrassed and not knowing quite what to do. Beatrice came over to him, standing so close that her breasts brushed against him.

'It was to be expected,' she said. 'Don't let it bother you. Stay and have dinner with us – they'll be back in a few minutes. We can get better acquainted.'

Her voice hardened suddenly, and she added, 'It's what always happens to fools.'

171

THIÈS

The Return of Bakayoko

The stars were strewn across the sky like some golden seed sown by the wind. The earth cooled beneath the touch of a night breeze from the north, heralding a change in the season. The insects and the birds of the tropics sang their nocturnal hymns.

The darkness was so thick that it was impossible to make out the features of the man who was walking, quickly and surely, through the tangle of alleyways, the jungle of straw huts and wooden cabins. He was whistling a cheerful little tune and stopped from time to time to listen to the mewling of a cat or the sonorous snoring from a near-by house. He was very tired, and his mind was occupied with the thought of where he might go to rest. 'I would go to the office, but I don't like to wake the men . . . But if I go to Uncle Bakary's, I think it would please him . . .'

When he came to the end of a pathway he seemed to know well, he stopped and lit a cigarette lighter. The flame fell across a section of the wall of a modest house which had been opened out and shored up with timbers. Between the timbers there was a little window. The man knocked on the wooden shutter and then moved over to stand before the door of the house, which was hung with an old blanket.

'Who is there?' a voice from the interior called, and the words were followed by a spasm of coughing.

'Ibrahim Bakayoko, son of N'Fafini Bakayoko and of Niakoro Cissé.'

'*Lémé, lémé!* My child, my child!' old Bakary cried. 'Come in, quickly! When did you arrive?'

'Your threshold is the first I have crossed, Uncle.'

'You have done well. It is to me that you should have come first: Have you eaten?'

'Yes, Uncle, I have eaten.'

The two men went into the cabin, and by the light of a candle set in the middle of the floor Bakayoko could make out the sleeping form of an old woman, lying with her back to him.

Bakary sat down on the edge of the bed. 'If you have eaten, there is no need to wake your aunt Fanta now. But how are all of your people – your mother, your wife?'

'When I left they were well; but for some time now I have had no news, except for a letter from Ad'jibid'ji, telling me about the Diara affair.'

'Yes, we know about that. It was a sorry business, my son . . . but it has turned out well, it seems. For an old man like me, who is not accustomed to the new ways, it is still surprising to see that the young people can understand each other so well and act together.'

Bakary had been studying the man before him as he spoke. On entering the house, Bakayoko had placed his short upper tunic, of the type called a *froc*, in a corner with his walking stick and pack, and now he was wearing only a pair of white trousers, striped in black. His soft sandals were the kind worn by Peul shepherds, with leather straps that laced high on the ankles. A straw hat with a wide brim to shade his eyes from the sun hung down across his back, supported by the thong knotted beneath his chin.

'I must let you sleep, and I am tired myself,' Bakayoko said. 'I will sleep in front of the door.'

'Sleep here,' Bakary said, indicating the ground beside his own bed. 'I will get you a cover.'

'Thank you, Uncle, I have everything I need. Pass the night in peace.'

Bakayoko lifted a corner of the blanket, which served as a door, and looked out at the stars. 'I can still get two hours of sleep,' he thought. 'That's better than nothing.' He took a large square of cloth from his pack and spread it out on the ground, unlaced his sandals, placed the straw hat beneath him as a pillow, and stretched out. Three minutes later he was asleep, for he was among those men who can sleep whenever they will.

◆

Although Bakary rose early the next morning he could find no trace of Bakayoko's visit. He looked through the other rooms of the little house and questioned his wife, Fanta, but she had neither seen nor heard anything. 'I know I wasn't dreaming,' he told her and went off to the union office in search of news.

Lahbib was there, but he knew nothing of Bakayoko's arrival, and when the word of Bakary's story got around, the younger men began to make fun of him, saying that he was getting so old he was beginning to have visions. Bakary never liked being called old, particularly when the young men, who spoke the word in French, accompanied it with others whose meaning he could not understand. And this morning the situation was made worse when Samba was sent to look for Bakayoko and returned without having found any sign of him.

The union office was already beginning to be crowded, since this was the final reunion of the strike committee before the meeting with the representatives of the company in the afternoon. All of the delegates were there, including the group from Dakar of which Beaugosse was a member. When Edouard, the personnel director, who had been appointed intermediary between the strikers and the management, arrived, the door to the office was closed.

But in the meantime a crowd had begun to gather in the square outside and in all the neighboring streets – a crowd whose many colored garments seemed even more vivid in the morning sun, a crowd dominated by women and animated by the sound and movement of the children and the steady drumming of the tam-tams.

Bakayoko had to thrust his way across this shoal of people to reach the union building. They recognized him by the wide-brimmed straw hat, and he was constantly forced to pause by the press of hands held out in greeting. Samba N'Doulougou, who was on the porch, saw him approaching.

'*Hé, Bambara dyion!* – you slave of Bambara! There you are at last! So old Bakary isn't crazy after all!'

The staircase was crowded with strikers, obstructing the steps to the door, and Bakayoko's passage was interrupted again by the numbers of men who wanted to shake his hand. Finally, however, he reached the top, and Boubacar, who was standing guard, seized him by the shoulders in a giant embrace.

'*Hé, Bambara dyion* – you haven't gotten fat!'

But before Bakayoko could answer, the sound of voices raised in chorus interrupted him, and they both stood motionless, listening. Led by Penda and Dieynaba, the women had formed into a solid rank and were improvising words to a chant dedicated to their men:

> The morning light is in the east;
> It is daybreak of a day of history.
> From Koulikoro to Dakar
> The smoke of the savanna dies.
> On the 10th of October, fateful day,
> We swore before the world
> To support you to the end.

You have lit the torch of hope,
And victory is near.
The morning light is in the east;
It is daybreak of a day of history.

When the singing had ended, a great clamor of voices and the beating of the drums filled the air.

'They are all here,' Boubacar said. 'The white man, too.'

'A white man?'

'Yes. The one they call the work inspector.'

Bakayoko listened to the voices from the streets for a moment longer and then pushed his hat back from his head and went into the office, followed by Boubacar.

A dozen or so men were seated around the table, and he went directly to an empty chair next to the one occupied by Edouard.

'Excuse me for being late,' he said as he sat down.

Doudou was presiding over the meeting. 'Do you know Ibrahim Bakayoko?' he said, speaking to the white man. 'He is the chief of the trainmen's group, as well as the delegate from the Sudan region. Bakayoko, this is Monsieur Edouard, the personnel director of the company, who was sent from Dakar as a mediator between the management and ourselves.'

Bakayoko cast a rapid glance at the other delegates around the table, satisfying himself that he knew them all except the handsome young man who was seated between Lahbib and Balla. Edouard seized the opportunity to study his neighbor. The thick lips, marked by little slanting ridges and pressed firmly together, gave the man's face an expression of hardness which was borne out by the narrow, deep-set eyes. A long scar, reaching from the left side of his nose to the underpart of his jaw, seemed only to accentuate the severity of his features.

'Shall we go on?' Bakayoko said, not wanting to prolong the silence which had fallen in the room.

'We are listening to Monsieur Edouard,' Lahbib said.

The personnel director was ill at ease, and Bakayoko's presence at his side embarrassed him even further. As he came into the room he had accidentally stepped on Samba N'Doulougou's foot, and he could still hear the little man's jeering words: 'As if walking all over the colonies wasn't bad enough, now they have to trample on the colonials!'

'I was just explaining,' he said, 'that I am only here as an intermediary between the company and you. Your demands have been thoroughly and conscientiously studied in Dakar. There are some of them that we think are legitimate, but there are also some very real problems. The figures for last year's operations are not good, and for that reason we must, for the time being, set aside the matter of family allowances. The matter of pensions will have to be studied in relation to the technical employment level of all parties concerned; and lastly, any increases in salary and payment of back pay on such increases must be considered in relation to the cost of living. If you are in agreement that, for the time being – and I repeat, for the time being – these three points can be set aside, we can adjourn this meeting to the company's office right now. What do you think, Monsieur Bakayoko?'

'I am not alone here, monsieur,' Bakayoko said and began filling his pipe.

'You have all heard what Monsieur Edouard has proposed,' Lahbib said. 'He suggests that we suppress three of our demands.'

'It seems to me that it would be advisable,' Edouard said quickly, 'and . . .'

'It seems to me that there wouldn't be much left of the things we have asked for,' someone interrupted.

'But I am sure that if you will restrict your claims now, the management will do everything in its power, after you return to work. Things will get better gradually, and all of the questions held in abeyance can be worked out by degrees. Ask your own delegates from Dakar – they will tell you that I am your friend, and that I am doing my best to arrange it.'

Lahbib looked at Doudou, who was even more uneasy, in his role as presiding officer, than the personnel director.

'We could take a vote by a show of hands,' he suggested.

Bakayoko lit his pipe carefully, holding the bowl turned down. The flame from the lighter threw craggy shadows across his jaw line.

'Why vote yet, Doudou?' he said, blowing a cloud of smoke toward the ceiling. 'We still have a good many things to say.'

'There isn't much time,' Edouard said.

'That's true enough, but it isn't the people you are thinking about for whom there isn't much time. How long have you been in Africa?'

'Almost seven years.'

'Seven years you have been the personnel director? Seven years when you knew that the company was robbing us every day, and you never lifted a finger? And now you expect us to believe that you have fallen from heaven to be our savior?'

Bakayoko paused for a moment and looked directly at his neighbor, but

176

the expression in his eyes made it clear that he expected no answer. He turned back to his comrades and spoke clearly and distinctly.

'The question that we must consider here is whether we intend to be responsible for what we have undertaken in this strike. We have made some mistakes, and doubtless we will make others, but is that any reason why we should abandon now those who have followed us and trusted us, those who have gone hungry, and those who have been imprisoned or killed?

'This generous gentleman has come here to tell us that the question of family allowances must be thought of in terms of the figures for last year's operations. Wouldn't it be more accurate to say that they must be thought of in terms of the fact that some of us have more than one wife, and they don't want to give us the allowance for that reason? He tells us also that to be entitled to a pension the old men must pass tests to determine their technical employment level. But when they were recruited to work on the line twenty or thirty years ago, did anyone ask them about their technical level? The back pay due to us on our salaries apparently represents a very considerable sum, but in spite of the fact that they could easily afford to offer three million francs to Doudou, this must be considered in terms of how little we can live on.

'Let us look at it in another way. We are driving a train down the track, and ahead of us we think we see an obstacle which makes us afraid. Are we going to stop the train and say to the passengers, "I can't go any farther; I think there is something up ahead that frightens me?" No – we are responsible for the train, and we must go forward and find out if the obstacle really exists. The gentleman beside me here is the obstacle which has made us afraid, but we cannot let ourselves be stopped by it. Is he sincere when he says he wants to help us? I don't know, but don't ask me if I believe it! He must know, however, that after the times we have been through since this strike began it is impossible for us to think that he has been on our side all along.

'That is all I had to say, and I have said it in French so that he would understand me, although I think this meeting should have been conducted in Ouolof, since that is our language.'

Bakayoko's pipe had gone out while he spoke, and when he had finished he relit it and leaned back in his chair, with a slow, almost languorous movement. His heart held neither spite nor malice, but he had traveled over a thousand miles among the strikers and their families, and the sufferings, the privations, and the tragedies he had witnessed had shaken him more than he realized. He was astonished to note now that his pulse was beating in the same rhythm as the drums in the street. Even though the door and windows were closed, he could hear them plainly.

Beaugosse had been watching him closely, as had all the others, and found himself admiring the man's calm and self-assurance, in spite of the jealousy he felt toward him. As for Edouard, he had been more surprised than shocked by the harshness of Bakayoko's words. He had also understood very well that his last phrase signified that his presence in the room was no longer desired. He had only to take his briefcase, get up, and leave, but he was incapable of doing it and sat rigid in his chair. It was at his own request that the management had appointed him as mediator, and he had done his best to merit the confidence they had shown him. But he had also tried to understand these men with whom he was sitting now, and they had answered by turning him away. He was frustrated and hurt by the failure of an effort in which he had honestly believed.

At this moment the door opened slightly, and Samba N'Doulougou said, 'It's old Bakary.'

Bakayoko gestured to the old man to come in and spoke a few words to him in a dialect which no one else in the room understood. Then, speaking to Edouard, he said in French, 'Would you be so kind as to wait for us outside, monsieur? We still have a few things to discuss among ourselves.'

His forehead red with anger, the personnel director seized his briefcase and followed Bakary, who smiled broadly as he held the door for him, delighted that he had been entrusted with a mission he could talk about later.

When they were alone, Bakayoko asked in Ouolof, 'Is there anyone who does not approve of what I said?'

'I approve of him leaving,' Balla, the welder, answered. 'We're old enough to know what we have to do.'

'So do I – so do I,' several other voices agreed.

'I think we are all in agreement not to change anything in our list of demands,' Lahbib said, and since there were no dissenting voices he added, 'In that case, we can go over to the company's office now. However, the delegation is supposed to be only six, and there are ten of us.'

'We'll have to select the ones to go,' the delegate from Saint-Louis said.

'There's no necessity for that. They didn't set any limit on the number of representatives they would have,' Bakayoko said. 'We'll all go over together.'

As they got up from their places around the table, Bakary reappeared. 'My son, the *toubab* you told me to accompany has left the building,' he said.

'So much the better, Uncle.'

One by one the delegates filed out of the office and down the narrow staircase to the street.

It was a ten-minute walk from the union building to the offices of the company, and the crowd had formed a noisy, living hedgerow along both sides of the streets. The women seemed the most excited and were constantly taking up again the refrain they had sung in the square that morning. Doudou marched at the head of the delegation, with Lahbib at his right and Bakayoko on his left. Lahbib was wearing a white drill suit of European cut and rumpled black tie; Bakayoko had put the big straw hat back on his head and had not abandoned his pipe. Behind them came Balla, Samba, Beaugosse, Boubacar, and the other delegates. The crowd closed in behind them as they walked, forming a long procession. A cordon of troops stood guard in front of the Dakar-Niger building. The soldiers parted to let the delegates pass and then reformed their ranks.

'We'll wait here until they come out,' Penda shouted.

'But they may be in there all afternoon,' the sergeant of the militiamen said. He did not like the idea of being faced with this unruly mob of women.

'We have been waiting for this day for months,' Penda said. 'We can wait an afternoon.' Then she climbed up on a stone marker and gave a signal to start the singing:

> The morning light is in the east;
> It is daybreak of a day of history.

The other women took up the chorus, and the drums began to beat again.

The meeting between the management and the strikers was to take place in a conference room on the second floor of the building. Dejean, the director, and his closest associates had been there for some time, and the waiting was playing tricks with their nerves. With the exception of young Pierre, who had had the feeling for several days that he was watching a play whose plot he did not fully understand, every man there was living through a period he had never expected to see. It was probably Dejean, however, for whom the crisis was not only the most unexpected but the most totally incomprehensible. A discussion between employer and employees presupposes the fact that there are employees and there is an employer. But he, Dejean, was not an employer; he was simply exercising a function which rested on the most natural of all bases – the right to an absolute authority over beings whose color made of them not subordinates with whom one could discuss anything, but men of another, inferior condition, fit only for unqualified obedience.

Standing by one of the windows, holding the curtain aside, he could see the crowd that had invaded the street, their faces gleaming with sweat, their tunics and headcloths a weird medley of colors; and he could hear the insistent drumming of the tam-tams and the singing of the women.

In an effort to break the gloomy silence in the room, Victor returned to a subject they had already discussed. 'We've got to get rid of Leblanc. It won't do to let him be seen around here any more.'

'Doctor Michel is going to take care of it,' Isnard said. 'I telephoned him and he knows all about it. That jackass – sending money to the Negroes! That's a real case of sunstroke.'

'Good,' Dejean said absently. 'I know Michel – he'll do whatever has to be done; he knows the ropes. But it won't be just a case of sunstroke – Leblanc had another disease long before he arrived in Africa. It will cost the company less that way.'

He leaned closer to the window, trying to get a better look at a man in a pith helmet who was having difficulty trying to force a passage through the crowd.

'It's Edouard,' he said, and then added, 'Name of God, he's alone!'

The door had scarcely closed behind the personnel director before he was surrounded by the others. He took off his helmet and wiped his forehead.

'It was that bastard of a Bakayoko who ruined everything,' he sputtered. 'The others understood why I was there; they were even beginning to listen to my advice, but as soon as he came in the whole thing changed! He's just against all white men – one of those dirty nationalists. He even sent some old gorilla with me to watch me. But the last straw was when he told them they shouldn't be speaking in French . . .!'

The anger Dejean had been trying to stifle for days burst out at last. 'Ah, that one . . .! He's going to find out what I'm made of! He'll speak French, and so will they! I should have had him hanged in 1942! If only the directors had listened to me . . .!'

Since he understood little of what they were talking about, Pierre had gone back to the window and was watching the spectacle in the street. Some groups of men and women were dancing, and the young man remembered having been told at school in France that, for the Negroes, the slightest pretext was good enough as an occasion for singing and dancing. Thinking of the letter he would write to his family at home, he tried to catch some of the words to the song that came up to him from the crowd. He turned to the group of men standing around the green-covered table.

'Do you understand what the women are singing? It may have something to do with the strike.'

'Don't be a fool,' Isnard snapped. 'It's just shouting and yelling, as usual. What do you think they know about the strike? They're just making noise because they like to make noise.'

Pierre did not answer. He had just noticed that the crowd was opening up to make way for a little group of ten men and then closing in again behind them.

'There they are!' he cried.

They all raced to the windows then and pulled the curtains aside. The windows were closed, but in spite of this the shouts and the singing, which seemed to have become a kind of hysterical chanting, invaded the room. In a voice he strove to keep calm, Dejean called the others back to order.

'Take your places, gentlemen,' he said. It was not until he had seated himself in his own chair at the head of the table that he realized he had broken the frame of the eyeglasses clenched in his fist.

Just as Pierre was sitting down – last, since he was the junior among them – there was a rap on the door and Lahbib came in.

'Good day, gentlemen,' he said; but the only answer he received was a vague murmur which might have been a series of groans. Without waiting to be invited, the delegates from the union took their places in the empty chairs. Balla, the welder, found himself seated next to Dejean, who was presiding. It was the first time he had ever been this close to the director, and he glanced down at his hands and then looked furtively around at his companions, as if reassuring himself that they were still there. Doudou, between Lahbib and Bakayoko, was seated directly across the table from Isnard. After the brief scuffling noises of chairs being moved, a weighty silence ensued. The personnel director thought it his duty as mediator to speak first.

'We will use French for this meeting,' he said, looking at Bakayoko.

'Since we are all Frenchmen,' Victor added, with a mirthless smile.

It was Lahbib who answered. 'Since there is no intermediary language, we will use French.'

But Edouard insisted. 'Do you agree, Monsieur Bakayoko?'

Bakayoko was sitting in the relaxed position which seemed to be his habit, leaning slightly to one side and far back in his chair.

'I am not alone in this strike,' he said, looking at the personnel director, 'but since your ignorance of any of our language is a handicap for you, we will use French as a matter of courtesy. But it is a courtesy that will not last forever.'

They all stared at him. Dejean's face turned purple, and Victor half rose from his chair.

'Be careful what you say – your words may cause you trouble!'

'Monsieur,' Bakayoko said, 'we are here for a discussion among equals, and not to listen to your threats.'

The negotiations had started badly, and now a thick wall of silence seemed to rise up as the men on either side of the table took each other's measure.

It was Dejean, mastering his anger, who broke through it first. 'Very well,' he said. 'Let's get down to this list of grievances.'

'They are not grievances,' Lahbib said. He was too simple a man to amuse himself with a game of words, but he respected them and did not like to see them misused.

Dejean went on as if he had not even heard him. 'Re-evaluation of salaries . . .'

'A twenty per cent increase all along the line,' Doudou said automatically and began distributing some sheets of paper to his comrades, although he knew perfectly well that at least half of them did not know how to write.

'Annual paid vacations, pensions, family allowances . . .' Dejean continued.

'Payment of back wages, based on the settlement with French railway workers in July 1936; contractual bonus of six thousand francs to the trainmen, at the same rate of interest paid by French trainmen,' Doudou said, spreading a year-old copy of the *Journal Officiel* on the table.

'That's all?' Dejean demanded. 'Don't you think it's a little too much?'

'And you, monsieur?' Bakayoko said. 'Don't you think this thieving has lasted long enough?'

'You are not in charge here!'

'If you look at the list of delegates, you will find my name.'

'I'll warn you just once more – if you go on in this manner I shall adjourn the meeting.'

Doudou leaned toward Lahbib and said in Ouolof, 'It would be better if Bakayoko would be quiet. The red-eared men are going to get angry with him and use it as an excuse to send us all away. They're just waiting for the chance.'

'It's true, Bakayoko,' Balla said. 'Don't answer him again, or they'll break up the meeting.'

182

Pierre had followed the earlier discussion excitedly, and now, almost without thinking, he demanded, 'What are you saying? I can't understand you.'

'If we are content, we speak French and you understand. If we are not content, you can't understand,' Balla said, summoning up his best French. Pleased with this answer, he looked around the table at his comrades, seeking their approval.

Bakayoko's heavy lips sketched a smile. He leaned back in his chair, took his tobacco pouch from his pocket, and began to fill his pipe.

'It doesn't really seem as though you came to this meeting with good intentions,' the personnel director said unhappily, 'so how can we expect that anything will come of it?'

'We must all do our best to see that something does, Monsieur Edouard,' Lahbib said earnestly.

'Very well then,' Dejean said. 'Let us consider this matter of good intentions. You certainly must recognize that the matter of family allowances cannot be considered.'

'Why?' Doudou asked.

'Simply because you are all polygamous,' Victor said. 'How do you think we could possibly recognize all of those children?'

'And with the money you got, you would just go out and buy more wives and have more children,' Isnard interrupted. 'The Dakar-Niger isn't nursery school, for God's sake!'

'But in France everyone gets it!' It was Beaugosse who had spoken, somewhat to his own surprise. Crossing the square amid the enthusiastic acclaim of the crowd a few minutes ago, he had suddenly felt the surge of a courage and spirit he did not know he possessed. 'The time of the knights has returned to us,' he had thought, 'the time of the *Damels*, the warrior-knights of Sénégal.'

But Victor just snorted, 'In France there are no such things as concubines!' and Beaugosse could think of nothing to answer.

'Then we are not to have the family allowances?' Doudou asked.

'No, no, and again no!' Dejean intervened angrily. He knew that he was going to be forced into some sort of compromise; the peanut season was over, and the harvest had to be brought into the factories and terminals at Dakar, Rufisque, and Kaolack. The manufacturers, the merchants, and even the stockholders in the railroad had already been bringing pressure to bear on him. But to give in on the question of family allowances was much more than a matter of agreeing to a compromise with striking workers; it would amount to recognition of a racial aberrance, a ratification of the customs of inferior beings. It would be giving in, not to workers but to Negroes, and that Dejean could not do.

He scarcely noticed that Lahbib was speaking again. 'Polygamy is a matter which is of concern to us, too; but your concern with it now has never prevented you from making use of it when the need arose. When it is a matter of recruiting young men for work on the line, you don't bother to ask them if their father has one wife or two. And the line itself was built by the hands of the sons of what you call concubines . . .'

Lahbib never finished the little speech he had been preparing for so long. Dejean had stood up and was shouting at him. 'I know that pack of lies – I've heard if all before! You are led by a bunch of Bolsheviks, and you are sitting there insulting a great nation and a great people!

'*Monsieur le directeur*,' Lahbib said, 'you do not represent a nation or a people here, but simply a class. We represent another class, whose interests are not the same as yours. We are trying to find a common meeting ground, and that is all.'

Seeing that Dejean was about to lose his temper again, the personnel director said hastily, 'If we cannot arrive at an understanding here, why don't we select one of your deputies to the National Assembly and ask him to serve as mediator?'

At the mention of the word 'deputies', Bakayoko, who had said nothing since his comrades urged him to remain calm, leaned forward in his chair.

'Our deputies,' he said, with an ironic smile which stretched his mouth to the line of the scar that split his face. 'Our deputies. Do you know what we think of them? To us, their mandate is simply a license to profiteer. We know them, and that is what we think of them. There are some of them who, before their election, did not even own a second pair of pants. Now they have apartments, villas, automobiles, bank accounts, and they own stock in companies like this one. What do they have in common with the ignorant people who elected them without knowing what they were doing? They have become your allies, and you expect us to let them be the judges of our differences? Oh no, a thousand times, no! With that much – or should I say that little – imagination, Monsieur Edouard, you should have understood long ago that you can only negotiate with us.'

Dejean had apparently not even heard what Bakayoko said. He was still caught up in his anger with Lahbib. 'Where would you be without France and the French people?' he demanded suddenly.

'We know what France represents,' Bakayoko said, 'and we respect it. We are in no sense anti-French; but once again, *Monsieur le directeur,* this

184

is not a question of France or of her people. It is a question of employees and their employer.'

The heat and his own anger had turned Dejean's face the color of red brick. He rose heavily from his chair, walked over to the windows, and opened the big central bay. The singing and the beating of the drums struck him like a blast of wind.

'Can't you make them be quiet?'

'You can always refer the matter to their deputies,' Bakayoko said.

Dejean did not answer. He closed the window and started back to the table, as if he were returning to his place, but when he passed Bakayoko's chair he stopped abruptly and, before anyone could have stopped him, he slapped him hard across the face. The big trainman leaped to his feet, overturning his chair, and seized the director by the throat. Their neighbors hurled themselves at the two men, trying to separate them.

'Take your hands off him, Bakayoko!' Lahbib cried in Ouolof. 'That's what he was looking for! In the name of the workers, take your hands off him!'

Doudou was trying to tear Bakayoko's clenched fingers from their grip on the director's neck. 'Can't you see he's already half dead with fear?' he shouted. 'Let him go!'

Clutching at his throat, Dejean staggered backward, his mouth hanging open. If Lahbib had not caught him, he would have fallen. The brief flurry of oaths, exclamations, and insults that had broken out around the table died down, but as Dejean collapsed back into his chair the silence was heavy with hatred and confusion.

Doudou began to gather up the papers scattered on the table. 'Well,' he said, in a voice muffled with apprehension, 'what about our demands?'

It was Dejean who answered, still gasping for breath. 'Nothing! Absolutely nothing! Zero! And I'll have every one of you discharged!'

'Unless you leave yourself!' Bakayoko said, bending over to pick up his pipe.

It had been almost two hours since the cordon of police opened to allow the delegates to enter when it opened again so that they could leave. The noisy, motley crowd was waiting for them, and Bakayoko raised his arms for quiet.

'You will know everything that happened! Let us pass now – we are going back to the union office. There will be a meeting in the Place Aly N'Guer in half an hour.'

In a fog of dust still hot from the last rays of the sun, the crowd stepped back to open a path.

FROM THIÈS TO DAKAR

The March of the Women

The crowd had preceded the delegates to the Place Aly N'Guer. Weary with the long hours of waiting, first at the union building and then before the offices of the company, most of them were sitting on the dusty ground, but others gathered in little animated groups, discussing the events of the day, while the sun blasted their sweaty shoulders and arms and skull with the last of that day's fires. Penda, Dieynaba, and Mariame Sonko tried as best they could to maintain some semblance of order among the excited women, but it was not until the delegation arrived and took up its position at the center of the square that the clamor finally subsided.

Lahbib spoke first. He gave them all of the details of the meeting with Dejean and his associates, but he was a bad speaker and he knew it, so he performed his duty as rapidly as possible and turned the platform over to Bakayoko. The trainman waited until the murmurs which had followed Lahbib's account died down. His voice was clear and distinct and could be heard at the farthest corners of the square. Since they already knew what had happened that afternoon, he spoke first of other things, beginning with a brief history of the events which had brought the line into being, and then speaking of the strike of September 1938 and of the men who had died in it. He knew that he would provoke the anger of the crowd when he concluded, 'And now they refuse to give us what we are asking for, on the pretext that our wives and our mothers are concubines, and we and our sons are bastards!'

Again he had to wait for silence, and then he said, 'Well, we are not going to give in to them and go back to work! And it is here that this strike must be won! In every town I have visited in these past months I have been told, "If Thiès can hold out, we will hold out." Workers of Thiès, it is here, in this city, that there is a Place du Premier Septembre, in honor of the men who died in 1938, and it is in their name that you must hold out now. You know that there is support for you everywhere – from Kaolack to Saint-Louis, from Guinea to Dahomey, and even in France

186

itself. The time when we could be beaten by dividing us against ourselves is past. We will maintain the order for an unlimited strike, and we will continue to maintain it until we have won!'

Shouts and roars of approval came back to him from the crowd, where even the few who had remained seated were standing now and waving their fists with the others. But in the midst of this unleashed tumult, a little group of women managed to make its way through the crush and approach the delegates. Bakayoko saw them and raised his arms, calling for silence.

'Our gallant women have something to say to us,' he cried. 'They have the right to be heard!'

It was Penda who addressed them, hesitantly at first, but gathering assurance as she spoke.

'I speak in the name of all of the women, but I am just the voice they have chosen to tell you what they have decided to do. Yesterday we all laughed together, men and women, and today we weep together, but for us women this strike still means the possibility of a better life tomorrow. We owe it to ourselves to hold up our heads and not to give in now. So we have decided that tomorrow we will march together to Dakar.'

For a moment Penda's voice was lost in confused murmuring that linked astonishment and misgiving, and then she spoke again, more firmly.

'Yes – we will go together to Dakar to hear what these *toubabs* have to say and to let them see if we are concubines! Men, you must allow your wives to come with us! Every woman here who is capable of walking should be with us tomorrow!'

Again there was murmuring and shouting, and some applause, but there were also cries of remonstrance and protest. Bakayoko took Penda by the arm.

'Come to the union office with us,' he said. 'Your idea is good, but you can't start on something like this without thinking it over carefully.'

As they crossed the square, through the gradually scattering crowd, they passed dozens of little groups discussing this new development. It was the first time in living memory that a woman had spoken in public in Thiès, and even the onslaught of night could not still the arguments.

The discussion at the union office was no less heated. Balla expressed the opinion of many when he said, 'I'm against letting the women go. It's normal that they should support us; a wife should support her husband, but from that to a march on Dakar . . . No, I vote against it. The heat or their anger or something has gone to their heads! Lahbib, would you take the responsibility for letting the women go?'

'We can't possibly listen to everyone's ideas or opinions about it. If you wish, we can take a vote.'

Bakayoko interrupted the argument that threatened to break out. 'We have no right to discourage anyone who wants to strike a blow for us,' he said brutally. 'It may be just that blow that is needed. If the women have decided, all that is left for us to do is to help them. I move that the delegates from Dakar leave immediately to warn the local committee of their arrival. You're from Dakar, aren't you?' he asked, speaking to Beaugosse for the first time. 'How long do you think it will take them to get there?'

'I've never gone to Dakar on foot,' Beaugosse answered, 'but I don't think it is anything for women to try. Besides, there is no water there; when I left, Alioune and all the other men were scouring the city for a cask or even a bottle of water – which is what the women should be doing. Instead of that, they have been battling troops in the streets and starting fires. Now the soldiers and the militia are patrolling everywhere. You would be sending those women straight into the jaws of a lion.'

'You can keep your French for yourself,' Bakayoko said. 'The men will understand you better if you speak their language. As for the men in Dakar looking for water for their families, the time when our fathers would have considered that demeaning is past. If all the workers thought like you, we might as well say good-bye to the strike and to all the months of sacrifice.'

'All right, Bakayoko,' Lahbib said. 'Calm down, and let's get back to practical matters. If the women have decided to go, we must help them and prepare an escort for them. We'll have to do something about the children, too – at least about those whose mothers will be leaving. I suggest that we try to find some trucks and send them into the villages in the brush country. Everyone here has relatives in the villages. As for you, Penda, you will have to be sure that the men who come with you do not bother the women; and if you find that this march is too hard for the women, stop them and make them turn back. There will be no shame in that, and no one will hold it against you.'

If the truth be told, although Bakayoko, with his manner of disregarding destiny or bending it to his will, was the soul of this strike, it was Lahbib, the serious, thoughtful, calm, and modest Lahbib, who was its brain. Lahbib counted each one of God's bits of wood, weighed them, and balanced them, but the strength that was in them came from Bakayoko.

While the men discussed the measures to be taken at the union office, the women prepared for their departure. An inky night flowed through the

188

city, somber and viscid, as if the heavens had decanted a layer of crude oil across the earth. The cries and shouts that pierced the darkness were like fitful flashes of lightning, but the ceaseless sound of the tam-tams seemed to carry with it a promise that dawn would come.

The compound of Dieynaba, the market woman, had been turned into the major place of assembly, although she herself was not to leave because Gorgui was dying. Shadows came and went in the courtyard, challenging and calling to each other; the squalling of children and the excited chattering and laughter of the old women who were being left at home added to the hubbub and confusion, but at the same time there was a steady trampling of purposeful feet, like the sounds of a legion lifting camp.

Another group was making ready in the Place du Premier Septembre, just across from the militiamen who stood guard in front of the police station. Prevented by their orders from talking with the women, and uneasy in the flickering light of the lanterns they had brought from the guardhouse, they watched this gathering of shadows without knowing quite what to do, but there were some among them who listened to the drums and knew what was in the air.

At last, toward two o'clock in the morning, when a few venturesome stars had succeeded in stabbing through the obscurity, the two groups came together. A cloud of white dust, pushed up and out by a lazy wind, rose to the sky and a meeting with the darkness.

'Now we are leaving!' Penda cried.

Like so many echoes, hundreds of voices answered her. 'Now we are leaving . . . leaving . . . leaving . . .'

Preceded, accompanied, and followed by the beating of the drums, the cortège moved out into the night.

At the first light of morning, some of the men who had gone out with the women to speed them on their way turned and went back to Thiès.

'Do you think they will get there safely?' Bakary asked.

The bowl of Bakayoko's pipe glowed briefly in the gray dawn. 'Yes, Uncle,' he said. 'We have faith in them.'

To observe the ceremony of the women's departure properly, Bakary had girded his arms with amulets and fetishes. His upper arms were completely covered by circlets of red, black, and yellow leather, and his forearms with bracelets made of antelope horns edged with horsehair or covered with red cloth sewn with *cauris*, the little shells which once had been used as money. On the index finger of his right hand he wore an enormous ring of raw metal. He had sworn that none of these charms would leave his body until the women's journey had ended.

189

When he returned to his home, he found a letter from Bamako waiting for him. As soon as he had read it he went out again, hurrying to the union building as fast as his decaying lungs would permit, in search of Bakayoko.

'There is bad news from Bamako,' he told the trainman. 'Read it – it's a letter from Assitan. The police came and took Fa Keïta away. Your mother is dead, and little Ad'jibid'ji was hurt.'

Bakayoko recognized the handwriting of Tiémoko. Assitan must have dictated the letter to him.

'You will be leaving for home, my son?'

'I must go first to Dakar, Uncle. Preparations have to be made for a meeting after the women arrive.'

'My son, there is no longer a man in your house. You have read the letter – your family needs you.'

'There are many houses such as mine, Uncle; houses in mourning, as there were in 1938. We must fight for the living and not give our time to thinking of the dead.'

'Sometimes,' Bakary murmured, almost to himself, 'I wonder if you have a heart.'

His tired old eyes studied the precise features and well-shaped profile of the man before him, seeking out some sign of emotion and finding none. Suddenly he reached into the folds of his tunic and brought out a long dagger. It was a beautiful, pointed blade, sharp as a razor and sheathed in elaborately carved, curving horn.

'Here,' he said. 'Take this, you may need it.'

'But, Uncle, I am going to Dakar – if I should be taken with that, I will be sent to prison.'

'My son, my son – I have had this blade for almost fifty years. It sees the sunlight only on Fridays, when I use it to trim my hair. It has never been used to kill anyone, and if you should meet a *toubab* who asks questions about it, give him my name and tell him that I will explain.'

Bakayoko accepted the old man's gift, and then, before leaving the city himself, he went with Lahbib to see Aziz, the shopkeeper. They wanted to borrow the Syrian's truck, but the matter was not easily arranged. Lahbib, in fact, was forced to resort to blackmail. For some years he had been going to the shop of the Syrian once each week to keep the accounts in order, and it was not until he had alluded, very politely, to some transactions that might be of interest to the police that the old Chevrolet was grudgingly rented to them.

With the matter of transport to carry the children to the outlying villages thus arranged, the two men left. When they arrived at Dieynaba's house to pick up the articles Bakayoko would need for his journey, they found the usually bustling and noisy courtyard silent and empty. The market woman was seated on the ground beneath the little projecting roof of her cabin. Her pipe hung loosely in her hand, and she was staring unseeingly at the jumble of walls. She turned her head when she heard the whisper of their sandals on the hard-packed ground.

'Are you at peace, Dieynaba?' Lahbib asked.

For a long time she did not answer, but simply stared at the two men as if she were searching for something beyond their figures. They could see that her eyes were streaked with red. At last, with a sound like a sigh that had welled up somewhere deep within her, she murmured, 'Gorgui is dead. His leg rotted away, and it rotted all the rest of his body.'

Bakayoko walked over to her. 'Give me your pipe,' he said gently.

'I have no more tobacco.'

Bakayoko took the pipe from her hand, drew a leaf of tobacco from his pocket, and crumbled it carefully between his palms before filling the pipe. Then he lit it himself and handed it back to Dieynaba. For a moment his hand rested on her shoulder, and then he went into Penda's cabin, where he had left his pack.

'We will bury him tonight,' Lahbib said.

'He is the son of true believers, from both his father and his mother, and he is unclean . . .'

'Don't think about that. I will find some men and we will bathe his body and dress it as it should be before it is put into the earth.'

Dieynaba did not appear to be crying, and yet, one by one, tears rolled down her cheeks and dropped to the cloth that covered her breasts. She murmured, 'Why can't we just kill all the white men?'

'Woman,' Lahbib said, 'you must not let hatred enter your heart. We want no more blood, we want no more children killed, but hatred cannot be our guide. I know that it is difficult . . .'

Bakayoko came out just then, with his pack on his shoulder and his walking staff in his hand. He had heard Lahbib's last words, and he looked at him in astonishment, muttering between his teeth, '. . . and turn the other cheek . . .' He shook his head angrily and said aloud, 'It would be better if you arranged to bury him tomorrow morning – it will be too late today. I must leave now – I want to arrive in Dakar before the women.'

He looked down at Dieynaba, whose shoulders were now racked with sobs, and turned to go, but he had walked only a few steps when Lahbib rejoined him.

'Write as soon as you can,' he said, 'and take care of yourself.'

Lahbib had put his hand on Bakayoko's arm, and the trainman sensed the warmth and friendship in the gesture. It did him good. Certainly he was one of them, he was fighting for them and with them, and yet sometimes he felt himself far from them, very far away, and lonely.

◆

Ever since they left Thiès, the women had not stopped singing. As soon as one group allowed the refrain to die, another picked it up, and new verses were born at the hazard of chance or inspiration, one word leading to another and each finding, in its turn, its rhythm and its place. No one was very sure any longer where the song began, or if it had an ending. It rolled out over its own length, like the movement of a serpent. It was as long as a life.

Now the day had come. The road was too narrow for them, and they moved forward spread out in the shape of a fan, so that some walked in the dust and others in the dry grass beside the road, while still others followed the tracks of the railroad, and the younger ones amused themselves by leaping from tie to tie. The colors of waistcloths and blouses and headcloths flowered across the landscape. Dun-colored burlaps and striped and checked drills and ticking mingled with bright splashes of prints and the faded cottons of old tunics. Open collars and rolled-up sleeves revealed well-rounded shoulders and elbows, blanched with a film of dust, and hitched-up skirts betrayed slender, handsome legs as well as hammy thighs.

The sun was behind them, beating ever harder on their backs, but they paid no attention to it; they knew it well. The sun was a native.

Penda, still wearing her soldier's cartridge belt, marched at the head of the procession with Mariame Sonko, the wife of Balla, and Maïmouna, the blind woman, who had joined them in the darkness without being noticed by anyone. Her baby was strapped across her back with an old shawl.

The men of the little escort group followed at some distance behind the women, and several of them had brought bicycles in the event that they should be needed. Boubacar had strung a necklace of cans and gourds filled with water from the framework and handlebars on his. Samba N'Doulougou was perched like a scrawny bird on an elegant English machine. His rump beat irregularly against the saddle, and his feet parted company with the pedals at every turn.

They were traveling across a countryside laid waste by the dry season. The torrents of the sun had struck at the hearts of even the grasses and the wild plants and drained away their sap. The smallest leaves and stalks leaned toward the earth, preparing to fall and die. The only things that seemed alive were the thorny plants that thrived on drought and, far off toward the horizon, the lofty baobabs, to whom the comings and goings of seasons meant nothing. The soil was ridged and caked in an unwholesome crust, but it still bore traces of ancient cultivation; little squares of earth pierced by stumps of millet or corn, standing like the teeth of a broken comb. Once, a line of thatched roofs had been drawn here, against the bosom of a rich, brown earth; and countless little pathways – coming from no one knew where, going no one knew where – crossed this master road, and the hundreds of feet that trod them raised a cloud of reddish dust, for in those days there was no asphalt on the road from Dakar.

Quite early on the first night they came to a village. The inhabitants, bewildered at the sight of so many women, plied them with questions. But their hospitality was cordial, although a little ceremonious because of their surprise at such an event. At dawn, their thirst assuaged, their stomachs calmed, their feet still sore, they left again, to a concert of compliments and encouragement. Two hours later they passed the bus to Thiès, and some of the women performed a little dance in the road to acknowledge the cheers and waving of the travelers. Then they took up their march again.

And the second day was very much like the first.

◆

It was at about noon of the third day that their fatigue began to show itself. They had passed through Pouth, where the villagers formed a double rank to applaud the singing women, but little by little after that the procession had lengthened out. The sun upended its caldrons of live coals on the earth, and the movement of their knees and ankles became steadily more difficult and painful. Like a river which, having amassed all its strength to pass through a narrow gorge, spreads out and moves sluggishly when it has reached the plain, the troop of women straggled across the landscape.

Maïmouna, who was still walking with the group in the lead, put her hand on Penda's shoulder. 'I don't hear the singing any more,' she said.

'That's true – I hadn't noticed. How long has it been?'

'Since we saw the snake that had been crushed by an automobile,' Mariame Sonko said, and she sat, or rather, fell back against the rim of the embankment.

Penda studied the horizon. 'Get up, Mariame. This isn't a good place to rest; there are some trees up ahead.'

'They are a long way off, your trees!'

The little group started out again, but they had gone only a short distance when Boubacar came up to them on his bicycle, with four of the other men following.

'There's a whole group back there that won't go any farther,' Boubacar said to Penda. He had shown so much enthusiasm for his role as her assistant that even Maïmouna had began to wonder about the reasons for it.

'They must go on,' Penda said. She gestured to the men with Boubacar. 'You – take the water cans and go on ahead to those trees; and don't give anything to drink to anyone until they get there. And you, Boubacar, take me back to that group.' She climbed on the back of his bicycle, and they set off toward the rear of the column.

Most of the women were walking by themselves, in Indian file, too tired even to group together and gossip. The largest and heaviest seemed to be suffering most; little rivers of sweat rolled down their faces and arms and naked thighs. They had pulled their skirts up high around their waists in the hope of making movement easier, and some of them had cut branches and walked like old people, leaning on their canes. When they passed a clump of bone-white, skeletal cade trees and a flight of vultures rose heavily into the air they were seized with panic, and those who had been walking in the grass hurried to join the others on the road. In all of their ancient legends these birds and these trees were the living homes of evil. Their presence together could be nothing but a warning of disaster to come.

A little beyond this point Penda and Boubacar came across the group of the younger girls, led by Aby, who had been one of Penda's assistants at the distribution of rations. They, too, were tired, but they were still laughing and talking as they walked. Boubacar braked the bicycle and put out his enormous feet to steady it.

'You can do better than this,' Penda called out. 'You're not old women!'

'We're not the last,' Aby said.

'I know, I know, but keep going just the same. We'll rest up ahead in the shade – and sing; it will help you and it will help the older women.'

194

A few voices picked up 'the chant', but it was a scattered, half-hearted effort. Penda shook her head, and they went on to the rear, pausing frequently to encourage women who were walking alone and urge them to join with one of the little islands into which the whole column had now broken. When they finally arrived at the group which had refused to go farther, almost an hour had elapsed since they left the head of the column.

Something like a hundred women were sitting or lying along the shoulders of the road or the slope of the railway embankment. Branches thrust into the ground and strung with skirts and blouses formed makeshift shelters from the sun, and some of them were sleeping with just their heads inside the little patch of shade. The rest of the men of the escort were waiting a little farther on, seated on the edge of a shallow ravine.

'All right,' Penda said sharply, as she got down from the bicycle. 'You have rested long enough. Now we have to go on.'

'Go on? With a sun like this? Do you want us dead?' It was Awa who had spoken, the wife of Séne Maséne, the foreman carpenter. Comfortably installed, with her back resting against the embankment and her head in the shade of a little shrub, she looked like a queen bee surrounded by her drones.

'Get up,' Penda said, striving to remain calm.

'We are tired. What difference does it make whether we leave today or tomorrow? If you're in such a hurry, go on ahead – we'll see you in Dakar.'

'No – there can't be any stragglers; we must all arrive together. If there are some of you who want to go back, do it now, but the others will go on.'

'Hé!' Awa cried. 'You're not the one to give orders here! My husband is a foreman . . .'

'Awa, I warn you, don't start that with me again! You have a short memory if you've forgotten already what happened at the ration distribution.'

Awa turned her head slowly on her enormous shoulders, as if calling on her companions to witness what she was about to say.

'I am staying,' she announced. 'We don't have to obey Penda. It's just because she can't have children that all the men run after her. And there are *deumes* in that group with her! Yes, there are women possessed of the evil spirit, and she wants us to mix with them! Well, piss on her!'

Penda could no longer control her anger. She strode rapidly over to the embankment and began kicking down the branches and snatching away the skirts and blouses. The women cried out in protest, and Awa screamed,

'The whore won't dare to touch my cloth!' but Penda went grimly on with her work until she had destroyed the last of the flimsy shelters.

Then she looked around her and, seeing that some of the women were still lying or kneeling on the ground, she began to count them out, lifting her fingers one by one.

'One, two, three, four . . .'

'Witch!' Awa cried. 'You have no right to do that!'

'No, no! Don't count us, please!' Séni said, getting quickly to her feet. 'We are God's bits of wood, and if you count us out you will bring misfortune; you will make us die!'

'I want to know how many of you are against the strike,' Penda said. '. . . five, six, seven, eight . . .'

'Stop!' Awa cried, scrambling to her feet. 'We will be eaten alive! My dream was true! I dreamed that spirits carrying pointed knives came and cut me in pieces to devour me!'

With fear and anger dividing their hearts, the women gathered together their clothing, knotted the cloths around their heads, and went back to the road. The men followed at a little distance, led by the giant Boubacar.

◆

When the stragglers rejoined the other women, they were given a surly welcome. The trees in the area Penda had chosen for the halt were few, and there was little shade. Most of those who had arrived first were already sleeping, and they were angry at being disturbed.

'*Hé*, you're the last to get here, and now you want all the best places!'

'We've been walking through hell – we want to rest!'

'And what about us? We didn't walk through hell?'

'Just move over a little.'

'*Hé*, look where you're sitting! You've got your ass in my face – if you farted, you'd smother me!'

'Awa, just because you're so fat doesn't mean you can do anything you please. Move your big ass!'

'Watch your words, Yaciné!'

'And you watch where you put that big rump, Awa!'

'Look out there! You're stepping on me!'

'I'm swimming in my own sweat – I don't need yours!'

'Is there anything to drink?'

'No; the water is all gone. The men have gone to look for some.'

At last, however, the newcomers settled down as best they could.

196

Fatigue overcame irritation, nerves and muscles relaxed, and the women slept.

Maïmouna had managed to save a little corner of shade for Penda, and the exhausted girl lay down beside the blind woman. She unfastened the buckle of the cartridge belt and pulled her skirt up high above her knees, sighing with relief, but just as she allowed her head to sink gratefully into the dry grass Boubacar appeared.

'Penda, Penda . . .'

'Now what?'

'The men who went for the water haven't come back yet,' the smith said awkwardly. The warm scent of female bodies and the sight of all these recumbent sleeping women made him uneasy. He lowered his eyes, trying not to stare at the long legs of the girl on the ground beneath him.

Penda propped herself up on an elbow. 'Well, send some others then. If there are no more bicycles, they'll have to to go on foot. We can't stay here long, and we have to have water before we leave.'

'I've already sent a second group.'

'Then why are you bothering me? Tell Samba N'Doulougou I want to see him; I have something to tell him.'

Boubacar did not answer. He stood there for a moment longer, then turned his massive back and disappeared among the trees, walking cautiously to avoid stepping on the women.

Maïmouna had trembled at the mention of Samba's name, and Penda had noticed it at once. She lay there, motionless, watching the blind woman. The sighs and snores of the sleeping women seemed enormous in the silence of the torrid afternoon. Séni was sleeping at Penda's feet, a little thread of saliva bubbling from the corner of her lips.

'Penda,' Maïmouna said gently, 'why are you so hard on Boubacar?'

'What do you mean? I'm not hard on him. Is he the father of your children?'

'No. Why is it that people who have eyes can never see?'

'Well, if he isn't the father, why is he always hanging around you?'

'Penda, could it be that there was always only one place in your heart, and now Bakayoko has taken it?' Maïmouna was speaking very softly, not wishing to disturb their neighbors. 'That man will occupy your heart, and then pass through it, leaving nothing but bitterness. He will destroy everything. You see, with us – with women – we love a man when we know nothing of him, and we want to know everything. And we will pursue the one we have chosen no matter what happens, no matter how he treats us. But when we have learned what we want to know, and there

197

is nothing left, no longer any mystery, then our interest is gone. The ones like Bakayoko will always be our bane. They do with us as they will. Before you have time to say "no", you have already said "yes".'

Penda was studying the face of the blind woman as she spoke, searching for the thoughts behind the sightless eyes.

'How do you know all this?' she asked.

'I haven't always been blind. After I lost my sight, my ears replaced my eyes. I have learned to know what people are thinking, and to understand what is said between the words that are spoken, and I tell you this: in Bakayoko's heart there is no room for anyone. He is blinder to his neighbor than I am . . .'

'Who is the father of your children?'

'You are just being stubborn. That is of no importance any longer. I was not betrayed by that man. He thought that he was possessing me, but it wasn't true; my flesh was calling out to be satisfied, just as his was. I knew that he would abandon me, and in my heart I had already abandoned him. We will be in Dakar soon, and I shall stay there. I will be among my brothers, the beggars, and with my child, who will always be mine. A child may not know its father, Penda, but what child can question the body in which it lived for nine long months?'

'You will stay with me,' Penda said.

The blind woman was silent for a moment. 'Rest now, Penda,' she said at last. 'Soon the wind will come up, and there will be a great storm.'

◆

It was during the next stage of the march that the crisis occurred which seemed certain to bring about the failure of the whole enterprise.

It had not been easy to rouse the women, who groaned and complained bitterly, pressing their hands against their aching limbs and backs, trying to rid themselves of the stiffness brought on by an hour's rest. Penda tried to cheer them up by joking with the group of younger girls.

'Be sure you don't let the men get too close to you. I don't want to have to answer to your families when your bellies start to swell!'

'We haven't done anything,' Aby said indignantly.

'And I suppose if you did you would come and tell me about it right away, *hé*?'

But no one was in a mood to laugh. Water had become the only thing they thought about. The few cans Boubacar's men brought back had been enough to supply only a few drops to each person.

'I'm as filthy as a pig,' one woman said, displaying the scales of dried sweat, caked with dust, that had formed on her legs.

'I'd like to get in the water and stay in it, like a fish!'

'When I get to Dakar, I'm going to do nothing but drink for the first hour!'

'Those beautiful, well-scrubbed boys in Dakar won't be interested in our dirty bodies!'

Little by little, however, the column reformed. There was no laughter or singing now, but a curious new thing seemed to have come to them: the sort of hope, or instinct, that will guide an animal searching for a new place to graze.

More and more often now, Penda left her own group and walked back along the length of the column, gathering in the stragglers, stopping to talk to the old and the more feeble, encouraging them to go on. On one such journey she heard Awa talking to a group of her friends, in a loud, frightened voice.

'I swear to you, there are evil spirits among us. My dream came back while we were resting – but I've taken precautions; they won't want me.' Saying this, she untied a corner of her skirt, which she had made into a large knot. 'Before we left, I covered myself with salt, and every now and then I eat a little of it. That way, when the *deumes* come to devour me, they will find that they don't want me.'

Several of the others held out their hands eagerly, and Awa gave them each a pinch of salt. In their fatigue and discouragement, the women were beset again by all the fears instilled in them by age-old legends. The sky itself seemed to threaten them; little clouds the color of Dahomey ivory, bordered in dark gray, raced across the horizon, throwing the bony fingers of the cade trees into stark relief.

'You are right, Awa,' one of the women said. 'We must be very careful. These offshoots of hell can change themselves into grains of dust, or into ants or thorns, or even into birds. I'm going to warn my sister.'

'You're a bunch of fools,' Penda said angrily, 'and you ought to . . .'

But she was interrupted by a piercing, disjointed shriek, followed by the sound of hysterical screaming from the rear of the column. She began to run in that direction, and a few of the more curious among the other women followed her, but most of them remained frozen where they were, and some even fled in the opposite direction.

Séni was rolling in the dust in the middle of the road, her limbs writhing horribly, her back arched and twisted in convulsions. Her skirt had been torn off, a slimy foam dribbled from her mouth, and her eyes rolled back into her head until only the whites stared out.

'I told you!' Awa cried. 'It's a *deume* who is devouring her! We've got to find it!'

The great orbs of her eyes, rolling in terror, suddenly came to rest on the tiny figure of Yaciné, seated by the side of the road a few feet away. The old woman had cut her big toe, and since it was bleeding profusely, she was trying to bring her foot up to her mouth to suck the blood away.

'There she is! There she is!' Awa screamed. 'Look – she is sucking Séni's blood through her feet!'

Twenty mouths screamed with her now. 'There she is! There is the *deume*! Catch her, catch her!'

Yaciné leaped to her feet, panic-stricken, and tried to run, but she was caught in an instant. A dozen hands seized her roughly, and others hurled branches and stones at her.

'You've all gone mad!' Penda shouted, trying to protect the old woman, whose face had been gashed by a stone and was beginning to bleed.

Awa was still screaming hysterically. 'I told you so! I told you so! We have a *deume*, and Séni is going to die!'

'*Fermez vos gueules!*' Without realizing it, Penda had spoken in French. 'You're the ones who are *deumes*! Let this woman go, or I'll eat you alive myself! Mariame! Go get Boubacar and the men and bring Maïmouna, too!'

She succeeded at last in freeing Yaciné, half dead with fright, her clothing almost torn from her body. Séni was lying on her back in the road, surrounded by a circle of women. Her legs were straight and stiff, and her teeth were chattering violently.

Boubacar arrived, followed by five or six men on bicycles, one of them carrying Maïmouna behind him. She leaned over the prostrate woman, her fingers moving swiftly over her face and feeling for her pulse.

'It isn't serious,' she said. 'It's just the heat. She'll have to inhale some urine.'

'All right, some of you sluts go and piss!' Penda cried.

Some of the women climbed over to the other side of the embankment, and Maïmouna followed them. She came back a few minutes later, carrying some clods of humid earth. Seating herself in the road, she kneaded them into little balls, which she passed back and forth under Séni's nostrils, while Penda held up the unconscious woman's head.

In all this time, Awa never once stopped shouting. 'There are others! I tell you, there are others! Séni is going to die – I can smell the odor of death from her already. They brought us out here because it would be easier to devour us here – it's just like it was in my dream!'

Penda could no longer control herself. She rested Séni's head on the knees of the blind woman and hurled herself at Awa.

'Now, you are going to be quiet!'

Her fists were as hard as a man's, and she hammered at the other woman's face and stomach until she stumbled and fell against the foot of a tree, screaming with pain and fear.

Then, her anger drained out of her by this explosion of physical energy, Penda walked over to the giant smith, who had been watching her in amazement.

'Boubacar, some of the men will have to carry the women who are sick,' she said, pointing at Awa, the weeping Yaciné, and Séni, who was now sitting up, with her head resting calmly on Maïmouna's shoulder, next to that of the baby sleeping on her mother's back.

The men lifted her from the ground and installed her on the seat of a bicycle, where they could support her as they pushed it along. Boubacar took Awa on his powerful back, and the column formed up once again. All of the women seemed to want to walk behind Maïmouna, as if she trailed a protective wake in which they would be safe. The wind she had prophesied earlier was rising now; huge black clouds, running before it, cast fitful shadows across the road, frightening the marchers. Disembodied twigs and leaves danced across the earth, carried by waves of dust.

And suddenly, as the road twisted around a little hill, a man's voice called out, '*Tialaverd, Tialaverd, ban'ga!* Here comes the storm!'

It was really just a minor whirlwind, and not the great storm Maïmouna had predicted. As it approached them, three columns of dust twisted up to the sky, flattening the grasses in their paths and tearing the leaves from the bushes and shrubs. The terrified women flung themselves into a near-by ravine flattening their bodies against the ground and burying their heads in bushes or clumps of grass. Their headcloths were whipped away and carried up into the trees, catching against the branches and streaming out like pennants. One woman's waistcloth was torn from her, and she was hurled, naked, against the trunk of a eucalyptus tree.

They had all seen hundreds of dust storms just like this one, but their nerves were already stretched to the breaking point, and even after it had passed their despair persisted. Penda went from one group to another, encouraging them, pointing to the columns of dust vanishing in the distance, urging them to get up and go on.

Boubacar was still carrying the mumbling and cursing Awa, Yaciné was still weeping, and Séni, held in the seat of the bicycle by two men, kept murmuring. 'My heart . . . my heart . . .' Even the men were beginning to complain. Only Maïmouna, her baby strapped across her back, walked steadily forward, humming one of her endless refrains.

'What a blind woman can do,' Penda said, 'the rest of you should be able to do!'

At last, just as night was falling on the weary and haggard procession, they heard a joyful beating of drums approaching them. The people of the village of Sébikoutane, told of the women's arrival by their children, were coming out to meet them. In gourds, in tin jugs, in cooking pots, and in old cans they were carrying water.

◆

The last two stages of the march, from Sébikoutane to Rufisque, and from Rusfisque to Dakar, were almost a promenade. The reception given the women at Sébikoutane had been magnificent. The earth of the village square was red with the blood of sheep slaughtered for the feast, and the celebration had gone on until far into the night. But best of all had been the water; all the water they could possibly drink. The 'marchers', as people now called them, learned that they were rapidly becoming famous; the newspapers, and even the radio, had mentioned them. Those who had never ceased complaining while they were on the road preened themselves and strutted now, inventing vicissitudes they had never undergone and risks they had never run. Even Awa succumbed to the fever of good will, and just before their departure from the village she sought out Penda.

'I'm not going back to Thiès,' she said. 'I'm going on with you, Penda. I promise that I won't cause you any more trouble, and to prove it I am going to ask Yaciné to forgive me for what I did.'

Penda was massaging her swollen feet, but she got up instantly. 'I'll come with you – I want to see this . . .'

Seeing Awa approach, Yaciné shrank back in fear, but the carpenter's wife fulfilled her promise.

'Yaciné,' she said, 'I came to ask you to forgive me. Out there I was tired and out of my head with the heat, and I lied. You are not a *deume*.'

Yaciné began to laugh and cry at the same time. 'Do you hear that, all of you?' she shouted. 'I am not a *deume*! Now I can return home without shame, and with my head high! Oh thank you, Awa, thank you!'

Just after that, the long procession set out again. The waistcloths and blouses and headcloths had all been washed, and a sky swept clean of even

202

the smallest cloud by yesterday's winds smiled down on the colorful horde. Between Rufisque, their last stopping place, and Dakar, they breathed the fresh sea air of the Atlantic for the first time. The ranks of the original column from Thiès had been swollen by women from the villages, and by a delegation from Rufisque; and a large group of men had reinforced the escort. The women sang again and laughed and joked.

'We will surely see some beautiful houses at Dakar.'

'But they are not for us; they are only for the *toubabs*.'

'After the strike we will have them, too.'

'After the strike I'm going to do what the wives of the *toubabs* do, and take my husband's pay!'

'And if there are two of you?'

'We'll each take half, and that way he won't have anything left to spend on other women. We will have won the strike, too!'

'The men have been good, though. Did you see how the smith was sweating while he was carrying Awa?'

'Bah! For once he had a woman on his back. They have us on our backs every night!'

In the last miles before they reached their goal they passed a point from which they could see the island of Gorée, a tiny black dot in the green expanse of the ocean; they saw the vast Lafarge cement factories and the remains of an American army camp. As they approached the first buildings of Dakar's suburbs, a breathless boy on a bicycle raced up to meet them, leaping off his machine in front of the little group at the head of the column.

'There are soldiers on the road at the entrance to the city,' he gasped. 'They say that the women from Thiès will not be allowed to pass.'

The laughter and the singing stopped abruptly, and there was silence. A few of the women left the road and took shelter behind the walls, as if they expected the soldiers to appear at any minute; but the bulk of the column stood firm. Penda climbed up on a little slope.

'The soldiers can't eat us!' she cried. 'They can't even kill us; there are too many of us! Don't be afraid – our friends are waiting for us in Dakar! We'll go on!'

The long, multi-colored mass began to move forward again.

Maïmouna, who was walking a little behind Penda, suddenly felt a hand on her arm.

'Who is it?'

'It's me.'

'You, Samba? What's the matter?'

'There are soldiers . . .'

'Yes, I heard.'

Samba N'Doulougou did not understand too clearly what force it was that had compelled him to come here now and seek out this woman whose body he had enjoyed one night. Was it pity for the weak and infirm, or was it for the mother and the child? He remembered the shame he had lived with for months, as he watched her working in the sun while her belly grew large with the child, his child. And he remembered the way he had tried to alter his voice so she would not recognize him.

'Give me the child,' he said. 'It will be easier for me to avoid the soldiers.'

'You want your child?' the blind woman said.

'The soldiers are going to be there . . .'

'And after that? . . . A father may die while a woman is big with child, but that does not prevent the child from living, because the mother is there. It is up to me to protect this child. Go away now. After I get to Dakar you will never see me again; and I have never seen you. No one knows who is the father of this child – you can sleep peacefully, and your honor will be safe. Now go back to the men.'

Just outside the big racecourse of the city, the column confronted the red tarbooshes of the soldiers. A black non-commissioned officer who was standing with the captain commanding the little detachment called out to them.

'Go back to Thiès, women! We cannot let you pass!'

'We will pass if we have to walk on the body of your mother!' Penda cried.

And already the pressure of this human wall was forcing the soldiers to draw back. Reinforcements began to appear, from everywhere at once, but they were not for the men in uniform. A few rifle butts came up menacingly and were beaten down by clubs and stones. The unnerved soldiers hesitated, not knowing what to do, and then some shots rang out, and in the column two people fell – Penda and Samba N'Doulougou.

But how could a handful of men in red tarbooshes prevent this great river from rolling on to the sea?

DAKAR

The Meeting

As soon as the news of Beaugosse's return to Dakar became known, a crowd began to gather in the Place M'Both, in front of the union building. While the members of the committee met inside to hear the delegates' report on the breakdown of the talks at Thiès, the people in the square stood about waiting restlessly. They knew already that the meeting had ended in a defeat for the strikers, and their faces were hard and determined, their fists clenched against their thighs.

For several days the atmosphere in the city had been growing steadily more oppressive. Since the fire and the attack on the *spahis*, the authorities had considerably augmented the security forces, and now soldiers and sailors as well as police and militiamen patrolled the streets constantly. Protective cordons of troops formed a virtual barricade between the native quarters and the residential and commercial avenues of the European quarter, and the enforced segregation had created strain and unrest on both sides of the wall.

For the strikers and their families, life became more difficult with each succeeding day. Their bodies grew weaker and the lines in their faces were etched more deeply; but for many of them the ordeal they were passing through was taking on an even greater significance than the rites of initiation to manhood that they had undergone in their youth.

Alioune had succeeded in persuading a considerable number of the men that their old feudal customs had no place in a situation like this. Now, husbands, sons, and even fathers could be seen every morning, leaving their homes in search of water and returning at night, triumphantly pushing a barrel or carrying a sackful of bottles. At last the men had found something to do which not only occupied the long, empty hours but helped to relieve the scarcity of food and thereby made it possible to carry on with the strike. They sought out their friends among the fishermen on the ocean front, and small fish caught with a line or tuna trapped in the great nets began to replace the vanished meat and rice on their tables.

The union building had become the center of all activity. Benches and chairs were crammed into every possible corner, and blankets, sheepskins, and strips of matting were strewn on the floors to provide places to sleep. Since the electricity had been cut off, they were forced to work at night by the light of strips of cloth set in bowls of palm or fish oil.

And there was a great deal of work to be done. A campaign to demoralize and undermine the unity of the strikers – and particularly of their wives – had been undertaken by the men who were their 'spiritual guides', the imams and the priests of other sects. After the prayers and religious services all over the city, there would be a sermon whose theme was always the same: 'By ourselves, we are incapable of creating any sort of useful object, not even a needle; and yet you want to strike against the *toubabs* who have brought us all of these things! It is madness! You would do better to be thanking God for having brought them among us and bettering our lives with the benefits of their civilization and their science.'

Infuriated by the workers' resistance to their injunctions, the imams turned the full force of their wrath on the members of the strike committee, accusing them of responsibility for every crime they could think of – atheism, alcoholism, prostitution, infant mortality. They even predicted that these infidels would bring about the end of the world.

But there was another matter that was more serious than this . . .

Alioune had gone to see Gaye, the secretary of the metal-workers' union, which was a branch of the powerful Confédération Générale du Travail, in the hopes of obtaining a promise of mutual assistance. He had not been well received.

'You don't belong to the C.G.T., and I don't have anything to do with the men on the Dakar-Niger,' Gaye had said. 'You wanted your independence, and you have it . . .'

'There is something you don't understand . . .'

'Just let me finish, Alioune. You don't want to go by the union's general policies, and we won't have anything to do with separatists and deviationists. Your union is autonomous, and that's the way you wanted it, so don't come crying to me about it now.'

Alioune knew that Gaye had only to say the word and the other branches of the confederation would join with the trainmen, but he also knew that he would not do it without attaching his own conditions.

A day or so before 'the marchers', as the women of Thiès were now known all along the line, were expected to arrive in Dakar, Gaye came to see Alioune at the office of the strike committee.

'Well,' he said. 'It seems that the women will be here tomorrow or the day after. What about this matter of mediation you were asking for?'

'You know perfectly well, Gaye, that it isn't a matter of mediation. The management on one side and ourselves on the other; that's all we want. We could accept your mediators for the meeting itself, but we would have to talk to the other branches of the confederation first.'

'That's just what I thought you would say! You want to involve everyone else, but keep the settlement in your own hands! Well, that's not the way it's going to be. We've already talked it over – the masons, the coal miners, the men at Shell Oil, even the civil servants – and we have agreed to a meeting, with the governor-general, the deputy, and the Imam presiding. Now it's up to you.'

Alioune knew that he was trapped. Gaye had brought together a group that was too powerful to fight against alone.

'Very well,' he said. 'Tomorrow night we'll discuss it with the other unions and plan the meeting for the day after.'

'Why wait?'

'No reason, Gaye, except we work as a group here, and I have to discuss this with the other members of the committee.'

'All right then. Tomorrow night.'

Alioune was still a victim of his anger and his sense of frustration when he rejoined his comrades. His desperate play for time had only been made in the hope that Bakayoko might arrive before the following evening and find some way of getting out of the trap.

'I'd like to see him buried in molten lead!' he said, as he came into the room where the others were gathered. 'There's no way of backing out of it now – he has everyone on his side!'

'It is the will of God,' Arona said.

'Oh shut up with your talk about the will of God!'

◆

When Bakayoko arrived that night, the union building and its little courtyard were already deep in shadow. Men were sleeping on army cots and on the ground, and here and there the glow of a cigarette pricked the darkness of a corner unreached by the feeble light of the lamp. Bakayoko sat down on the cot next to Alioune, who was wearily removing his canvas shoes. He listened without interrupting as Alioune poured out the story of his meetings with Gaye.

207

'We are finished,' he said, when at last he had heard it all. 'We've been wrapped up as neatly as dough in the hands of a cook.'

'It's my fault,' Alioune said. 'Until now I've always just followed instructions from Thiès. I knew that one day or another we would go back, and that we might not even get everything we asked for – but I didn't know that, just by talking with the others, I would be responsible for bringing the governor and the deputy into it.'

'You did what you could. The thing that made us strong in the first months was that we were the ones who were controlling what was happening. Now it seems as if events were controlling us. But what can you do – we're not rich enough – and we can't pass out either titles or villas. But we can still hold onto our faith in the future; this is just a temporary halting place, and we will get what we are asking for yet. For the moment, the best thing we can do is sleep – I haven't closed my eyes in two days, and I don't imagine you have either.'

The silhouette of a crouching figure moved by them in the shadows. It was Deune, following his nightly habit of gathering up the cigarette butts.

'Don't waste time crying about it,' he grunted. 'If it doesn't work this time, we'll just start again another time.'

Stretched out on his cot, Alioune could hear Bakayoko's regular breathing, but in spite of his own fatigue he could not sleep. He was thinking of a painful scene that had taken place that morning.

Beaugosse had come to the committee's office, looking for his comrades. He had seemed embarrassed and uneasy, and before anyone had had a chance to say, 'Good morning,' he had announced, 'I wanted to let you know that I'm leaving the D-N; so don't count on me being here after today.'

At first everyone had thought it was a joke, and Deune had clapped him on the back and said, 'He's trying to be funny again.'

'No, I'm not trying to be funny; I'm leaving. I'm going to work as a storekeeper in the tool sheds at the port.'

'But why should you leave now?' Idrissa demanded. 'You've just come back from Thiès; you took part in the meeting there . . . and we still need you. There aren't that many of us who know how to read and write! I don't understand you . . .'

'There's nothing to understand. I'm leaving, that's all. I have the right to do what I want for myself, don't I?'

Deune had walked over to the window where the young man was standing. 'But what you are doing now is not a good thing, little one,' he

208

said. 'We're not as intelligent as you are, and you make us wonder about a lot of things. Did you tell us the truth about what happened at Thiès?'

'Yes, I told you the truth. You gave me a job to do, and I did it honestly. I'm leaving now for personal reasons.'

'You're betraying us; that's what you're doing!' Deune's rumbling voice had risen almost to a shout. 'We were proud of you – we were proud that we could point to you and say, "Look at that little one; he is educated and intelligent, but he still prefers to stay with us and fight with us" – and now you're quitting us. It isn't easy to get a job in the port – you must have been to see the *toubabs* . . .'

'Calm down, Deune,' Alioune had said. 'You're exaggerating.'

'I'll say what I have to say! I trusted this boy; I voted for him to be our delegate at Thiès. And now he's quitting us! You all remember that quitter who was tried by the men in Bamako, don't you? You approved of that, didn't you? Well, make him turn in his card right now!'

Without a word, Beaugosse had taken his wallet from a pocket of his linen jacket, drawn out a gray pasteboard card, placed it on the table, and left the office.

'I don't know if I have the right to do this,' Deune said, 'but I'm going to do it anyway'. He picked up the card and tore it into little pieces.

The scene had troubled Alioune greatly, and as he lay there, trying to sleep, he could not help thinking about it again and again. Suddenly he realized that Bakayoko was sitting on the edge of his cot, lighting his pipe.

'You're not asleep, Alioune?'

'No, I was thinking – about some difficult things. Did you meet Beaugosse at Thiès?'

'Yes; he doesn't like me. But I don't like him either. Tell me; who will be the delegate for the masons?'

'His name is Seydou. They trust him, and he is a good speaker,' Alioune said curtly. He was annoyed by the way Bakayoko had spoken about Beaugosse, because he knew the story of N'Deye Touti and the boy. He lay down again and said very softly, as if he were talking to himself, 'You know, the difficult thing about you is that although you understand the problems very well, you don't understand men – or if you do understand them, you never show it. But you expect them to understand every word you say, and if they don't, you lose your temper. Then they become timid, because they know they are not as intelligent as you are, and they don't like to be made fools of. So the result is that no one dares to do anything when you are not around . . . I ought to tell you that I wrote a letter to

Lahbib about it. You were already on the way here when it was sent, but now you won't be surprised if he mentions it to you.'

'You did well,' Bakayoko said. He rapped the bowl of his pipe against the foot of the cot and was silent for a moment. 'I wish I could make you understand something, too. When I am in the cabin of my engine, I take on a sense of absolute identity with everything that is in the train, no matter whether it is passengers or just freight. I experience everything that happens along its whole length. In the stations I observe the people, but once the engine is on its way, I forget everything else. My role then is nothing except to guide that machine to the spot where it is supposed to go. I don't even know any longer whether it is my heart that is beating to the rhythm of the engine, or the engine to the rhythm of my heart. And for me, that is the way it has to be with this strike – we must all take on a sense of identity with it . . .'

A voice from the other side of the office interrupted him. 'What you are saying is very interesting, but it is also tiring. Tomorrow is going to be a hard day.'

Then there was silence in the little room – silence and the heavy odor of sleeping men.

◆

When it was announced next morning that the women of Thiès would arrive early in the afternoon, the city was galvanized into action. Everything that could be used to carry the precious water the men had brought in was filled, because 'the marchers' were sure to be thirsty. In every house and courtyard the women were busy sweeping, cleaning, and preparing lodgings. At N'Diayène, the central courtyard was transformed into one great kitchen. Knives in hand, all the housewives of the neighborhood were cleaning and scaling fish and tossing them into a collection of giant kettles.

'I feel as if there were fish swimming around inside of me,' Mame Sofi said. 'Fish in the morning, fish at night – if this keeps up much longer I'll have a fish tree growing in my belly.'

'Stop grumbling,' Bineta said. 'If it weren't for them we would all be dead by now, and the children with us. And the women of Thiès will be hungry. Someone told me that it's a girl named Penda who is leading them.'

'Ah! I know that one – she's a prostitute. They shouldn't have let a woman like that be the leader of honest women.'

'Oh Mame Sofi, you and that tongue of yours! Can't you ever find anything good to say about anyone?'

But Mame Sofi had already found another target for her malice. N'Deye Touti had just come out to the courtyard, carrying a little bundle of damp laundry.

'Look at that! Just look at that!' Deune's first wife screamed.

'What's the matter now?' Bineta and the others demanded, looking around to see what had annoyed Mame Sofi this time.

'What's the matter? Can't you see? No one has enough water to drink, but our *"Mad'mizelle"* has enough to wash those indecent clothes of hers! It's immoral to walk around like that; it's only fit for the white women!'

'Oh, let me alone, Aunt Mame Sofi! I had some dirty clothes and I washed them; that's all!'

The neighbors had stopped their work and were watching delightedly. Seeing Mame Sofi in a good argument was a spectacle they had not enjoyed in a long time. But Ramatoulaye intervened.

'Be quiet, both of you,' she said. 'N'Deye Touti, go fix the milk for Strike; and as for you, Mame Sofi, you would do better to get on with your work and not talk so much. A man just came by to say that the women of Thiès are already entering the city.'

It was the middle of the day now, and the sun was doing its work. The crowd was already gathering, from the avenues and from all the streets and alleys, turning its back on the white stone buildings of the European quarter and moving towards the Moslem district. The avenue Gambetta was a black river of people. Trainmen were busy everywhere, handing out leaflets urging everyone to stop work for the rest of the day and come to the meeting. Sometimes the police tried to stop them, but the crowd always opened up and swallowed them, laughing happily at the frustration of their pursuers.

'The marchers' came in through the suburb of Hann, across the bridge at the entrance to the city. The strikers who had been assigned to maintain order tried desperately to keep the crowd formed in a double rank along the sides of the street, so that they would have room to pass. The mingling of sound from this mass of people – a drumming of thousands of heels, ringing of bicycle bells, creaking of cart wheels, shouting and singing, and the cries of cripples and beggars – could be heard as far away as the docks. A vast echoing dome seemed to cover the entire city.

'Stop pushing! They're going to pass right by here; you'll see them!'

'Is it true they walked all that distance without food or water?'

'The poor things – that's more than the men could do!'

211

'They're coming to see the deputy – to arrange with him about the strike.'

'If you ask me, the strike is a matter for the men to settle themselves.'

'You're right there, brother – this is nothing but politics. These women are all Communists.'

'But they aren't doing anything except trying to help their husbands.'

'And where will that get them? It's just as the Imam says – they don't know what they're doing. Look around you, woman – there are soldiers everywhere. You wait and see; there's going to be trouble at the meeting. I know what I'm talking about; I work in their offices.'

This was the sort of thing everyone was saying as they waited for the women to arrive. The air was filled with curiosity, speculation, excitement and fear.

The reception committee, with Mame Sofi and Bineta at the head of the women's group, was stationed at a grade crossing near the bridge. In addition to the women, it was made up of Bakayoko, Deune, Arona and Idrissa, who seemed to be squinting even more than usual. Bakayoko was wearing the old, wire-brimmed straw hat again and, clinging to his arm, chattering excitedly, was a very old woman whom everyone called Grandmother Fatou Wade. No one knew how old she was; she was no longer sure herself, but wherever anything happened in the city, she could always be found.

'Look,' she said, proudly holding up a blue, polka-dotted waistcloth of the kind that had been made in the old days when all the dyeing of cloth was done at home with indigo. 'This cloth is older than I am. It came to me from my mother, who got it from her grandmother. In those days, when they wanted to honor a guest they spread cloths like this on the ground, for the guest to walk on. I brought it with me today so we could receive these women properly.'

Just at this moment, from the angle of the avenue el-Hadji-Malic-Sy, a cry went up from a thousand throats, 'They are coming! They are coming!'

With their arms linked together and their backs turned to the crowd, the trainmen, joined by contingents of men from the masons and dock workers, struggled to hold back the pushing, shouting masses of people. Mariame Sonko was at the head of the column of marchers, with Maïmouna, the blind woman, at her arm. In the group just behind them were Awa, Séni, and the young girl Aby, walking proudly and laughing. Boubacar and some of the men of the escort walked on either side of them, screening them from the crush with their bicycles.

As they approached the grade crossing, Grandmother Fatou Wade

212

pushed forward to meet them. She waved the cloth above her head and then spread it across the street in front of Mariame Sonko, who paused in astonishment.

'No, no!' the old woman cried. 'Come ahead, come ahead, and walk over the cloth. In the old times, that is how the warriors were received when they returned to their homes!'

There were shouts of enthusiasm from the crowd, and the other women began to follow her example. In a few minutes the pavement was strewn with handkerchiefs, headcloths, and even blouses, and the great, multicolored carpet made the arrival of the women seem like a kind of carnival.

While the other members of the strike committee were directing the marchers to the compound of N'Diayène, where food and water were waiting for them, Bakayoko went to talk to Mariame Sonko and Boubacar. It was only then that he learned about the death of Penda and Samba N'Doulougou.

One of the men with Boubacar was pushing an English bicycle whose handle bars had been turned up as high as they would go. 'It's Samba's,' he said. 'We kept it, and I suppose I could ride it, but I can't seem to bring myself to get on it. I don't know . . .'

Bakayoko said nothing. The news of these deaths oppressed him, and for the first time he was afraid of losing his confidence in the future. 'Penda, too . . .' he murmured, and suddenly discouragement stabbed at him like the claws of a hawk plunging on its prey. Was all of the learning he had managed to acquire, all of the effort of a mind he had harnessed so rigidly to the service of this cause – was all of that to vanish now, before the specter of these two corpses?

A strong hand clapped him on the shoulder, and a laughing voice rang in his ears. 'Man, we are going to win!'

'Man, we are going to win!' he answered; but as he walked along with the column his head was bowed.

◆

Never before had such an enormous crowd assembled at the racecourse in Dakar. In addition to the strikers, there were the dock workers, the fishermen from N'Gor, from Yoff, and from Kambaréne, and the workers and office staffs of all the big factories. Seen from the height of the grandstands, the assortment of head covering – turbans, fezzes, tarbooshes, white and khaki pith helmets, and brightly colored handkerchiefs, starched and knotted at the corners so that they stood up like rabbit's ears – made

213

the crowd resemble a moving mosaic, dotted here and there with the blacks and whites of umbrellas and parasols.

Soldiers, militiamen and policemen were standing guard before the gates to the field itself, and at the foot of the stands there was an imposing array of security forces. The first delegation to arrive was the group led by the Imam. He was followed by El Hadji Mabigué, in his finest tunic and wearing all of his medals. As they made their way across the field to the stands, stopping every now and then to respond to the greetings of the faithful, he held an umbrella carefully above his master's head. A non-commissioned officer of the police conducted them ceremoniously to the places reserved for them in the central pavilion of the grandstand.

A few minutes later a murmur of excitement rippled across the crowd, as the women of Thiès came in through the main entrance gate. Their long journey together had been an effective training school; they marched in well-ordered ranks, ten abreast, and without any masculine escort now. They carried banners and pennants printed with slogans, some of them reading, EVEN BULLETS COULD NOT STOP US, and others, WE DEMAND FAMILY ALLOWANCES.

Behind them came the mass of the strikers, led by the members of the committee. They, too, were carrying banners: FOR EQUAL WORK, EQUAL PAY – OLD AGE PENSIONS – PROPER HOUSING, and others. In spite of their brave appearance, no one could help noticing the fatigue and hunger in their faces and bodies.

Bakayoko and Alioune were standing together, near one of the betting booths of the race track.

'Take a look at your protégé,' Bakayoko said ironically.

Standing beside a tree a few feet from them was Gaye, accompanied by the personnel director, Edouard, the chief of police of the Moslem quarter, and young Pierre. With them, and dressed as they were, in European fashion, was Beaugosse.

'Look,' Edouard said, gesturing towards Bakayoko. 'It's our orator friend.'

'Is he going to speak?' Pierre asked.

'I hope not,' Gaye said.

Bakayoko turned his back to them.

'Don't worry about Beaugosse,' Alioune said. 'He'll come back to us. I know what's wrong with him.'

They were interrupted by the arrival of Grandmother Fatou Wade. 'I have been looking for you, my son,' she said to Bakayoko, 'to ask you something. Do you still have your mother?'

'No, Grandmother. She was murdered by the police while I was away from home.' Bakayoko looked at the old woman steadily as he spoke. She reminded him of Niakoro. He remembered the words Bakary had said to him and a little twinge of regret caught at his heart.

'From today on, then, I will be your mother,' the old woman said, taking his hand and holding it for a moment. 'My husband died in the first war and my oldest son in the second. And now they have taken my other son. Look here – this is all I have left of them.'

She untied a knot in a corner of her waistcloth and took out three medals: a Croix de Guerre, a medal for service in the colonial armies, and a medal awarded to soldiers who had been wounded in the service of France. 'Since there has been no food, I've tried to sell them, but none of the shopkeepers will buy them. I wonder why the *toubabs* give out such things – to me, they are just symbols of death.' She sighed and put the medals in Bakayoko's hand. 'If you stay in Dakar, my son, come to live with me. There will always be a place for you.'

She walked off and left them, sucking at her cheeks as Niakoro had done, filled with joy at having found a son to replace her own.

'Alioune,' Bakayoko said, 'if they should try to stop me from speaking later on, round up some of the men – and especially some of the women – and tell them to shout like they have never shouted before!'

◆

N'Deye Touti had followed the women of Thiès on to the field of the racecourse. She was upset, and in a bad humor. Just outside the entrance gate she had encountered Mame Sofi, who smiled at her sarcastically and said, 'Which one are you looking for – Bakayoko or Beaugosse? They're both inside. If you want to make yourself useful, you can help us take the collection after the meeting . . .'

She seemed unable to prevent herself from thinking about Bakayoko. She had tried to speak to him at N'Diayène, but he had been busy with the women of Thiès, especially the blind one. At one moment, however, he had put his hand on her shoulder and said, 'Your eyes are still like two moons in a single night.' She had drawn away, thinking that he would follow, but he had not.

'Where are you going, N'Deye Touti?'

The voice startled her, and for a second she hoped that it might be Bakayoko, but it was Beaugosse.

'I was looking for a place to sit,' she said.

215

'Come with us. Monsieur Edouard, this is the girl I was telling you about.' He looked at N'Deye Touti. 'These are my friends; they can be very helpful to you.'

The chief of police came over to her and said, 'Mademoiselle, let us forget about what happened the other day. You are a sensible girl – and I am not always on duty.'

'Oh yes,' Edouard said, 'after Beaugosse spoke to me about you, I talked to the directress of your school, and there is no reason why you can't go back. Everything can be arranged; I'll take care of it myself.' He patted N'Deye Touti's hand. 'I'm delighted to see that you have chosen Beaugosse: he's a fine young man and should have a splendid future. But, come, we had better take our places now. You come with us, mademoiselle.'

The central portion of the grandstand had been divided into sections for the Europeans and the various delegations and officials. As they made their way up the steps, there was a series of strident blasts from the whistles of the policemen at the entrance gate, and a platoon of troops of the 'Red Guards' swept on to the field, preceding the official cars. The red and white of their flowing burnooses contrasted vividly with the coal black of their splendid horses, and gold stars glittering fiercely on their tarbooshes.

The governor-general and the deputy, who was also the mayor of the city, got out of the first car, and a group of their assistants from the second. They walked rapidly up the steps and took their places in the first row of the stands, behind a battery of microphones.

The first three speeches were brief. It was the Imam, in his capacity as spiritual guide to a large part of the community, who opened the meeting by repeating the theme of all of his recent sermons. He warned the faithful in his audience against evil influences from 'abroad' and spoke glowingly of the governor and the deputy, thanking them for honoring the meeting with their presence, in spite of their heavy responsibilities. To give even greater effect to his words, he concluded by reading the first two verses of the Koran.

The governor spoke next, adopting a paternal tone and telling them how he had spent thirty years of his life in the study and administration of colonial problems. At this point he caught himself quickly and changed the phrase to 'African problems'. This strike had been especially difficult for him, because it indicated that there had been regrettable misunderstandings on both sides, but he promised to study the demands of the strikers carefully. 'I know you are all aware,' he said, 'that a great many things have changed for you since my appointment here – and always for the better. Still others will change in the future, and the changes will always be to your advantage. But time and patience are necessary, in order for such progress to be made and to be advantageous to everyone. The workers on the railroad can go back to their work tomorrow morning. Contrary to rumors spread by a few malcontents, no sanctions will be taken against the strikers, and I personally promise all of them that their requests will be studied and satisfied insofar as possible, in the near future.' He concluded by reminding them that the ties which linked Africa to the homeland were the ties of blood shed in a common effort.

He was heard respectfully and loudly applauded, although a good half of his audience had not understood a word he said. Gaye, who followed him, had been charged with speaking specifically to the workers. He first went into a summary of his own union activities and then explained how the other unions had adopted an attitude of 'wait and see' toward the strike, since they regarded it as a 'political maneuver' and felt that any attempt at a 'separatist' policy in the workers' movement must be avoided.

When he had finished, Alioune came hurriedly down the steps from the grandstand and went over to Bakayoko.

'They are never going to let one of the trainmen speak!' he said angrily.

'All right, then, just do as I told you. Get everyone to shout until they can't even hear the loudspeakers. Then we'll see what happens.'

It was now the turn of the mayor-deputy, and his speech was a great deal longer than any of the preceding ones. He spoke, in fact, for almost an hour, reading his text through a pair of heavy, horn-rimmed glasses perched carefully on his blunt nose. When he opened his mouth, the gold caps of his two front teeth sparkled brilliantly in the middle of his round and sweating face. His hair was turning gray and cut so short that it was little more than a stubble. He spoke in French, placing a considerable distance between each of his words.

'I greet you, peaceful friends,' he said, 'and thank you for listening to me. When a child climbs to the top of a tree, he tells no one what he is about to do, but if he falls, he cries out and everyone comes running to help. That is the way it is with this strike. When the workers on the Dakar-Niger decided on it, they did so with no warning to the people best qualified to help them, and with no thought of the consequences of their action. And now, you see the results. There is no water and no food in *our* homes, and the shopkeepers refuse to give *us* credit. And yet, this strike is the work of a few black sheep, acting on the advice of foreigners, because such a way of acting is not in keeping with *our* habits or *our* customs.

'When I was asked to come back here and take a hand in resolving this crisis, I thought at first of refusing, but in the end I accepted, because it is my duty to help you in any way I can. I have already proposed some decrees, and even some laws, to govern such situations, and I am sure that they will be granted, but time is needed in matters of this kind. If you, the strikers, are not concerned by this, at least do not stand in the way of others. Your strike endangers the progress of everyone and can even retard it. The management of the railway has already consented to some of your requests, and the rest will have to come from the National Assembly in Paris, since it is within their jurisdiction.'

The deputy paused to wipe his streaming forehead and clean his glasses.

'Why doesn't he speak in Ouolof?' demanded Grandmother Fatou Wade, who was once again leaning on Bakayoko's arm. 'I can't understand anything he's saying.'

The Bambara did not answer. His teeth were tightly clenched, and the expression on his face was one of thinly controlled fury. He gestured suddenly to Deune, Alioune, Idrissa and Boubacar, who were standing near him, and the four men vanished into the crowd.

At last the deputy was concluding his speech.

'... It seems that some of you have been thinking of calling for a general strike. In my capacity as mayor of this city, as well as your deputy, I forbid it. It would destroy everything we are working for. I am speaking now directly to the leaders of the unions, and I tell you this: you know that we do not have many votes in the National Assembly, and because of this we must always work carefully. We are trying to do our best, and so are the toubabs, but you will accomplish nothing by defying them. I have given my word that work will be resumed tomorrow, and then the discussions will go on. The rest is up to me. Once again, I ask you to have confidence in me.'

After acknowledging the applause for a moment, the deputy turned back to his chair, mopping at his face with his handkerchief; but he had not even sat down before Bakayoko was on the stand before the microphones. Gaye tried to interfere, seizing him by the arm.

'You certainly aren't planning to speak after the governor and the deputy!' he cried.

In the crowd, however, a few voices could already be heard, shouting, 'Baillika mou vahe, baillika mou vahe! Let him speak, let him speak!'

That governor whispered a few words in the deputy's ear, and the latter turned to Bakayoko. 'You may go ahead and speak,' he said, 'but don't be long, young man.'

The crowd was roaring louder now. 'Baillika mou vahe!'

Bakayoko swept the straw hat from his head, leaving it dangling across his back, and took up the stem of one of the microphones. When he began to speak, his words came slowly, almost as if he were matching his rhythms to the ponderous departures of his locomotives.

'I thank you for having let me speak,' he said, in Ouolof. 'It would have been very strange if everyone had been able to speak here except the men who are on strike. What I have to say, then, I say in their name. For more than four months now we have been on strike, and we all know why. It has been a hard life in that time – without food, without water, without even fire. It is a hard path for a man, and harder still for the women and the children, but we chose it and we have trod it. There is no longer any water in the whole district where we live. But among the men who spoke to you before me, did anyone tell you why? No one is questioning the words of these men, but what *did* they tell you, and to whom were they talking, in a language most of you do not understand? The Imam spoke to you of God. Does that mean he doesn't know that people who are hungry and thirsty are likely to forget the way to the mosque? You were told also that the governors have brought you many wonderful improvements and changes. It is true that I am young, but I haven't seen very many of them, and I could call on the older workers to tell us what they have seen! We can't feed our families with projects! And you were also told that there would be no sanctions against us – but did anyone say whether there would be sanctions against those who have killed women and children?'

Bakayoko repeated his last sentences in Bambara, and then in French. He felt no fear at all. It was no longer the crowd he saw in front of him, but two shining rails, tracking a path into the future. Even his voice seemed turned to steel.

'It seems that this strike is the work of a little group of black sheep, led by foreigners. If this is so, there must be a lot of black sheep in this country; and you, who know us all, look at me and tell me who are the foreigners. It seems also that we are incapable of creating anything by ourselves, but we must be of some use because, since we stopped working, the trains have stopped running. We are told that some of our demands will be satisfied, but which ones? We have asked for pensions, for family allowances, for raises in pay, and for the right to have a union which is recognized by the company. But not one of the men who spoke before me even mentioned a single one of these words. Why not? They are simple enough. Our deputy told us that he had come here to help *us*. Ask him then why he cannot apply in his own country the same social laws he votes for in a country far from here. Ask him how he lives, and how much he

219

earns. But perhaps you find all of these questions boring and want me to be quiet now?'

There was a clamor of voices from the crowd. 'No, no; go on!'

The governor and the European members of the delegations had understood very little of what Bakayoko was saying and, therefore, were undisturbed, but Gaye and the deputy were fidgeting uneasily in their chairs.

'Since you want me to go on. I have one thing more to say. When we had our discussion with the management, they told us that our demand for family allowances could not be considered because our wives and our mothers are really only concubines. But when it was a matter of going off to be killed in the war, did anyone ask the patriots who volunteered if they were legitimate or illegitimate? Ask your deputy to answer that question, too.

'I can't speak any longer now, but before I go I still have one thing left to do. *Monsieur le gouverneur, Monsieur le député*, the old lady you see there before you is Grandmother Fatou Wade. She lost her husband in the first war and her older son in the second. They gave her these medals, which have no value to her, and now they have put her younger son in prison because he was on strike. She has nothing left. *Monsieur le gouverneur, Monsieur le député*, take back these medals and give her her son and her daily rice in exchange!'

Once again he repeated his words in Bambara and in French, and this time, when the Europeans understood what he was saying, their eyebrows came together and their expressions hardened. Bakayoko had opened his hand to show the medals as he spoke, and now he closed his fist around them again.

'Mother,' he said in Ouolof, 'I have done as you asked. Now it is up to the rest of you – masons, carpenters, fitters, fishermen, dockers, policemen and militiamen, civil servants and office workers – to understand that this strike is yours, too, as the workers in Dahomey, in Guinea, and even in France have already understood it. It depends on you, workers of Dakar, whether our wives and our children will ever see a better life. There is a great rock poised across our path, but together we can move it. As for us – the trainmen will never go back to work until our demands are met!'

Bakayoko ran quickly down the steps of the grandstand, experiencing again his old familiar urge to get away and be alone after a moment such as this. On all sides of him he heard shouts and cries, gradually becoming louder and more distinct: 'The masons will go out, too! ... The dock

220

workers want to vote! . . . The metalworkers! . . . Strike! Strike! . . .' Then, above all the tumult, the chant of the women of Thiès could be heard:

The morning light is in the east . . .

Crossing the field, Bakayoko almost collided with Alioune. He took both of his friend's hands in his.

'Forgive me, brother,' he said, 'if I had to say these things, but it was the only way. After what we listened to out there, there was no hope of any honest discussion. Now we will have a common front – there will be a general strike. We had to do it – it was the only way.'

Outside the gates, the women of Dakar, with N'Deye Touti among them, were passing among the crowd, taking up a collection.

'For the strikers . . .'

'To help the women of Thiès return to their homes . . .'

'For the children . . .'

And small change and coins, and even a few bills, were dropped into the brightly colored scarves and aprons and handkerchiefs that were held out to receive them.

The next morning a general strike was called. It lasted for ten days, the time required before pressure from all sides forced the management of the railroad to resume the discussions with the delegates of the strikers.

When the women of Thiès started out on their journey home, the drivers loaned them trucks, and, since the fishermen had voted to turn over an entire day's catch to them, one of the trucks carried nothing but fish.

Maïmouna, the blind woman, remained behind, in the compound at N'Diayène. She still had milk and had begun to nurse the baby who had been called Strike. 'I am nourishing one of the great trees of tomorrow,' she told herself. At night she liked to sit in the courtyard, surrounded by the children, singing one of her old songs to them or telling them the story of the girl and the curious little man who had lost their lives on the road at the entrance to the city.

DAKAR

The Edge of the Sea

Bakayoko and N'Deye Touti were resting on the fine warm sand of the beach, between two long fishing boats hewn from great logs and propped up on lengths of smaller ones. The girl was sitting with her legs stretched out before her and her back against one of the boats, while the man, lying on his stomach with his head supported in his hands, was watching a group of children who were setting traps for sea birds. One of them, a sickly little creature, was running after a sand crab. When at last he had caught it, he crushed it with a blow of his heel, and Bakayoko smiled. N'Deye Touti could see nothing of him but the top of his head and his left ear and hand.

'Will you be staying here for a while?' she asked.

He did not reply. His attention had just been caught by a gray-winged bird moving with precise little hopping steps towards one of the traps. There was a sound like the creaking of a pulley, a brief flutter of wings, and the bird was caught up by one leg. The young hunters gathered in a circle around it, shouting aloud in triumph.

'They are happy,' Bakayoko said, turning over on his back and clasping his hands behind his neck.

N'Deye Touti looked down at him thoughtfully, studying the high, clear forehead, the close-cropped hair, and the scar, which always seemed to her to be so virile. For several days now she had basked in the warmth of this new intimacy. Sometimes she found herself counting on her fingers, as she had done in school, but now she was saying, 'I'll sleep with him, I won't sleep with him, I'll sleep . . .' She knew that everyone at N'Diayène already regarded her association with him as the beginning of a liaison and considered it with indulgence. She was happy to have him near her and to be alone with him, but she could not help asking, in that gentle little voice that jealous women love to use, 'If you leave, when will you come back?'

'I don't know; I'm waiting for that boat the fishermen told me about.'

'A boat, as far as Bamako?'

'No, I'll get off at Kayes, and then I can go with the fishermen as far as Bapoulaba . . .' He traced the route for her in the sand with the tip of his fingers. 'From there, I'll have to go by the rapids of the Félou . . .'

'That doesn't tell me when you will come back.'

'I can't tell you. I don't know myself.'

◆

They did not return to N'Diayène until after nightfall. The authorities had made no move to apprehend him, but Bakayoko thought it wise to remain out of sight as much as possible. The stars were beginning to come out. They could overhear the conversation of two sailors who were walking just ahead of them.

'What do you think of that little slut? She told me to come, I took off without permission to get there, and then she had gone off with some civilian! I'll smash that bastard's face if I ever get my hands on him.'

'If you haven't got any money, you might as well get used to it. I've got one lined up for tonight, though – on credit. If this strike goes on, they'll all come around to that . . .'

'Don't tell me about the bitches! And tomorrow we've got to be on guard at the station at the crack of dawn . . .'

N'Deye Touti slowed her pace until the sailors were a good distance ahead and then said, 'Why don't you ever talk to me about Penda?'

'She's dead. Did you know?'

'Yes, I knew. Did you know her well?'

'I knew her. Why do you ask?'

'She was a whore.'

'Who told you that?'

'All the women in the compound know it. They say that the only thing that was never on top of her was the railroad. I just wondered how . . .?'

N'Deye Touti left her question unfinished, and Bakayoko did not reply at once.

'You will probably never be worth as much as Penda,' he said at last. 'And I know what she was worth. She was a real friend, and she lost her life because of it. There are a great many ways of prostituting yourself, you know. There are those who do it because they are forced to – Alioune, Deune, Idrissa and myself all prostitute our work and our abilities to men who have no respect for us. And then there are others who sell themselves morally – the ones like Mabigué and Gaye and Beaugosse. And what about you?'

223

He stopped to light his pipe.

'Let me do it,' N'Deye Touti said, but at the first puff she coughed violently and spat. 'It's disgusting – how on earth can you smoke that?'

They walked on again in silence. To their left there was a long wall of hard, white clay, and on their right a field of guava trees.

'Do you want me to tell you something?' the girl asked suddenly. 'I would like to be your second wife.'

'What?' Bakayoko stopped short, as if he had been struck on the head.

'I've thought about it very seriously and asked myself a lot of questions; and I told myself that if you refused it would be because it would be difficult for you to reverse yourself now, after you have always said that you were against polygamy. And I know that you are really against it. I was, too; it was one of our customs that I could never understand, that I hated even. But it happens sometimes that you come to like something you thought you hated . . . And at least I can tell myself that since I was born a Moslem, my religion authorizes it. You told me once that these old feudal customs would only really disappear when Africa was reborn and free. In the meantime, while we are waiting for that time to come, I want to be your second wife. I know of another "emancipated" girl who has done it. Why shouldn't I? . . . And I wouldn't be jealous of Assitan.'

N'Deye Touti paused, a little breathlessly. She had been speaking very rapidly, in French. Bakayoko had no immediate answer, because as she spoke myriad thoughts and memories had been flashing through his mind, vanishing as quickly as they appeared. Traveling constantly, from one end of the line to the other, he had known a great many women, and he had approached them as a thirsty traveler will seize upon fresh water, but he had never attached much importance to the act of sex. For what else there was to marriage, there was Assitan, and that was enough.

He stopped, and N'Deye Touti turned to him and came back to where he stood. In spite of the darkness, he could see that her eyes were shining, and he could feel her breath on the naked flesh of his chest. With a familiar, almost brotherly, gesture, he took her head in his hands and tilted it gently to the side. N'Deye Touti lifted her head to his and closed her eyes.

'Will you?' she asked.

'No.'

◆

All the rest of the way, past the rows of straw huts and cabins, dotted now with flickering yellow lights, neither of them said a word. When they arrived in the courtyard of N'Diayène, they found Alioune waiting for them.

'Ah, if it isn't our great leader,' Bakayoko said, laughing.

'Don't joke with me now! The news is very bad – from everywhere, it seems. At Thiès, Doudou is dead. A bad attack of the fever, from what Lahbib wrote me. And at Bamako, they have arrested Konaté and taken him to the camp where they are holding Fa Keïta and the others. About the only good thing is that your boat has arrived. It leaves again tomorrow at dawn, and it would be safer if you embarked tonight. Only . . .'

'Only what?'

'Someone will have to go to Doudou's funeral.'

'Me? Oh no, I'm not going to Thiès. Doudou may have died of the fever, but it was a fever brought on by hunger and overwork. Now if there had been doctors for the workers . . . In any case, you are in charge here; appoint someone. I'm leaving. There is no one at all in the Sudan.'

'Sometimes I wonder,' Alioune said, 'if you don't carry things a little too far . . .'

N'Deye Touti interrupted him. 'He has no heart,' she said, 'and he wants everyone else to be like him – inhuman!'

She ran off into the house, leaving Bakayoko to say his good-byes to the women who had gathered in the courtyard and thank them for their hospitality.

'We have done nothing,' Ramatoulaye said, 'and it is a sad thing that we could do so little for a man like you in such a time. There is nothing to thank us for.'

He rested his hand on the shoulder of the blind woman, who was nursing Strike. 'Peace be with you, Maïmouna.'

'Peace be with you, man, and with all of yours.'

After a last glance around the courtyard, Bakayoko strode rapidly into the house and went directly to the central room where he had left his things. Naked children were sleeping on the bed and on strips of matting unrolled across the floor. N'Deye Touti was waiting for him, holding his old straw hat and his walking stick in one hand and his pack in the other. The room was lit by a single candle set in a jug on the floor, and the light, striking upward, formed pools of shadow on the girl's face. 'She looks like the bronze masks of a goddess of Ife,' Bakayoko thought, and it occurred to him that N'Deye Touti might have chosen her position carefully. Her eyelashes were fluttering nervously, and her lower lip trembled. As they stood there looking at each other in the half light, a tear glinted in the corner of one of her eyes, then rolled down her cheek, and, for an instant, hung sparkling at the tip of her chin.

The sight of a woman weeping was a thing to which Bakayoko was a stranger. He took his traveling gear from her hands, put on the straw hat, and tied the leather thong at his neck.

'I wish . . .' he began, but then he stopped abruptly, turned, and left the room. As he crossed the courtyard he said again, 'Ramatoulaye, may peace be with this house.' Then he disappeared into the night.

N'Deye Touti had followed him to the door, still hoping for some word or gesture. When he had gone, and the darkness had engulfed his figure, she muttered furiously. 'The pig! The filthy pig!' and now she made no effort to control her tears.

◆

Bakayoko's fleeting appearance in her life was destined to have consequences for the girl which she could have had no way of foreseeing on that last evening. As the earth hardens beneath the harsh suns of the dry season, the heart also hardens in the flames of unhappiness. For days after he had gone, she seemed completely indifferent to everything that happened around her. The great dark eyes, which once had sparkled wide at the slightest emotion, moved from one object to another, from one face to another, as if the outside world no longer existed, and everything now centered on some interior vision from which she drew a kind of morbid pleasure.

She had an attack of fever which lasted for several days and left her very weak, but as soon as it had subsided she was seized with a fever for work. None of the things she had once disliked doing any longer repelled her; she cared for the children and washed their clothing and went on long errands in the heat of the day, in search of a handful of rice. Sometimes she would sit for hours bent over a schoolbook of geography, studying out every detail of her country in one map after another. And often the multi-colored lines on the page would seem to be drawing the face of a man.

One day, as she was wandering absently through the courtyard, carelessly dressed and wearing a pair of old sandals and a hat that had long since lost its brim, Mame Sofi said, 'What are you looking for, *mad'mizelle?*'

'I'm looking to see if there is still any water, Aunt.'

'You're not going to tell me that you're going to the well for some, like the men?'

'Why not?'

And she left, pushing an old barrel before her, watched with amusement by the other women, who lost no opportunity to make fun of her.

When she returned, several hours later, she was unrecognizable. Her face was haggard and drawn, her clothing was plastered to her body with sweat, and she had lost both the sandals and the hat. Ramatoulaye went out to help her.

'No, Aunt! I got this far, and I can manage the rest of the way.' Bracing her feet in the sand, she pushed the heavy cask into the courtyard.

'I'll go again tomorrow,' she said.

'I'll come with you,' the blind woman murmured.

And so, each day after that, accompanied by Maïmouna and little Anta, she rolled the big cask to the well, filled it, and brought it back to N'Diayène. Everyone still called her '*mad'mizelle*', but now there was admiration and affection in their use of the word. One morning, when there was no paper to light the fires, she gave them all of her notebooks except one. That night, alone in the light of a candle, she took out the single one she had hidden and wrote a poem which might have been the swan song of her youth.

◆

Bakayoko left the boat at Saint-Louis on the same day the strikers tore up a long stretch of track on the main line of the railroad. He had had nothing to do with this act of sabotage, but considering his reputation he decided that it would be best to take no chances and went on immediately into the interior. The fishermen put relays of boats at his disposal, and with them he went up the Sénégal and Bakoy rivers as far as Kati. There he bade farewell to his rowers and set out for the Sudan, traveling always on dirt paths and little-used roads.

One morning, as he was nearing home, he paused to rest, driving his walking stick into the ground and draping his hat on it. Then, having removed his outer tunic, he stretched out in the shade of a baobab tree and took a folded paper from his pocket. It was a letter from Lahbib which had been delivered to him when he left the boat. He wanted to re-read it.

My brother,

I am sure Alioune must have told you the news of Doudou's death.

227

There were a great many people at his funeral, but I was not surprised that you were not here. Do you know what has happened to Aziz, the Syrian? The police came and closed up his shop – because of the truck, I imagine. His father-in-law was ill, and his wife was weeping. It was not a pretty sight, and I felt a little ashamed. And you?

The women got a big welcome when they came back, of course, but now the men are having all sorts of trouble with them. At first they even pounced on me like tigresses – they wanted to start running everything! But things are a little calmer now – the children have not come back yet, and the women go out to the lake every day. In future, though, we will have to reckon with them in whatever we do.

The death of Samba N'Doulougou upset me terribly. And Penda's, too. She was a brave girl. I know that you knew her better than I. I don't know of anything we can do for her now, but if you should know of something I do not, tell me.

And now, come home. Bakary told me once that you had no heart, and sometimes I think he is right. I suppose there must be men like you at a time like this – it is very difficult to fight without being able to hate the person you are fighting. I have some time to read now, so try to bring me some books – novels, not too obvious, but not too difficult either – and especially some books about the lives of men in other countries.

Your family needs you, too, so come home soon.

Sidiame dome n'deye – peace be with you, my brother.

Lahbib.

Stretched out beneath his tree, Bakayoko felt very much alone, and he thought about Penda. He might have made her his second wife, and now he found himself wondering about the nature of the feelings that had drawn him to this girl. Could it have been the fact that she, like himself, was a traveler from one station to another? He was really only sure of one thing; his feelings for her had stemmed from what was best in himself.

A breeze crackled through the leaves of a bush, startling him, and he leaped to his feet and seized his walking stick. A few feet from where he stood a sparrow hawk had plummeted on a rat.

'You bastard, you frightened me!' he laughed.

He turned back to his resting place and saw that, in getting up so suddenly, he had dropped his tobacco pouch, and now the wind was scattering the shreds of leaf through the grass.

'If I can't smoke, I'll die!' he said aloud. 'I guess I had better hurry and get home, hadn't I?'

But only the bird was there to answer him, lifting its wings to carry its prey into the morning sky.

BAMAKO

The Camp

It was impossible to approach the camp without being seen, since it stood in the middle of a naked plain and was dominated by four observation towers where sentries were stationed day and night. Behind the double fence of barbed wire, and in front of the only gate, native auxiliary troops stood guard. They had all been brought here from Central Africa, and none of them spoke any of the three languages of the Sudan: Bambara, Peul, or Sonrhaï.

There were three buildings at the center of the enclosure: the quarters of the 'commandant', the barracks for the guards, and the common-law prison. Nothing much was ever seen in the camp of the inhabitants of this building. They left in the early morning, surrounded by militiamen, to work on the roads, and they did not return until after nightfall. Sometimes there would be one who did not return at all.

Slightly apart from this central group, and also surrounded by a barbed-wire fence, was a square, flat-roofed building on which stood a kind of sentry box built of mud and branches. Here, too, one of the auxiliaries was always on guard.

It was to this building that Fa Keïta had been brought. His hands were untied just before the sheet-iron door was opened, and then he had been pushed inside to a darkness as black as if he had fallen into a pit. The first thing that struck him had been the odor – a sicklysweet smell, mingled with an acrid reek of ammonia that burned at his nostrils.

He tried to move forward a step and collided with a metal container of some sort, which overturned noisily. He sprawled on the ground in the midst of a spreading liquid, and when he groped his way to his feet he realized that his tunic was soaked.

'What is that liquid that smells so bad?' he asked gently.

'What's the matter, man, can't you see?' a voice answered from somewhere in the darkness.

'God is my witness that I can see nothing at all, though I am not blind.'

230

'You've turned over the crap bucket,' another voice said. 'The flies' dining room. Do you have a stone in place of a nose?'

Fa Keïta was so overcome with shame that he was incapable of speech. In the days of his retreat, before he was arrested, he had purified not only his soul but his body; he had felt himself clean and fresh as a newborn child, and now he was soiled and polluted. Hastily he began to recite a prayer.

'*Lai illaha illaïaou!*'

He was interrupted by a kind of bleating sound. 'L-l-listen to this t-t-true believer who drops on us from h-h-heaven and walks on our f-f-feet!'

'If I have stepped on you, I ask you to forgive me,' Fa Keïta said.

He understood now that there were several men in the room, and since their eyes were accustomed to the darkness, which was pierced only by the needles of light from two tiny loopholes in the walls, they could see him fairly clearly while he could still not even make out their figures.

'Is there any place to sit down?' he asked.

'Only by the dung you just turned over, man. You had better stay where you are.'

He felt himself brushed by a human form and heard the sound made by a stream of liquid striking against metal. His feet were spattered with urine, and then the man who relieved himself farted loudly.

'At least,' the stammering voice began, 'if we d-d-don't eat, we can still fart and the *toubabs* won't know it. But where I come from, it's more p-p-polite to belch.'

Fa Keïta was indignant. He had seen and heard a great many things in his long life, but never before had he come across such vulgarity and lack of respect in the presence of an old man.

'These are men of low birth,' he thought. 'Oh God, hold out your hand to me, I implore you! Lend me your protection and your grace! What have I done to deserve such a punishment?'

Tears rolled down his cheeks. He tried again to move, and this time he collided with a man's leg.

'Man, we told you once to stay where you were. If you step on us again, you'll see what will happen!'

Fa Keïta summoned up all of his courage. 'I am Fa Keïta, who is called the Old One,' he said. 'I'm from the "smoke of the savanna", and we are all on strike there. I do not know why the *toubabs* came and took me away during the days of my retreat, but I am here and I am very tired.'

'Why didn't you tell us that at once?' one of the voices said.

231

Now he was surrounded by shadowy figures, and hands reached out to touch his, in token of friendship and respect.

'All of us here are strikers,' a voice said, 'and all from the Sudan.'

'I knew that from your accent,' Fa Keïta said.

'And I am from Ny-Ny-...'

'He is from Nyamina. Tell us, Old One, is it true that they have gone back to work?'

'Men, no one has gone back to the shops.'

'Do they ever speak of us?'

'I have heard nothing, except that some of the strikers were in prison and that they were badly treated.'

'Do you hear that? They know outside how we are being treated. I told you so – Bakayoko knows everything that happens. That man is a real Bambara!'

'And what about the *toubabs*? What are they doing?'

'Nothing that I know of. We never speak of them.'

'Has Bakayoko come back to Bamako yet?'

'No, he is still in the countries to the west. Perhaps he has gone to see the chiefs of the "smoke of the savanna".'

Fa Keïta felt a little reassured, and now he was even beginning to be able to distinguish among the figures of his companions. He told them everything of what little he knew, including the story of Diara and of the trial. The reactions to this were violent.

'The son of a bitch! To do a thing like that while some of us are here, dying of hunger and thirst, buried alive! Tiémoko should have had him stoned in the market place!'

One of the prisoners came over and took the old man by the hand. 'Come over here,' he said. 'It's a little cleaner. You can sit down here and rest against the wall.'

Toward the middle of the day, the guards brought their daily ration of food: an old tub that had been cut in two, containing some sort of blackish, pasty substance and a tin can of water.

Several days passed with no change in this routine. Fa Keïta seldom mingled in the conversations of the other prisoners, which invariably hinged on the same subjects – the strike, food and lice. He had begun a period of meditation again and had even tried to carry out the ritual prayers, but the man from San said, 'Old One, it is too filthy here for you to put your forehead to the earth. God will wait until you are in a more fitting place.'

'How long have I been here?' Fa Keïta asked, almost as if he were talking to himself.

'Each time the guards come with the tub, you can mark one day. For you, it is ten now – for the rest of us, much longer.'

And then there was silence again, troubled only by the hoarse breathing of sleepers and the constant sound of scratching.

◆

One morning the door was thrown wide open, allowing a brutal sunlight to flood the room and releasing a wave of nauseous air which made the guards recoil. It was the periodic 'promenade' organized by the 'commandant', an ex-sergeant major in the colonial forces named Bernadini. Since he had long since been retired from the army he was no longer subject to military authority, but only to that of the colonial police administration; and the men under his orders as 'commandant' of this camp were auxiliaries and not regular troops. He was a hold-over from a time that was gone and a breed that had almost disappeared, but he had been kept on, in the thought that he might some day be needed . . . A Corsican, and the product of a series of foundling schools, he hated all *macacos*, as he called the Negroes.

He stood in the sun in the center of the enclosure, his head protected by an old-fashioned conical helmet, tapping the naked thigh beneath his army shorts with the tip of a riding crop, waiting for the prisoners to file out.

They were lined up in ranks in front of him by the guards, seeming, with their jerky steps, their hairless legs and fleshless bodies, more like an assembly of locusts than of humans. The sun burned at their eyes, and when they closed their lids a round, black spot pulsed violently at the center of a red cloud.

The man from San leaned towards Fa Keïta and whispered, 'That one is the worst of all the *bilakoros*, of all the unclean infidels.'

'*Macou!*' the chief of the auxiliaries shouted.

'Silence!' Bernadini repeated. 'Now who was talking? No one, of course! I am accustomed to that. But let me tell you that I was in the camp at Fodor, in Mauretania, and I swear to you that no one who was with me there is likely to forget it!'

He went over to the stammerer, who seemed to be muttering something to himself, and lashed at his face with the riding crop. 'That's just in case it was you who was talking! If you open your mouth again, I'll plant my foot here!' He flicked at the man's groin with the butt of the whip. 'That should make you come, *macaco*! All right, chief, on with the promenade!'

There were about forty of the prisoners, Fa Keïta discovered as they began circling around the enclosure, walking in single file, one behind the other. On each turn they left behind them in the sand a faint, circular track, like the tracks of circus horses around a ring. And as they walked, the heat of the sun aroused their lice, and the itching in every portion of their bodies drove them to such frenzy that they scratched until the skin was raw.

In the center of the circle they marked out, there was a shallow pit about the size of a man's body, marked at its corners by four pegs about six inches high. Resting on the pegs was a sheet of steel pierced with holes.

Bernadini had walked off with two of the guards, and, when he saw this, Salifou, the man of San, turned his head slightly towards Fa Keïta.

'If you want to talk, Old One, keep your teeth together and don't move your lips, and then they won't see you.'

'Man, what is that pit?'

'It's for the ones who are tired and can't walk any longer – that's the way he describes it, a place to rest! And I was the one who had to dig it! When I finished, he put me in it. When they took me out, I was pissing blood!'

'*Thié!*' Fa Keïta exclaimed.

'Man!' Salifou repeated. 'You are right – but that is the way that *bilakoro* is. Today he is pleased with himself, though – it seems he has a new prisoner.'

'Do you know who it is?'

'*Macou!*' One of the guards came running toward them, his whip brandished threateningly above his head.

They said no more, and the silent circling in the burning sand went on.

A short time later, Bernadini came back to the center of the circle, with the two guards pushing another man between them. It was Konaté, the secretary of the union local at Bamako. His hands were tied tightly behind his back.

'Well,' Bernadini said gleefully, 'what do you think of your charges now, secretary of my ass? They are pretty, aren't they? And I am here just to satisfy all of their demands – even the ones they haven't made! I even give payments on account. Here, would you like one?'

His fist crashed against Konaté's nose.

'Try to organize a meeting here, and you'll see what I give you to discuss! You think you're a big man, but you're just as much of a fool as the rest of them. And as for your Bakayoko, we'll catch him, too, and he'll be brought right here to complete my little collection of monkeys!'

Konaté was not listening to Bernadini. He had been watching the men circling around him, and when he saw Fa Keïta his heart seemed suddenly wrapped in iron bands.

'Well then, secretary, what about this strike? You can see for yourself that the men have everything they need – fresh air for their promenade – good food, instead of the cockroaches and vultures they eat at home . . .'

'You have no right . . .' Konaté began, but he was never able to finish. The riding crop slashed brutally across his face.

'How dare you interrupt a white man, you stinking pig! The right here belongs to me, and don't you forget it! You do nothing but obey, *macaco*!'

Konaté hurled himself at the man, but the guards moved more quickly than he and dragged him back.

'Chief!' Bernadini shouted. 'Throw him in the pit!'

Konaté struggled violently, but the guards stripped off his clothes, bound his legs with heavy cord, and rolled his naked body into the pit.

Bernadini walked over and grinned down at him. The sun's rays struck Konaté's body only in the spots where holes had been pierced in the steel, patterning it with rows of little yellowish disks.

'So you wanted to show off before your friends, eh, secretary? But you see who is master now, don't you? I've screwed tougher ones than you, you know.'

He leaned over and touched a finger to the steel plate, but withdrew it hastily. The metal was burning. 'All right, chief,' he said. 'Let's give him a little water.'

Very slowly the guard began pouring water from a gourd. On contact with the metal, it made a little hissing sound, a faint white vapor steamed up, and the scalding water rolled across the surface of the steel plate and began to fall, drop by drop, through the holes. With implacable regularity it burned and bit into the skin of the man beneath.

'You've got guts, my little secretary,' Bernadini said. 'You're doing better than most of them – we'll see how long you can hold out. Chief, a little more water.'

Grimly, desperately, Konaté struggled not to cry out, but no matter how tightly he clenched his teeth he could not prevent a moan from escaping as the drops continued to fall. The other prisoners were still circling around him. Fa Keïta was not even watching the scene at the pit. His eyes were lifted toward the east, above the thorned wire of the fences, beyond the reach of the savanna and the great trees shouldering the sky, far off to the line of the horizon. His eyes were lifted toward a meeting with the only thing truly worthy of any form of suffering – a faith in God. The debasement of which human beings were capable was a thing he could neither conceive nor bear. He had never shared the feelings which had brought the men around him to where they were now, but he was beginning to wonder if his wisdom had been only ignorance.

Two times more he made the seemingly endless round, and then he took the decision he had been reflecting on all this time. Since he could not pray in the filth and stench of the prison, he would profit from the chance that had been offered him now. With slow, deliberate steps, he left the file of prisoners and began walking towards the fence that surrounded the camp. At a little distance from the circle, he paused, gathered up a handful of sand for his ablutions, and stood up again, girding up the cloth around his waist. Facing towards the Kaaba, his palms turned outwards, he began to pray.

'*Allahou Ackabarou . . .*'

'What!' Bernadini roared. 'What's going on here? . . .' The guards had already raced over and seized the old man. 'No, let him alone,' he ordered. Then he turned to Fa Keïta. 'Go ahead . . .'

The old man stumbled a few paces toward the fence.

'Well,' Bernadini said, 'are you going to pray, or am I . . .?'

And as Fa Keïta began to kneel, the 'commandant's' boot caught him in the kidney and hurled him head first into the strands of barbed wire. Little drops of blood flecked the skin of the old man's shoulders and back and sides.

The prisoners had stopped, as if their feet had suddenly been trapped in the sand.

'Get them moving!' Bernadini shouted to the guards. Then he turned back to watch Fa Keïta, who was trying as best he could to free himself from the barbs. His hands were bloody, and scarlet threads ran down from the dozens of points where his flesh was torn.

'Well, are you going to pray some more?' Bernadini asked.

'How far will God lead me?' Fa Keïta thought. Again he lifted his palms and began to bow down, and again the 'commandant's' boot flung him into the steely-pointed wires. More slowly this time, he freed himself, but no sound at all came from his lips. With his arms stretched out before him, he knelt again, his forehead resting on the sand.

Bernadini put his foot on the old man's neck, like a hunter posing for a photograph. 'Just look at how well he prays,' he said. 'He's a real saint, this one.'

Suddenly, then, he seemed to lose interest in the man kneeling beneath him, in the men still shuffling around their circle, and in the man in the pit, who was screaming now with every drop of water that seared his skin.

'I've seen enough of their dirty faces,' he said to the chief of the guards. 'Take them back where they belong.' He thrust the riding crop under his arms, as he had once seen English officers do, and strode off toward his quarters.

In the time they had been in the sun the prisoners had lost the habit of darkness, and they had difficulty finding their old places when they were herded back to the stinking room. Fa Keïta let his body slip down beside the wall. Salifou, the man of San, had managed to pick up Konaté's caftan as he went by the pit, and he said, 'They'll be bringing Konaté in – we have to make a place for him.'

Fa Keïta's breath came out in a sigh. 'God knows I was not for this strike, for I do not like violence in any form, but if God is just, how can He let men be treated so? In all my life, and in the lives of my parents, we have done no wrong to anyone – why then should we be treated so? I do not know if the strike should go on, I do not know what must be done, but I know that something must be done so that we are treated with respect, as men . . .'

'We'll see what Konaté has to say,' Salifou said. 'Perhaps he will know something.'

◆

At almost the same moment when the prisoners were being returned to their dungeon, the union building in Bamako was the scene of an animation it had not known in a long time. Tiémoko was holding a telegram and wondering what to say to the excited group of men that surrounded him.

'Well,' one of them demanded, 'are you going to read it to us? Or do you want to keep the news to yourself? They say the strike is over. Is it true?'

'I think it's over, but let me go to Bakayoko's first. He's back at home, and he'll have to explain it – I don't understand some of the things that are written here. Don't say anything about it until I get back.'

He ran all the way to Bakayoko's house and found him in the central room, with Ad'jibid'ji seated beside him. Tiémoko handed him the telegram.

'Here, read this. I don't understand everything it says.'

Bakayoko read aloud:

'Conditions accepted. Strike terminated. Return to work tomorrow. Direct train Bamako–Thiès. Put conductor disposition Thiès committee. Lahbib.'

There was a moment's silence, and Bakayoko said, 'The strike is over.'

'Yes, but what does it mean by "direct train" and "put conductor disposition"?'

'That means that tomorrow you will take a train to Thiès, and you'll receive instructions about what to do after that from the committee there. I'll go to Koulikoro myself. But now let's get back to the union office. Ad'jibid'ji, tell your mother where I have gone. You can come over later.'

It had been two days now since Bakayoko returned from Dakar, and during these forty-eight hours he had remained at home with his wife and his adopted daughter. On the evening of the first day he had said to his wife, 'Assitan, would you like to learn the language of the *toubabs*?'

In her astonishment she had answered simply, 'If you wish me to.'

This wall that had always been between them was difficult to tear down. It had been built a long time ago, on the first day of the union that custom had forced on them. Months had gone by then before Bakayoko could bring himself to the accomplishment of his conjugal duties. But Assitan had been brought up according to all the ancient rules and customs. She lived on the margin of her husband's existence: a life of work, of silence, and of patience. It would have been hard to know whether Bakayoko ever felt remorse for his infidelities to her, for this man's thoughts were secrets from the world. But it was possible that the moral and material distress he had seen on every hand in the days of the strike had affected him more than he knew – had altered and matured him.

This very morning, rising early, he had seen Assitan take up his big traveling pack and start toward the river to wash it.

'Woman,' he had said, 'you have eaten nothing; you are too weak for such work. Wait until the strike is over, and there is food, and you are strong again.'

Assitan had said nothing. She had seated herself in the courtyard and set to work restitching the heavy material which formed the straps of the pack, but in her heart she had felt a warmth, a joy she had never known before.

When Tiémoko and Bakayoko left the house now, they found that the news had already leaked out, and crowds were gathering in the square in front of the station, as well as at the union building. They had difficulty forcing their way through the clusters of men and women, laughing, shouting, embracing, but at last they reached the meeting hall, and Bakayoko climbed up to the stage.

'The news has been confirmed,' he announced. 'The strike is over. Tiémoko will go to Thiès tomorrow. We must make up the train tonight.'

'But that's a twenty-hour trip!' Tiémoko said.

'So? You have done it before, haven't you? I won't go with you, though. It isn't worth changing my plans just to hit back at that *toubab* who slapped my face. If Lahbib had needed me, he would have said so. But, for the moment, all we are going to do is wait for the release of the prisoners, because if they are not released there will be no return to work.'

◆

But the prisoners were released before the afternoon was over. Their return confirmed the end of the strike better than any news could have done, and they were welcomed by joyful crowds. Fa Keïta returned directly to his home, while the others were taken to the union building, where a celebration had been organized in their honor. The old man said nothing to his wives of what had happened in the camp, but ordered them to put aside their mourning and then closed himself in his room to accomplish a long and careful ceremonial of self-cleansing. When this had been completed, he put on his finest tunic, returned to the central room, and seated himself cross-legged on the ground, his prayer beads in his right hand. The women and children took their places behind him, their faces seeming oddly distorted in the glow of the single oil lamp that lit the room.

One by one the men came in. Fa Keïta had asked them all to call on him at dusk, before they returned to their own homes. Several of the prisoners were there, including the man of San, the stammerer, and Konaté, whose body was swathed in bandages. Tiémoko was there, too, feeling awkward and embarrassed when he remembered his conflict with the old man in the first days of the strike. Bakayoko had put his pipe in his pocket, so that he would not forget himself and light it. He never smoked in the presence of the Old One.

When the men had seated themselves, Fa Keïta said, 'I am honored by your visit to my home. I have no kola to offer you, but I shall consider myself your debtor.'

'We have not come for that,' Salifou said. 'We know how things are today, and we shall regard the debt as a thing for better days.'

'You are truly a man of San; you know the laws of hospitality. But, as you say, it is not for that I asked you to come here before returning to

239

your families and your work. It was because I had something I wanted to say to you. Just before we parted a little while ago I heard some words that did not seem good to me. If I am mistaken, you may interrupt me . . .'

The old man paused for a minute and fingered his prayer beads thoughtfully. 'To kill someone is a thing that any of us can do. When I was in the camp, I, too, wished for the death of the "commandant", but something far worse than that also happened to me. I questioned the existence of God, and when these thoughts took possession of me, I wept with shame. I have been told, Bakayoko, that you were struck by a white man, and certainly the man who committed the act was guilty of a grievous affront. I do not know what you did when you were in the countries to the west, but I do know that it has contributed today to the happiness of a great number of families. In the streets outside, people are laughing and shouting with pleasure again. And yet you are not content.'

Bakayoko looked down at Ad'jibid'ji, who was curled on a strip of matting, seemingly asleep. He smiled to himself, because he knew that the child was listening to every word the old man said.

'A little while ago,' Fa Keïta went on, 'I heard Konaté and Tiémoko talking about killing the "commandant". But if you were to kill him, you should also kill the blacks who obey him, and the whites whom he obeys, and where would that lead? If a man like that is killed, there is always another to take his place. That is not the important thing. But to act so that no man dares to strike you because he knows you speak the truth, to act so that you can no longer be arrested because you are asking for the right to live, to act so that all of this will end, both here and elsewhere: that is what should be in your thoughts. That is what you must explain to others, so that you will never again be forced to bow down before anyone, but also so that no one shall be forced to bow down before you. It was to tell you this that I asked you to come, because hatred must not dwell with you.'

The men got to their feet slowly, with heads bowed, like a group of conspirators whose plans have just been forged. Suddenly they all heard the clear voice of Ad'jibid'ji, who had sat up on her mat.

'Grandfather, I know now what it is that washes the water. It is the spirit. The water is clear and pure, but the spirit is purer still.'

'You have heard our *soungoutou*,' the old man said. Then he took up his prayer beads again. 'You may go now. As for me, I owe too much to my God; there is not enough time left to me to thank Him. Men, pass the night in peace.'

'And you – pass the night in peace,' they said and filed out of the room.

Bakayoko walked with them to the porch, but his thoughts were far away. He had already heard a phrase very much like that – 'hatred must not dwell with you' – it was Lahbib who had said it. But how could a man take arms against injustice without hating the unjust? To fight well, it was necessary to hate.

He turned around suddenly and called, 'Ad'jibid'ji!'

'Owo, "petit père". I am here.'

'Where is your mother? Go and find her. There will be a great *bara* tonight in the square, and I want to take you – both of you.'

THIÈS

Epilogue

On the last day of the strike, the city of Thiès still wore the mournful look which had become its habit. Most of the children were still in the outlying villages, and a stranger might have wandered through the streets for a long time without encountering a living soul. Since their triumphal return from Dakar, the women had organized their lives in a manner which made them almost a separate community. Distances no longer inspired any fear in them, and each morning they left the city very early and walked the few miles out to the lake. There they installed themselves comfortably, bathed and did their washing, repaired the few shreds of clothing that remained to them, cooked their meager rations, and gossiped endlessly about the events of the famous 'march'. When night came, they returned to the city and the homes of their husbands or fathers.

At the union office, only the six members of the strike committee knew that the director-general of the line had signed the agreement with the delegates. Fearing trouble, Lahbib wanted to avoid any kind of spontaneous demonstration in this city, which had been at the very heart of the strike, and where emotions were still keyed to a fever pitch.

He did not succeed in keeping the secret very long. The news became known during the night, and, as soon as the sun was up, the union building was invaded by questioning, excited men, and crowds began to form in front of the station and in the market square and all of the neighboring streets. There were still a good many skeptics among them, and the few who owned radios were given an opportunity to hold lectures and give out all sorts of details, true and false. Someone even stated that, in future, a representative of the union would sit on the board of directors of the Dakar-Niger. Little by little, as the day wore on and it became apparent that the news was true, the scars and the wounds, the horrors of hunger and thirst, began to recede into the distance and be lost in the forests of forgetfulness.

On a corner of the table in the union office, Lahbib was writing, setting

242

down in a schoolboy's notebook the principal events of the day, as he had done every day since the strike began. He ran the tip of his index finger along the line of his moustache. In spite of the victory, he was anxious, thinking of the things that remained to be done before the men returned to work the next day. Since Doudou's death, a scant twenty-four hours after the departure of the women, almost all of the responsibility here had devolved on him.

His glance came to rest on Samba N'Doulougou's bicycle, hanging on the opposite wall, its tires flat, its saddle askew. One of the marchers had brought it back, and they had hung it there, as a souvenir of the little man who had so often amused them and helped to keep up their spirits. Thinking of Samba, he thought of Penda. Penda, the girl of easy virtue; Penda, the warrior with a soldier's cartridge belt around her waist. He wondered idly which of the two images would remain longer in his memory. 'Bakayoko must know the news by now,' he thought. 'It will be best if he doesn't come back here. We'll take care of Dejean ourselves.'

He got up from the table as the other members of the committee began to arrive. He had asked them to come so that he could give them their final instructions.

'Is everyone here now?' he asked, and then, noticing Bakary in a corner, he added, 'You can stay if you like, old man; we'll be glad to have you.'

Bakary closed the door and found himself a chair. It was the first time he had ever taken part in a meeting of the committee, and he struggled to repress a fit of coughing, so that he would not annoy his comrades.

'It's the matter of Dejean and Isnard I wanted to talk to you about,' Lahbib said. 'Dejean may already have left for Dakar, where he will ask to be replaced here; but, as for Isnard, it was made an unofficial condition of the agreement that he would be recalled. I want to be sure, however, that everything is done correctly.'

◆

Early the next morning the workmen began to gather in front of the gate to the workshops and the yards, preparing to return to work. Out of old habit, they grouped together almost automatically, according to their various trades and their separate crews. There were still many who were not there, those who had not yet returned from the villages, but the old atmosphere, the familiar framework of the past, was swift in re-establishing itself. A noisy, celebrating crowd thronged the adjoining streets and squares; the cohort of beggars, thinner than before, waited for the daily

243

distribution of soup; and the flies and the dust were back. The great iron gates were still closed, and there were two soldiers standing guard, but no one paid any attention to them.

'Where is Sounkaré, the watchman?' an old workman asked. 'Why doesn't he open up?'

Lahbib arrived just then, followed by Balla and Boubacar. The soldiers opened the gate for them, and the men streamed into the yard. Three minutes later the siren shrieked out its long, familiar call, after almost six months of silence.

The mechanics discovered the corpse of Sounkaré – or, more precisely, what the rats had left of the corpse of Sounkaré – in the bottom of a pit in the motor repair shop, lying in a film of dried and blackened oil. A delegation was formed to carry the remains away, but the funeral service was brief; he had never been well loved.

The workmen did not really work, either that morning or in the afternoon. They lounged about the benches and the forges and before their lathes. The mechanics counted out their wrenches and their pliers; in the marshaling yards they experimented idly with the couplings of the cars; in the huts along the sidings the switchmen played with the giant levers; and in the offices the clerks moved a few papers around.

Toward the end of the morning, Isnard came to make a tour of inspection, but everywhere he went he found nothing but tight-lipped faces and stony backs. At last he gave up and left the shops, hurrying back to the administration building. He found Edouard there, and Pierre, but since they both knew what had happened they could only stare at Isnard as they might have at a man they knew to be condemned. They went together to Dejean's office, and the director agreed to make one more effort. He picked up the telephone, called the shops, and asked for Lahbib.

'So!' he began angrily. 'This is the way your union operates! I am told that the workers are doing nothing! They've got to work now – and work hard! You don't think you're going to be paid for doing nothing!'

'*Monsieur le directeur*, you know the conditions of the agreement. We know that you are going to leave, but Isnard must go, too. As long as he is here, the men will be at their jobs, but they will not work.'

Just as Lahbib put down the telephone, the blast of a whistle shattered the silence, seeming to reach out from the horizon to embrace the city. A minute or so later, the train from Bamako, driven at reckless speed by Tiémoko, pulled into the station and screeched to a stop at the junction of the Sudan–Saint-Louis lines. It had picked up freight and passengers all along the line and now was just a confused jumble of cars of both kinds.

As Tiémoko leaped from the engine, the passenger cars began disgorging clusters of humans, who seemed to vanish without trace in the enormous crowds already flocking through the waiting rooms and across the tracks and platforms of the station. The din was indescribable. Pickpockets and thieves had a holiday, and a woman's voice managed to make itself heard, screaming, 'Someone stole my hamper!'

Twenty minutes after the first train, two other freight trains came in, and then a third from Rufisque, where it had been held up for a long time before the tracks could be cleared. The engineers, shouting to each other joyfully, pulled out the stops on their whistles, and the workmen in the shops, drawn by the general hubbub, joined in the crowd. The combined efforts of the train crews and two squads of militiamen were necessary before the doors of the freight cars could be opened.

And then the women arrived. Having heard the screaming of the whistles, and wondering what it signified, they instinctively formed in the order of their march to Dakar and marched on the station. The compact mass of their column forced a way through the mob which now covered the square, and when they reached the veranda they found Lahbib and Boubacar struggling to restore some kind of order.

'What's happening, men?' Mariame Sonko demanded. 'The strike isn't over?' The tone of her voice implied, 'If you still need us . . .'

'Yes, Mariame, the strike is over, but there is still the matter of Dejean and Isnard. Dejean is gone – I saw his automobile leave a little while ago, and his family is already in Dakar, but Isnard hasn't left yet.'

The women looked at each other.

'Let's go to "the Vatican",' one of them shouted. 'We'll dislodge that red-eared rat!'

'Let's go,' said Séni. 'When you can still see the toes after you have buried the body, you have to throw on a little more sand.'

'Let's go then,' Aby laughed. 'We'll throw on some more sand!'

'Don't go into "the Vatican",' Lahbib said, 'and stay away from the villas; there are soldiers there. Just go and get the drums and sing.' He turned to Bakary and Boubacar. 'Go with them, and don't let them do anything foolish.'

'Do you think they will listen to us?'

'Yes, old man; just tell them you are speaking in the name of the union.'

The long procession of women turned around and retraced the path that had brought them to the station. They had begun to sing the chant of the march from Thiès to Dakar, and a large part of the crowd followed them.

245

When they arrived in the district of 'the Vatican', Boubacar and Bakary, who were walking at the head of the column, encountered a cordon of soldiers aligned along the street that led to the homes of the white employees of the Dakar-Niger.

'Have no fear, men,' said the native non-commissioned officer who commanded the group. 'We have orders not to fire. Even if we did not, however, we would not fire. The honor you seek is our honor, too. But please, do not come any farther.'

◆

All of the houses of 'the Vatican' were closed and barred, almost as if they were in a state of siege. The whistles of the locomotives, and now the singing and the beating of the drums, were an almost unbearable strain to nerves already taut.

In the villa of the Isnards, the curtains were drawn and the bolts on all the doors were firmly secured. On the dining-room table, two Mausers, a revolver, and an open box of cartridges gleamed softly in the light from the overhead lamp. Isnard himself was seated facing the door, with a high-velocity pistol thrust in his belt. His hair was tangled and matted, his forehead streamed sweat, and he seemed to be scarcely breathing. Edouard and Pierre were seated near him, waiting; not knowing for quite what they waited, annoyed at being forced to be present at the end of the drama. All evening long, Isnard had been telephoning right and left – to his friends, to all of the other 'old hands', even to Dakar. And the response had always been the same, 'It's too late – I don't see what I could do now. Think about your own safety first, and we'll see what happens later. You should have warned us before this. If you have been recalled, just do as you're told – believe me, in your own interest . . .'

It was finished. He knew that he was going to have to leave, but he could not bring himself to move.

'The swine,' he muttered. 'The swine. After all I've done for them . . .'

Pierre found himself wondering whether he meant the workers in the shops or the stockholders in the railroad.

Edouard interrupted Isnard's rambling. 'Look, I know it's difficult, but there is nothing else to be done. I didn't believe it myself, but it happened. Dejean is already gone. And the whole line is blocked by their men. Bakayoko is in Koulikoro, Alioune at Dakar, and Lahbib here . . . The car is ready; all you have to do is go out the back way. We'll take care of your furniture.'

'But good God!' Isnard burst out. 'What's happening, that they let these savages, these children, decide? They don't even know what's good for them! Most of them don't know how to hold a hammer, and they call themselves workmen! You'll see, if this goes on, it won't be long before there isn't a single European left in Africa! The first one of them that sets foot in here I'll shoot in his tracks!'

'Now, now,' Edouard said. 'You've got to calm down. It's time to leave . . .'

In all the time they had been talking, Beatrice had been pacing back and forth, from one room to another, like a panther in a cage. When she heard the personnel director's last words, she fairly hurled herself at him.

'That's it, that's fine; you're dropping us, too! You're in a hurry to see us go, handed over as a sop to the Negroes! They've won, and because that makes you sick at your stomach, you're taking it out on us! We're the ones who built everything there is in this town. In the rain, in the wind, even when it was a hundred and twenty in the shade, Isnard was on the job. And the men knew it – they liked him! They all liked him, even the boys!'

She turned and ran out to the kitchen like a madwoman, returning in a moment, dragging the maid by the arm.

'Tell them!' she screamed at the terrified woman. 'Tell them that you liked us! Tell them you liked Monsieur! Say it; in the name of God, say it!'

Suddenly she stopped, passed a hand across her sweating forehead, and released her grip on the wrist of the trembling maid. Before any of the men could have stopped her, or even known what she was contemplating, she had seized one of the Mausers from the dining-room table, thrown open the door, and gone out to the garden.

Two shots rang out, followed by a brief hysterical burst from an automatic rifle, and one of the soldiers clapped a hand to his thigh. Beatrice seemed to leap into the air and roll over, like a rabbit brought down in full flight, and then she lay stretched on the gravel walk of the garden.

The three men went out, picked up the motionless body, and carried it back into the villa, carefully bolting the door.

◆

At the sound of the shots, an echoing silence had fallen on the crowd, as if they had written a brutal ending to a long, long story whose climax, until then, had been unknown. Even the drums were silent.

'What happened?' one woman's voice demanded.

'It was the wife of one of the *toubabs*,' Aby said. 'She has been shot.'

'Oh, that poor woman,' someone said.

As the crowd scattered into the shadows of the rapidly descending night, Lahbib heard someone singing. It was the *Legend of Goumba*, the old song of Maïmouna, the blind woman.

> From one sun to another,
> The combat lasted,
> And fighting together, blood-covered,
> They transfixed their enemies.
> But happy is the man who does battle without hatred.